med —

122

365

1st pub 1928,
ltd to 960 copies —

3 lines of title

fine in unequal dj

VENUS CASTINA

FACSIMILE EDITION

This edition of *Venus Castina* is a precise facsimile of the original Limited Edition published in 1928.

The first chapter is introductory and in some respects pertinent only to the time it was written. The main body of the book, however, is historical and as timely, valid and pertinent to our time as to any other time in history.

VENUS CASTINA

FAMOUS FEMALE IMPERSONATORS

CELESTIAL AND HUMAN

BY

C. J. BULLIET

WITH ILLUSTRATIONS BY

ALEXANDER KING

BONANZA BOOKS · NEW YORK

DEDICATION

To you who laugh in the Theater when a Male Moron puts on a Grass Skirt and dances a burlesque Spring Song in front of a Jazz Band;

To you who giggle when the handsome young Preacher pitches high his voice and mimics a hoydenish Maiden at a Picnic Chicken Dinner;

To you who find delight in the Girlish Pranks our College Boys are playing on each other and on their Girl Chums;

To you who applauded in the World War the efforts of our War Department to guard our Young Soldiers from Female Contamination, leaving them to Other Devices;

To you who have closed our Houses of Prostitution and bade Young Men forget Sexual Desire in Athletic Friendship;

To you who view with Equanimity the rapid spread of the "Scythian madness" in America since the World War—

To you, all and individually,
is dedicated

VENUS CASTINA.

CONTENTS

I   AT THE SHRINE OF VENUS CASTINA   1

II   THE HERO IN WOMAN'S DRESS—ACHILLES, HERCULES, SAMSON   13

III   THE GODS IN FINE LACES   26

IV   LOVES OF THE PHILOSOPHERS   45

V   ORGY OF THE CÆSARS   64

VI   VERSATILITY OF SATAN   90

VII   THE EVIRATI   103

VIII   THE BOY FRIENDS OF SHAKESPEARE   130

IX   PETS OF THE RESTORATION   161

X   PRINCES IN PETTICOATS   179

XI   CRIME IN FLUFFY RUFFLES   224

XII   PINK GARTERS FOR THESPIS' SOCK   261

XIII   THE BOY WITH THE "MONA LISA" SMILE   284

VENUS CASTINA

I. AT THE SHRINE OF VENUS CASTINA

HERE is the procession through the ages of votaries of the Venus Castina—that goddess supposed to respond with sympathy and understanding to the yearnings of feminine souls locked up in male bodies.

It is a curious throng, motley and miscellaneous: gods and demigods, coeval with the lovely Castina herself; kings and princes and heroes of old days and modern; frenzied priests and wild-eyed devotees; geniuses and morons, mountebanks, mystics, degenerates, practical jokers and buffoons, rogues and criminals, soft-eyed dreamers of a forbidden ineffable, warriors and poets, artists, statesmen, quacks, hoodlums and harlequins, sinners, and occasionally a saint.

Some of us fold tight our togas about us as they pass, fearing contamination. Many of us look on with lively curiosity. A few sit dazed and enraptured beside the shrine of Castina, and seek to understand.

It is to the curious onlookers the author belongs—a curiosity stirred first to action by observing—not the finest stage impersonator of female types of our time—but the effect his impersonations seemed to exert on the women and girls of his audience. Men chuckled at the satirical flings of Julian Eltinge at the foibles of fair feminine creatures, back in those days of his first tour with George M. Cohan's minstrel show, but women were stirred more deeply. A search for the wherefore resulted in this book.

An investigation of Eltinge's forerunners on the stage, particularly in the days of Queen Elizabeth when there were no female actresses to create Shakespeare's heroines, sent the author off into some amazing labyrinths of psychology, which led to a broadening of the inquiry to include not only the mimic stage, but the drama of the world of affairs.

Clews were run down, sometimes to the most obscure of odd corners of history. Literally hundreds of volumes have been consulted, sometimes the significant fact or bit of fact being found in microscopic print in a foot-note of some obscure book in the public library of New York or Chicago or San Francisco, whose yellowed edges and slightly stuck pages indicated it had not been opened in many long years.

The search, however, was not grimly systematic, nor was it pursued eighteen hours out of every twenty-four. The author has kept, all through, an easy feeling of curiosity—idle, at first; lively, thereafter, but never mounting to the frenzy of crusade. There was no definite thought of publication of the results.

Even now, though publication has been determined upon because of the rapid spread through America since the World War of the

"Scythian madness," the author has no sermon to preach. The growing effemination of our young American males—and the joke made of it by both them and their flapper friends—is no new phenomenon in history; and this survey of the procession past the shrine of the Venus Castina is the demonstration.

"I believe," wrote at the dawn of this century a well-informed American correspondent to Dr. Havelock Ellis, the supreme British authority on matters of sex, "that sexual inversion is increasing among Americans—both men and women—and the obvious reasons are: first, the growing independence of the women, their lessening need for marriage; secondly, the nervous strain that business competition has brought upon the whole nation. In a word, the rapidly increasing masculinity in women and the unhealthy nervous systems of men offer the ideal factors for the production of sexual inversion in their children."

This was an extraordinarily shrewd observation, made a quarter of a century ago, and before many of the factors that have since come into our national life were operating.

The World War has intervened since, for example, with our policy—growing out of the fetid, miasmatic Ohio swamp of reform—of protecting the morals of our lusty young soldiers in camp. Prostitutes were barred from administering sexual comfort, and the young men were left to work out their own salvation.

There is nothing in the known mental accomplishments of those responsible for the drastic moral and hygenic measures to indicate their ideas were scientifically any further advanced than Ohio psalm-

3

singing or Tennessee fundamentalism—but there are indications that they may have got results comparable with those arrived at by the Greeks of the classic period. It would be interesting to know just how much of the present rising tide of effemination of the American male can be traced to the camps of the World War, unadorned by the female fringe Napoleon so carefully conserved.

Taking advantage of the moral cowardice of "statesmen" in times of war, the reformers, too, closed tight the public houses of prostitution even to civilians—a move that, like prohibition, had already gained considerable headway and needed only a moment when fanaticism was rampant and experienced reason dormant to be made complete.

With females as difficult to obtain as bootleg liquor—fanaticism has not let go its grip in either domain—dormant tendencies have developed in young male America with the same scandalous rapidity they have long enjoyed in English boys' schools and in colleges of Continental Europe where dormitory rules are rigidly enforced.

Prohibition, too, may be playing its part, but the point is not here insisted upon—only the theory indicated. American flappers, who used not to know what strong liquor tasted like, since it was unmaidenly to go into a saloon, are as well supplied with pocket flasks as are the boys. It is even a smarter sin, now, to drink than it is to transgress the sex code. Heavy drinking, as every physician knows—and every prostitute—rapidly lessens the potency of the male, though it stimulates the desire of the female. With the boys maudlin from their hip flasks, the girls are comparatively safe. The sexual life, con-

4

sequently, may be growing more and more sterile, thanks to Volstead-ism, and sterility is a potent factor in the transformation we are investigating. The boys and girls are becoming boon drinking companions—the girls rising to male heights of aggressiveness, the boys descending to female, more rapidly and surely than a quarter of a century ago when Dr. Ellis' correspondent was making his observations.

But, whatever the causes—and the author is not here to argue but to record—the "signs of the times" are unmistakable.

The wrist-watch that came in with the war—as the female prostitute was passing out—probably had its points as a military necessity, but the fact that it was universally regarded as effeminate, and yet made its way into general army and civil use, despite the jokes of the wearers themselves, paved the way for developments now rapidly in progress.

The powder puff for men is becoming a commonplace in the flashy circles, and compacts and lip-sticks are now displayed in men's furnishing stores. Silk underwear, gayly colored, delicately embroidered and occasionally even narrowly laced, can be had in any smart shop for men—one manufacturer even labels the delicate garments "S-I-S," with an explanatory parenthesis "Step-in-Suits."

Permanent waves and marcelles are sold indiscriminately to the sexes in the barber shops, and, speaking of barber shops, there is a tendency again to separate the males and females, who swarmed in when the bob came into fashion. Only, in the separation, the men's shops are equipped even more elaborately than the women's with

5

beauty preparations, for nature, slow to wake up, still insists on a beard on a male face. And extra beauty lotions and pencils are necessary to hide the annoying hair or guide it into channels of beauty. Our barbers may yet learn the Roman art of depilation practiced on Julius Cæsar and the other gay, effeminate young blades.

Even so should it be, a Columbia University instructor is quoted as calmly telling a girl newspaper reporter. "In all periods of the world's history when civilization was at its highest point, cosmetics were used extensively" by men as well as women. "This was notably true during the Egyptian and Roman empires. But in the Middle Ages, when civilization was at low ebb, cosmetics were practically unknown."

In another newspaper report, a woman beauty expert sounded an alarm: "Now that men have decided to try our lip-stick, rouge, eyebrow pencil and perhaps our curling iron, to point up the shapeless face and head, we women may have to look to our laurels."

One young man proved the good sense of the alarm by entering, for a lark, a female beauty contest in a Lowell, Mass., school, and, though he appeared in decolleté, he all but captured first prize when the late Rudolph Valentino, one of the judges, discovered the joke. In another beauty contest, in Chicago, the joke never was discovered, and female friends of a young man who had entered the contest at their instigation and who came near winning, had some bad moments fearing they had aided and abetted an imposture that might have a police court ending. They were overjoyed when their champion lost by a point or two.

6

In European art shows, there is a rapidly growing percentage of male nudes in both painting and sculpture, in comparison with female, indicating a reversion to the Greek preference for the athlete as a model over the girl of the hetairæ. In a German stadium there has been installed a workshop for sculptors, where they may study the athletes in action, as did Phidias.

In Germany, the question of the effeminate man, which is still more or less of a joke with us, has long been taken seriously, and the "intermediate sex" has been fighting for its rights, social and even political, as determinedly as women have fought and won in America.

Our American joke gets broader and broader as the years flit by. The theater fairly reeks with this brand of "humor." Female impersonation is no longer confined to the delicate, sly satire of a Julian Eltinge or the slap-stick burlesque of a George Munro—men imitating and good-naturedly making fun of the foibles of women.

The stage is full of chorus men, with all the symptoms of homosexuality worn on the sleeve. The comedians of the musical revues can hardly escape wearing a red necktie in some skit or other, with the broadest hints of its acquired significance, and they and the vaudeville comedians are continually invading more and more the regions of the pathologically effeminate. Disagreeable homosexual suggestion is so prevalent in the programs of the "jazz bands" as to become almost an identification mark.

This book is not a treatise, however, on the homosexual—in the early stages of the investigation, in fact, the pathological significance in female impersonation was excluded. The author was seeking only

7

men who had masqueraded in female clothes for some dramatic reason, either on the stage or in life—as Commodus, the Roman Emperor did, for example, to complete the illusion that he was Hercules reincarnated, or as Achilles was forced by his mother to do to avoid draft for the Trojan war. This rigid exclusion was found, after a while, to be impracticable, and, though the book will be discovered, in its overwhelming percentage, to be anecdotal of exploits of the female masqueraders, considerations of homosexuality are not dodged when apparently necessary.

Inversion, undoubtedly, or a strong tendency in that direction, is the mainspring in the vast majority of cases under consideration, but there is just as certainly a radically different factor that satisfactorily explains others. Dr. Bernard S. Talmey, of New York, who has had five men of this type among his patients, some of them female impersonators on the professional stage, names the impulse "transvestism" —a "desire for cross-dressing," that is for the male to dress like a woman, or the female to dress like a man.

"The longings for cross-dressing in our cases"—the five cases to which he has devoted acute attention, and which he minutely analyses in his book entitled "Love"—"may be best explained, that the feminine strain, normally found in every male, exists here in greatly exaggerated form. Every normal woman attributes an exaggerated value to clothes and, Narcissus-like, is more or less enamored with the female body. The same exaggerated value to female clothes is attributed by the male transvestites."

In my investigations, I have found very little popular interest dis-

8

played either in actresses playing men's rôles on the stage or in women assuming male attire in real life, in comparison with the opposite phenomenon. About the only brilliant exceptions are Mlle. de Maupin and Joan of Arc. Sex scarcely enters into the consideration of Joan— she remained feminine in male armor, and her exploits are those of a woman of fine courage, not of a man. Mlle. de Maupin, however, matches for interest any of the males who stepped into petticoats. Becoming a man, La Maupin was fierce as a lover—fiercer still as a duellist—as fierce, in this latter respect, as was the Chevalier d'Eon, who so frequently forgot his woman's attire when provoked to draw his sword. Maude Adams as Peter Pan, Sarah Bernhardt as Hamlet have none of the interest of Julian Eltinge or Edward Kynaston. They are accepted as sexless and mild—to be considered as artists, not as persons.

Maybe Dr. Talmey has hit upon the explanation. "The female transvestite," he continues, where we left off above, "on the other hand, thinks of clothes more or less as men do. Yet, the male strain in her, being a morbid phenomenon, dressing is of more importance to her than it is to the normal man."

In a foot-note Dr. Talmey sets out an analysis of the female mind worth quoting in its entirety, and going a long way to explain her deeper interest, as a general thing, in actresses than in actors—an interest that would account, as a corollary, for the hold Julian Eltinge once held on women playgoers:

"This" (her being enamored with the female body) "is the psychological explanation for woman's love of histrionic spectacles.

9

Almost two-thirds of all theatergoers are certainly women. Still so much demi-nude femininity is presented on the stage, presumably to amuse men and so few semi-nude men for the amusement of women. Why do so many women run to the theaters to see the nudity of their own sex? Men do not care for the sight of nude men. The reason is that feminine nudity is presented on the stage not for the amusement of the few men, but mostly for the amusement of the great throng of women."

(In further support of Dr. Talmey's observations, it may be remarked that when semi-nude men do appear on the stage, the women show mild interest, if any. Women generally are bored by athletes and "strong men" acts in vaudeville.)

"The female body," continues Dr. Talmey, "has a sexually stimulating effect upon woman. The pride of the female, says Weininger, is something quite peculiar to herself, something foreign even to the most handsome man, an obsession of her own body, a pleasure which displays itself even in the least handsome girl, by admiring herself in the mirror, by stroking herself and by playing with her own hair, but which comes to its full measure only in the effect that her body has on man. Woman desires to feel that she is admired physically. The normal woman regards her body as made for the stimulation of the man's sensations. This complex emotion forms the initial stage of her own pleasure. The female body has hence a greater exciting effect upon women than the male body has upon men. Female nudity produces a greater impression upon her than the male body ever does. Statues of female forms are more liable than those of male forms to

10

have a stimulating effect upon woman. The same emotions are evoked in woman at the sight of female clothes.

"Woman takes it for granted that her clothes, just as her body, have an erotic effect upon the male. Hence female clothes awaken in woman a complex emotion akin to the sight of the female body. Woman becomes sexually excited by her own clothes. For this reason clothes are to woman of the greatest importance. The desire for beautiful clothes is an irradiation of the sex instinct."

Julian Eltinge, therefore, in the most stunning gowns then to be seen on the stage of America—he had learned the art of female dress from Lillian Russell, a past-mistress—was, to the women and girls in the audience, a fashion plate, just as any equally stunning-looking female would have been. But there was something else. Eltinge was not wholly feminine, even when most completely submerged in his gorgeous finery. Always, there was a lurking touch of the male, poking the slightest bit of fun at the female. The women saw him as a caricature—a distortion just enough to expose their little tricks. It touched their ever-present sense of fun—not unmixed with a little anxiety— "Just how much do these men know?" I have seen little whimsical troubled looks flit across their laughing faces at a particularly daring challenge hurled across the footlights by Eltinge.

Further light—a whole flood of it—is thrown upon this attraction of the male in petticoats for the female, in the diary of the Abbé de Choisy, one of the most brilliant men-women of history, of whom we shall hear a great deal more later. The abbé, a churchman of Paris, was a constant masquerader in female attire. He lived in the days of Louis

11

XV, and was a great friend of Louis' brother, also addicted to women's clothes. A young girl, Mademoiselle Charlotte, thrown much into his company, fell desperately in love with the abbé, and when the affair had progressed to a liaison, the abbé asked her how she came to be won. Her answer is recorded in his diary, one of the liveliest documents in the literature of scandal:

"I stood in no need of caution as I should have with a man. I saw nothing but a beautiful woman, and why should I be forbidden to love you? What advantages a woman's dress gives you! The heart of a man is there, and that makes a great impression upon us, and on the other hand, all the charms of the fair sex fascinate us, and prevent us from taking precautions."

The abbé was duly grateful for the information, being a man possessed of scientific as well as merely human curiosity. He slept with little Charlotte for many weeks and then gave her—still a virgin, he swears—to a rival lover for wife. The abbé was too much engrossed with his own beauty, he explains, to molest hers.

With these little preliminary peeps into feminine psychology, let the procession of Venus Castina start. Maybe the world will watch, as well as America. For Pope Pius in his encyclical of May 12, 1928, just at hand, deplores the present education of male youth throughout Christendom, as "spoiled by too effeminate care."

II. THE HERO AS WOMAN—
ACHILLES, HERCULES, SAMSON

THE Hero as Woman—there's one Carlyle missed. Yet, had he chosen to consider that species, the Sage of Chelsea would have found in history an abundance of candidates for the honor of a not uncoveted spotlight. Warriors, there are, and statesmen, and kings, and prophets, and—gods. All masquerading in petticoats—a curiously vain herd—parading the vanity of muscular prowess in battle, of intellect in the forum—of perfumed, depilated beauty, swathed in soft silks, in the boudoir.

Of such, at the glimmering dawn of history is Achilles. The picture as we here redraw it is scarcely credible to the reader of rugged Homer. The old epic poet's son of Thetis, pursuing the brawny Hector thrice around the walls of Troy, breathing fiery vengeance for the murder of Patroclus, in no way suggests a painted chorus man in a Broadway musical comedy. Not so beefy, perhaps, as Ajax, swollen of muscle and ox-like of intellect, but spare, lithe

13

and sinewy as the winner of an Olympiad, before whose godlike form bend all maidens in abject worship.

And yet, it was among such maidens, and in the scanty flowing robes of old Greece that this same Achilles, ten years earlier, fooled so sharp an eye as that of Ulysses, wisest of men. (It would be interesting to see what Ulysses and Solomon could do with an examination for college entrance today.)

The tale is not in Homer, but is of a later time, when "higher criticism" dared start an investigation of the Homeric monopoly of things sacred just as we outside of Tennessee dare pry into the machinery of the Mosaic legend. Herodotus, for one, unearthed the astonishing fact that Helen was never taken to Troy at all, but was detained in Egypt, and was turned over to her outraged husband after the fall of the city of Priam.

Investigation, aided and abetted by vivid imagination, uncovered many interesting incidents in the life of Achilles, and the stories and scandals of his pre-Trojan days finally were crystallized in the "Achilleis" of the Roman poet Statius.

There it is disclosed that while the handsome boy, semi-god, was under the tutelage of the Centaur Chiron on Mount Pelion, his mother, the discreet sea nymph Thetis, hearing prophetic rumbles of the Trojan war, paid a visit to her old enemy. For it was Chiron who had taught the hot-blooded Peleus how to catch and tame the wily, resisting nymph and make her the mother of Achilles. She persuaded the Centaur to give up his pupil, whom she took with her through the seas to the Island of Scyros, where she attired him as a girl and set him free in the luxuriant gardens of King Lycomedes, her friend, to gambol with the king's fifty daughters.

If forty-nine of them were deceived, the lovely Deidamia was not so dumb—but list rather to the eloquence of the poet Bion, to whom Statius was indebted for certain of his material. Bion relates how the heroes of Greece were arming to proceed against Troy to recapture Helen and avenge the honor of Menelaus, so bitterly assailed by Paris—

"But Achilles alone lay hid among the daughters of Lycomedes, and was trained to work in wools, in place of arms, and in his white hand held the bough of maidenhood, in semblance a maiden. For he put on women's ways, like them, and a bloom like theirs blushed on his cheek of snow, and he walked with maiden gait, and covered his locks with the snood.

"But the heart of a man had he, and the love of a man. From dawn to dark he would sit by Deidamia, and anon would kiss her hand, and oft would lift the beautiful warp of her loom and praise the sweet threads, having no such joy in any other girl of her company. Yea, all things he essayed, and all for one end, that they twain might share an undivided sleep.

"Now he once even spake to her saying: 'With one another other sisters sleep, but I lie alone, and alone, maiden, dost thou lie, both being girls unwedded of like age, both fair, and single both in bed do we sleep. The wicked Nysa, the crafty nurse it is that cruelly severs me from thee. For not of thee have I. . . .' "

Only a fragment of Bion is preserved, and, of course, it has to

15

break off here. But, fortunately there is a preliminary stanza, in which Myrson supplicates Lycidas for the tale he proceeds to sing: "A song of Scyra, Lycidas, is my desire—a sweet love-story—the stolen kisses of the son of Peleus, the stolen bed of love; how he, that was a boy, did on the weeds of women, and how he belied his form, and how among the heedless daughters of Lycomedes, Deidamia cherished Achilles in her bower."

Later poets complete the story. The lovely Deidamia, who may have succumbed innocently to the wiles of Achilles at the outset, found him much more to her liking as a bed-fellow than her other sisters, after she had discovered his true nature, and she so utilized the discovery that a short time after the departure of Achilles, to whom she bade a tearful and passionate farewell, she gave birth to a son. This boy was the precocious Neoptolemus, who slew King Priam and became possessor of Andromache, widow of Hector, whom he made his mistress and his slave.

Returning to Scyros and the days when Achilles was lifting the beautiful warp of Deidamia's loom—in the daytime. The Greek princes, preparing to move on Troy, knew how invaluable would be the services of the strong young son of Thetis, and they sent Ulysses and Diomed in search of him.

After some difficulty, the emissaries learned of his whereabouts and of his mother's crafty move. Ulysses disguised himself as a merchant and sailed for Scyros with loads of silks and fine linens. Admitted to the garden of the king, and surrounded by the fifty-one eager girls, he began laying out his wares. The princesses crowded excitedly

16

around, fingering the fine textures in voluptuous delight. The fact that Achilles was not yet detectable, crushing in his hands the silks as eagerly as the rest, might argue for his fitness, in days of peace, as a chorus man.

But, among the textiles, Ulysses had hidden some pieces of armor. When these were disclosed, one of the girls suddenly lost interest in the gauzy gew-gaws, and sprang eagerly for sword and shield.

"Ah-ha!" cried Ulysses—or the Greek equivalent.

He took off his wig, disclosed his identity, made known his mission—and a few hours later, the prospective father of Neoptolemus was on the high seas, chatting blithely with the Prince of Ithaca, laying plans for the approaching war.

Non-Homeric as is this later embroidery of the Achilles legend, it does not conflict directly with the Homeric conception—there is something strikingly lady-like in "Achilles' wrath, to Greece the direful spring of woes unnumbered," the theme of the Iliad—a wrath petulant, if not silly, in view of the grave issues at stake.

Achilles, by the time Homer took him in hand, had abandoned ruffles, and was carrying on an intrigue with a Trojan damsel of high rank. He had a comrade in arms, the stern Patroclus—

Later poets and dramatists were not content with that Homeric conception, either.

Æschylus and Sophocles were among those who meddled, and from fragments of plays no longer extant is reconstructed a new Patroclus—a perfumed youth of mincing step, rival of Briseis, the Trojan damsel, daughter of Troy's high priest, for the affections of

17

Achilles. Because Briseis was taken from him by Commander-in-Chief Agamemnon, Achilles sulked in his tent, and let the Greeks all but lose the war. Because Hector slew Patroclus, Achilles arose again in his mighty wrath, avenged the blood of his comrade or his catamite in the blood of Hector—and then took unto himself a new comrade, Antilocus, son of Nestor.

Another pair of Trojan heroes later transformed into lover and beloved were Idomeneus, king and military leader of the Cretans, and Meriones, a handsome young noble in his ranks. In other lands and among other nationalities the same doubtful honor has been paid other comrades—David and Jonathan, for example, and Damon and Pythias.

Already it must begin to be apparent to the observant reader that Carlyle overlooked a bet, and we pass on now to Hercules, the prize strong man of Greece. Had there been a Tex Rickard extant, he would undoubtedly have been matched for the world's championship against the strong man of the Jews, Samson—who also, astonishing as it may seem, comes within the scope of our inquiry.

The Hercules legend is worthy the serious attention of the psychoanalysts. This heroic personification of rugged strength, this apparently pure type of animal masculinity, even to a bovine stupidity, nevertheless falls so far under the domination of a woman that he surrenders to her his club and his lion's skin, dons her habiliments, and sits spinning at her distaff. And furthermore, in an Achillean phase, he becomes the slave of an effeminate youth, for whom he undertakes the famous Twelve Labors.

The petulance of the pretty youth, Eurystheus, who could not be

18

satisfied with hardships already undergone by his bovine admirer and slave, but spurred him on and on for labor after labor, made him the model in after days of degenerate Greece and Rome for handsome boys who had in their toils warriors and knights to whom they assigned difficult undertakings.

The slavery to Omphale, queen of the Lydians, followed the release of Hercules from the witchery of the fair Eurystheus, and it was begun as an act of penance for the slaying of another youth, Iphitus (not unlikely, also, an Achillean friend) in a moment of blind rage.

Instead of undertaking another series of labors, Hercules decided to humiliate himself by donning women's garb and working for three years, giving the proceeds of his industry to the boy's father.

Omphale rather liked the arrangement, it would seem. She not only put on the lion's skin and brandished the club, but assumed a tone of Amazonian command, ordering her gigantic "maid" about the house, seeing that the slayer of the hydra polished the pans properly and making him quite an expert at spinning, weaving and embroidery.

The effemination of Hercules in the service of Omphale, as well as the conception of Eurystheus as a catamite are of the Greek decadence and do not belong to the original rugged legend, any more than does the conception of Achilles and Patroclus as lovers.

Moreover, the Hercules-Omphale legend has undergone a still further striking transformation in modern times, at the hands of a Continental playwright, who incorporated certain Sadistic and Masochistic elements.

Omphale, in the Greek, already mature and a widow, is made in

19

the modern version a beautiful young girl, playing with her sisters and slaves in the garden of her father, King Sardanus, to whom Hercules has been sold into temporary bondage to pay, with his labor, for the death of Iphitus.

A mischievous faun enters the garden, and with ravishing music and the languishing sighs of a lover makes a bold attempt to seduce Omphale. At first amused, the girl becomes indignant, and drives him away.

Hercules appears at this moment, clad in his lion's skin and brandishing his club. The girls are fascinated—none more so than Omphale, who sets about winning his attentions. Hercules at first assumes a stubborn resistance, but soon melts, and lies down at her feet. Overjoyed at her triumph, Omphale proceeds to show her companions how complete it is, and persuades the hero to exchange his lion's skin for her silken robe and his club for her distaff.

While they are caressing each other, back trips the impudent faun. Mistaking Hercules for Omphale, he rushes up to him, pushes away the lion-skin-clad princess, takes the hero in his arms, and whispers to him words of endearment. Indignantly astonished, Hercules springs to his feet, seizes the faun, hurls him high over the garden wall. Turning to the princess, he finds her laughing heartily at the escapade. This modern Hercules hasn't any lighter intellect than the bull-necked strong man of the Greeks. Wrathfully he seizes Omphale, strips from her the lion's skin, picks up a little whip with which she was toying just before the faun's reappearance, and proceeds to give her the lashing of her life.

This modern version, of course, has none of the flavor of the old Greek myth left, and the experienced reader will recognize in it the elements of degeneracy that go to make up the far finer "Salome" of Oscar Wilde.

In his affections for pretty lads, Hercules was more famous for the strength of his devotions than for their constancy to any one particular object. What jealousies must have assailed the hairless breasts of the pretty catamites.

In addition to Eurystheus and the ill-fated Iphitus, there was Hylas—"Beautiful Hylas—Hylas of the braided locks—never was he apart from Hylas." This youth accompanied him on the Argonautic expedition. In spite of their inseparability, celebrated by Theocritus, Hylas went without his mighty friend ashore on the island of Myria to draw water. Naiads spying the handsome youngster, kidnapped him in a frenzy of non-lymphatic passion, and hid him so effectually Hercules never was able to find him, though long he wandered up and down the island, "the cruel goddess of Love rending his heart within him."

Another of his favorites was Iolaus, his nephew and charioteer. "His passion for Iolaus was so famous that lovers swore their oaths upon the Theban's tomb." Iolaus survived the hero, and was the first to offer sacrifices to his manes as a demi-god.

It is significant of the general smirching of the name and fame of Hercules that the tainted Roman Emperor Commodus, puppet gladiator and inordinately vain stage player, should have hit upon the hero of the Twelve Labors as his model. The pronounced bias of fem-

21

ininity in the Emperor's nature was satisfied, along with his vanity to pose as a man of enormous strength.

The Hebrew Samson was effeminated by his Delilah much after the manner of Hercules by Omphale—one of many links in the chain forged by students in comparative religion connecting the Greek and Hebrew mythologies. Both Samson and Hercules have been identified, in etymological consideration of their names, with the sun. Instead of spinning, like Hercules, Samson was set grinding corn—distinctly a woman's work in those days.

The cutting of Samson's hair, too, is a symbolic act of effemination. "It is very interesting," says Freud in "Totem and Taboo," "that among primitive men circumcision is combined with or replaced by the cutting off of the hair and the drawing of the teeth, and that our children, who cannot know anything about this, really treat these two operations as equivalents to castration when they display their fear of them. Previously Dr. Freud had observed that "when children learn about ritual circumcision they identify it with castration."

It is a matter of common observation, in this connection, that little girls do not resist barbers as do little boys, and that since bobbed hair has become the style with mature girls and women they are far more docile under the annoying snip-snip of the scissors than are men.

The effemination of Hercules and of Samson may not be so much of a physical miracle or a psychological mystery as it appears on the face of the legends. It may be that the explanation is no more abstruse than this:

When they were put to the voluptuous test by passionate women

22

like Omphale and Delilah they were found wanting! These giants of strength were revealed as without sexual vigor to satisfy appetite so keen—to their disappointed mistresses they seemed worthy only of the kirtle!

"A hairy man is either strong or sensual," says a Latin proverb.

With this aphorism Ninon de l'Enclos, one of the renowned voluptuaries of history, was familiar. The great Condé, when a youth in the early flush of his victories in war, joined the multitude of moths that hovered quivering around the dazzling beauty. Nothing could be refused the handsome, gigantic prince by the ladies of the French court —least of all by the susceptible Ninon. One evening in bed, a few days after the beginning of the liaison, she gazed with admiration at his muscular arms and shoulders, and his hairy chest. "Ah Monseigneur," she sighed, "you must be very strong!"

Among the wild, nomadic Scythians the "female disease," as Herodotus calls it, was common. These powerful, hairy-chested warriors were effeminate to a marked degree.

"Plutarch repeats the old Greek statement that the Bœotians, the Lacedemonians, and the Cretans were the most warlike stocks because they were the strongest in love; an army composed of loving homosexual couples, it was held," according to Havelock Ellis, "would be invincible."

The Amazons were not women at all, but beardless young men "whose traditions made them shave their faces and wear their hair in braids," if a contemporary German archæologist, Dr. Emil Forrer, is not mistaken in his reading of certain Hittite clay tablets. According to newspaper reports of Dr. Forrer's discoveries, the Amazons "were merely the product of mistaken identity." In an age when beards proclaimed the fighting man, "it was natural that the Greeks should mistake these beardless warriors for virgins and that legends should grow up around them."

John Addington Symonds, examining photographs of a great number of modern athletes, so often pictured displaying their muscular charms, was struck with the frequency of signs revealing to his experienced gaze undoubted effeminacy.

When college boys engage in amateur theatricals, it not seldom occurs that the prettiest "chorus girls" are football or track heroes.

Every "female impersonator" on the professional stage is press-agented as an athlete—and not infrequently they are so.

On the American stage is a giant negro actor, whose swelling muscles have caused many chocolate female hearts to flutter, but who is insensible to their charms, and spends the time in his dressing room crocheting. His muscular strength is as real as it is apparent.

Any frequenter of prize fights, observant in matters of this sort, must have noticed the comparative frequency of unmistakable feminine mannerisms in contestants.

In Japan, the wrestlers knot their hair feminine fashion when engaging in a contest, and might well be mistaken for Amazons by strangers.

Breitbart, the Polish strong man, who could drive nails into heavy timbers with his bare hands, could use with those same hands a threaded needle very daintily. "He cooks, sews, darns hose, washes dishes and often puts his six-year-old son to bed," according to a newspaper report, which quotes his wife as adding, "He is as gentle as he is strong and takes a delight in doing the little things that most men despise."

"I like to embroider," Ray Pelkey, American light-heavyweight pugilist, is quoted in an interview. "Of course, if I were not a fighter I presume I would not have the courage to admit I like it."

"Since Rumania wrested Transylvania from the Austrians," reports the Associated Press, "efforts have been made to get the men to discard their skirts and wear modern masculine attire. But they have resisted all attempts to deprive them of their hand-embroidered shirtwaists and lace-trimmed petticoats." The courage of the men of Transylvania is no more questioned than that of the kilted Scotch Highlanders.

Achilles, Hercules and Samson—their psychology, if mysterious, is still not unparalleled.

III. THE GODS IN FINE LACES

THE priests of the gods, from history's dawn in Asia and Egypt down to the richly-robed Roman prelates of today, have set themselves conspicuously apart from their fellow males by the assumption of female attire—or attire approximating the feminine. Maybe the gods themselves are responsible—not only the sinful, gentle gods of the heathen but—

"The Lord God walking in the garden in the cool of the day" might have been dressed as appropriately in female garments as in male—that he had some clothes on is inferred from the fact that he didn't shock Adam and Eve, that morbidly modest pair who had hid their charms from each other with fig leaves.

"God created man in his own image; male and female created he them," the writer of Genesis states, and elsewhere repeats: "In the day that God created man, in the likeness of God made he them; and God blessed them, and called their name Adam." The insistence on the plural, including Eve along with Adam, has been taken to indicate, by certain thinkers in ancient times and modern, that both conformed to the appearance of their creator.

Moreover, the Talmud records that Adam originally was androgynous—that he was in the exact image of God—female as well as male. Philo, a Jewish philosopher who lived in the days of Jesus, re-affirms this belief, and goes on to relate that "God separated Adam into his two sexual component parts, one male, the other female—Eve—taken from his side.

"The longing for reunion which love inspired in the divided halves of the originally dual being, is the source of the sexual pleasure."

Philo seems to have borrowed his theory of love from Plato, and to have linked it up with the Talmudic fable. Plato, in turn, may have had access to the Jewish mythology, for he alleges the first human beings were androgynous and were separated by Zeus into unisexual halves.

The priest, then, in attiring himself to resemble his god, would be as rightfully entitled to female garments as to male.

Whether the gods were responsible, or more human causes that will gradually unfold as we proceed, it is certain that by the time of Moses the effemination of the priesthood of all the gods throughout Egypt and Asia had become a matter of scandal.

When Moses made himself the champion of Jehovah or Jah, the local god of Mount Sinai, and proclaimed him a "jealous god," threatening dire wrath on whomsoever should place any other god before him, he instituted some drastic reforms. The character of this god was to be sternly masculine. No one "who hath his stones broken" might come into his presence. The sins of Sodom were punishable by death. The priests, however hard up for money they might be (a chronic condition of the priesthood) could not accept "the hire of a whore or the price of a dog"—a terrible libel the translators in the days of good King James inflicted on the poor dog!

Moses thundered and his Hebrews trembled—but the gilded temptations flaunted by the heathen around them were as irresistible as a leg show to a village deacon. The Old Testament is as full of scandal from cover to cover as a New York tabloid.

Even those shining heroes, David and Solomon were human, and not infrequently fell from grace. David's ministrations as a boy musician to Saul and his friendship for Jonathan, "passing the love of women," have placed him under grave suspicions. His life, whether these suspicions be justified or not, was one long series of frenzied sins and bitter repentance.

Solomon, who had more "guts" than his father, and who would fit into the modern world as a gorgeous pagan, not only experimented freely in the choice of wives and concubines from all conceivable ranks of the heathen, but openly visited their "high places," as David doubtless had done secretly.

David had always on his neck the terrible Samuel, ready to rebuke him in the name of the Lord God for every transgression—as completely in God's confidence as a modern evangelist. When it came to such matters as "high places," Samuel knew whereof he spake, for, in his youth, he had been a "consecrated one," an expression that sounds pious enough, until somebody like Dr. Thomas Inman pries into the duties of such an one and find them to be "the service which the name Kadesh or Kodesh implies." This word "Kadesh" is translated in the Bible, according to Dr. Inman, as "Sodomite."

"The mind revolts at the belief that one thus debased could ever attain to a high political or religious eminence," pursues Dr. Inman, speaking of Samuel, David's mentor and tormentor. "But history tells us of more than one illustrious statesman, who has grovelled in the dirt that he might attain to dignity. The names of Alcibiades and Julius Cæsar are familiar to us all, but their early vices are known to few."

The "consecration" of Samuel was of a character for which the Levites became notoriously suspected in the decadent days of Israel— days long after the burial of Moses, days when the prophets thundered as even Moses had not.

The scenes that transpired in the "high places"—the groves of the heathen gods where Solomon went "slumming"—were reconstructed by a French writer in the Napoleonic era, and thus translated and transcribed by Dr. Inman:

"Atys sleeps, the Phrygians say, and he ought to awake with nature. The third day of the feast recalls his mutilation. At length joy breaks out, and is manifested by delirious movements.

"Then are to be seen the frenetic priests of Cybele rushing about in bands, with haggard eyes and hair disordered, like troops of Bacchanals, or foaming Pythonesses. In one hand they brandish the sacred knife, in the other they carry burning firebrands from the pine

29

tree. They dive into the recesses of the woods and valleys, and climb mountains, uttering while they do so the most horrible groanings. An intoxicating draught has carried madness to their brain; they turn upon themselves their active hands, and beat each other with heavy chains; they dance and regard with joy the blood which flows from their bodies, flagellate their backs, and at length mutilate themselves completely, in honor of the god whose coming they await, and they invoke his name while offering to him their gaping wounds and the bleeding spoils of their virility.

"These mutilations are also made in honor or commemoration of the dismemberment suffered by Osiris, Mithras, Adonis, Esum, and Bacchus; and by them is explained, in allegorical style, the cessation of the active male or fecundating power of the sun at the Autumnal equinox."

"The author then," continues Dr. Inman, "quotes Matthew xix. 12, where it is said approvingly, 'that some have made themselves eunuchs for the sake of the Kingdom of Heaven,' and states that 'Origen, one of the Christian fathers of the Church, reduced himself to the same condition as did the priests of Cybele.' "

When the participants in the Feast of Atys and similar wild orgies, common throughout Egypt and Asia, had recovered from the self-inflicted injury, they adopted female dress. Galli, these eunuchs were called.

Not only did the Jews tolerate the "high places" among them, but they so far forgot the stern masculine Jah of Moses as to imitate the rites. "There is little doubt," comments Dr. Inman, "that the

'Sodomites,' which are referred to in the 'Books of Kings,' were individuals who had been emasculated in wild orgies similar to those described, the intention being that they might conserve as long as possible the softness and graces of youths."

The Jews had traveled a long way from Jah of Sinai, who had admonished: "The women shall not wear that which pertaineth unto a man, neither shall a man put on a woman's garment: for all that do so are abomination unto the Lord thy God."

Moses, spokesman of Jehovah, wasn't speaking pettishly here, as we too often suspect he is doing until we look deeper into the matter. He was not worrying especially about the women, but he included them in his decree the better to protect the sex organs of the males—a constant concern of Moses, amounting almost to an obsession. In such orgies as we have witnessed thru the vivid lens of the anonymous Frenchman—orgies Moses had seen repeatedly with his own eyes—the women also indulged; and when the frenzy reached its height, it was no unusual happening for them to strip off their garments and give them to the men, who gave theirs in exchange. The assumption of women's garments had the effect of spurring on the male devotees to convert themselves as nearly as possible into women.

These eunuchs became the material from which the priests were made. It was such as they, wearing women's garments, that conducted the rites in the temples of the mysterious and potent Syrian goddess —Dea Syria—a goddess who particularly aroused the jealous, anxious wrath of Jah of Sinai. At the shrine of Venus in Cyprus, not only the priests but all male worshippers dressed as women. In processions in

31

honor of Bacchus, himself an effeminate god, Greek men were clothed in women's stoles. At Coos, the priest of Hercules sacrificed in female dress. The Argives, in celebration of rites in honor of the new moon, were clad as women. In Althis, the worshippers of Venus offered sacrifices in female attire.

It was into a world like this that Jesus made his advent.

For some reason or other, a holy dread of sacrilege prevents every attempt to assign masculine attributes to the Nazarene, and it has been so since about the third century of our era.

In those earlier days, however, there seems to have been circulated quite freely a tale to the effect that the lovely Mary Magdalen, before her conversion, "had a criminal intimacy with the Savior of the world" —a tale that even Voltaire shuddered to repeat. And yet, a general revival of that story might be salutary now, when Nietzsche's charge against Christianity, that it is morbidly effeminate, is felt vaguely to be true even by people who never heard of Zarathustra. In the late war, the attempts of the priests to convert into a Warrior God the gentle Prince of Peace, were peculiarly lamentable.

The spirit of effeminacy has been felt in religion from prehistoric times, arising out of the musings of eunuch priests and prophets— either physical castrates or mental—and Christianity is no exception.

Rather, this spirit reaches its climax in the religion instituted by Jesus, and made a practical going concern by St. Paul.

We have seen how Moses, reacting from effeminating rites about him, attempted to make a sternly male god of Jah of Sinai, and how he failed, because of the influence of the "heathen" upon his priesthood.

32

The interpretation and enforcement of the Mosaic ideal, reaffirmed by fiery prophets like Isaiah and Jeremiah, was a live question in the day of Jesus—the day, too, when Philo was speculating on the androgynous character of Adam.

Jesus repeatedly softened and nullified the Mosaic prohibitions, and one instance is of special interest for us here—"there be eunuchs, which have made themselves eunuchs for the kingdom of heaven's sake." He added with mysterious significance, that never has been cleared up: "He that is able to receive it, let him receive it."

It would have been interesting to watch the expression of his face at that moment—a daring speculation arises—did he think then of the Magdalen? In repentance, had he—"there be eunuchs, which have made themselves eunuchs for the kingdom of heaven's sake!"

The passage occurs after an argument of peculiar bitterness with the Pharisees on the question of marriage and divorce, and from the context there is no apparent reason for this outburst about eunuchs. Either Matthew was a bad reporter or something was preying on the mind of Jesus when the disciples took up the argument where the Pharisees had left off. "All men cannot receive this saying, save they to whom it is given," he told them confidentially.

The love of Jesus for his disciple John has been compared with the love of David for Jonathan, and, by a late writer, with the love of Shakespeare for the boy of the sonnets. This love stands out even more strongly than in the cases of David and Shakespeare, in view of the fact that Jesus appears, in the gospel narrative, peculiarly callous to women—a callousness so pronounced, in fact, that it would be com-

33

mented on freely in any other historical personage. The only offset to this general frigidity is the Magdalen legend.

Mithras, chief rival of Jesus for religious domination of Rome, was a castrate, and the rites in celebration of this Indo-Iranian sun god and "savior" were typical of those of all the effeminate gods of the East. It was only by the fantastic accident of the Emperor Constantine, a man of no religious conviction, of no morals and little judgment, deciding for Christianity against the equally potent Mithraism, that Christ instead of Mithras was enthroned. The apostate Julian attempted a restoration of the power of Mithras, but Christianity had gathered too much momentum during its protection by Constantine. The Christians accused—and still accuse—the devotees of Mithras of stealing their thunder. He was virgin-born, for example; he was mediator between God and man; he celebrated a sacred banquet of bread and wine; he washed away the sins of the world in blood—not in his own blood, as Christ had done, but in the blood of the sacred bull. I find no reference, however, to the castration and effemination of Mithras being suggested by any similar phenomenon in the life of Jesus.

The Mithras rites and the early Christ rites were so similar, however, and the two became so confused in the popular mind, that the effeminacy of Mithras may have crept into the early representations of Jesus in art. That the Christ figure as conceived by sculptors and painters throughout history has been generally effeminate—sometimes almost or quite to the point of the androgynous—is inescapable. This visualization of him, under sanction of Mother Church in the old

34

times, may have had a lot to do with the general feeling the world since has had with regard to him.

In the earliest days, when the only painters were the monks, the younger and handsomer monks of the monasteries served as models, not only for the Christ but for the Virgin as well. The traits that made a young monk popular in a community whence women were barred may, unfortunately, have helped fix the type of Christ in art. That the monkish models could pose for the Virgin, too, is significant.

Even in our late day, Christ has not lost the stamp early impressed on him. "Most pictures of Jesus during the last century give him a distinctly feminine look," writes the exceedingly erudite G. Stanley Hall. "The brow, cheek and nose, if all below were covered, would generally be taken for those of a refined and superior woman. . . . The beard is usually, though not always, light, exposing the upper part of the chin, and its scantiness, with the usually very copious hair of the scalp and the feminine features, sometimes almost suggests a bearded lady."

A portrait of Christ, with the feminine characteristics carried to the extreme, was exhibited in the Art Institute of Chicago for a few weeks some summers ago. The general appearance was in the Italian tradition, modified by the German, but the effemination was peculiarly exaggerated, aided by a smile playing around a pair of lips easily recognizable by anyone experienced in the psychology of degeneracy. The painter, a devout young man, seemed unconscious of the effect of his Christ on persons who knew, and the general public accepted the picture in the spirit of reverence in which it was painted.

Dr. Hall cites the Jesus in Liska's celebrated "Gethsemane"—"his

35

matted hair falls upon his shoulders, his face is turned upward, and his vestment also suggests feminine dishabille. The hair is usually wavy," he proceeds, "and sometimes, as in Reni's 'Ecce Homo,' almost suggestive of an Addisonian wig." Guido Reni, moreover, did a famous picture of Jesus as a boy with his inseparable companion—"John is splendidly virile, young as he is," comments Dr. Hall, "and Jesus looks like a beautiful, delicate, and precocious girl."

The Virgins of art, this psychologist suggests, "should not be superior to its Christs, nor the latter be more effeminate or bisexual in appearance than masculine. The lack of truly male Christs in art," he proceeds, "is now all the more significant, with the decline of dogma, religion is construed less in terms of intellect and more in those of conduct, and perhaps we might say that piety is now becoming more æsthetic even than ethical."

With another conclusion of Dr. Hall's, however, we are not inclined to agree. He had collected photographs and reproductions of some fourscore representations of Christ by painters of all ages, which he used to exhibit to his students at Clark University.

"I have often showed my collection of masterpieces to women, and while there are plenty of expressions of devout enthusiasm, those of indifference or even aversion seemed more honest. This certainly raises the question whether, as a whole, artists have done their duty to commend Jesus to women, who are his most devoted worshippers, making him conform to their ideal of what a manly man should be."

On the whole, Holy Church is wiser instinctively than Dr. Hall, however stupid it may be intellectually. This effeminate Christ, even

though his physiognomy, in some of the older representations, would "fit a criminal, weakling, or even idiot," as Dr. Hall further alleges, will hold the religious devotions of women far longer than a Christ with swelling muscles. Jah of Sinai never could have become popular with women. Hercules repelled them, but they followed Dionysius in vast, eager throngs all over Greece and Asia. Sandow today leaves our women cold—they want Valentino.

Whether or not the historical Jesus was a gallus, like Mithras, it is certain that only the feminine side of what may once have been a well-balanced genius has been preserved. Holy Church saw to that in the winnowing out of the many gospels, documents and letters once extant, and the condensation into the New Testament of all that was fit to give its devotees.

Of the effemination of the Hebrew strong man Samson we have already spoken, and of the services of the boy Samuel in the temple. Dr. Inman, in his epochal research, digested in two heavy volumes: "Ancient Faiths Embodied in Ancient Names," from which we have already quoted, made a startling discovery when he came to examine into the derivations of "Esau" and "Jacob."

The names of the twins, he found, signify literally "male" and "female"—"embodiments of the same idea as Adam and Eve, Mahadeva and Saraiswati, Abraham and Sarah," symbolizing, that is to say, "a man and a woman," with Jacob in the rôle of female.

"To allow the Jewish people to trace their descent from a male rather than a female," Dr. Inman goes on to state, "the appellation of Israel was substituted in later productions" of the mystic story.

But Jacob, even in the final version that has come down to us, is represented as smooth of face, soft voiced, an excellent cook, the favorite of his mother, and full of wiles of a characteristically feminine complexion.

Odd is this interpretation, in light of Dr. Otto Weininger's conclusions in his profound, if lurid and perverse, investigations into the psychic characteristics of the Jewish race (his own) that the Jew is intellectually and emotionally feminine—that his mental processes are those of a woman.

Placing his conclusions and Dr. Inman's side by side, it would almost seem that the father of the race, in his transformation from the woman Jacob to the man Israel, retained in his new body the female mind, and transmitted it to his posterity!

But, laying that fantastic speculation aside as only a curiosity, Jacob was undoubtedly of the ancient cult of phallic worshippers— a relic of his devotion is the stone on which he rested his head during his dream of the ladder ascending to Paradise. The stone is now in the British throne chair—and the ladder a very curious ornament in the theories of the psychoanalysts.

As a devotee of the phallic stone, perhaps as a priest, Jacob, in accordance with the custom of the East, would have worn the garments of a woman while at worship. This fact, which Dr. Inman has failed to note, while complicating the legend somewhat, makes easier to modern comprehension the sex duality of the patriarch. Dr. Inman makes him female from his mother's womb—the female who closely followed at birth the male Esau. A theory based on his habits as a

38

priest of the phallic stone, would make him only effeminate instead of physically female.

With their great ancestor, Israel, thus vaguely effeminate, is it any wonder the followers of Moses occasionally dared brave the wrath of Jah of Sinai—that even the priests stole away clandestinely from the Ark of Jehovah for the more inviting "high places" of the heathen? At any rate, so flagrant were the delinquencies that the whole organization of priestly Levites were under suspicion, not only of witnessing the revelries, but of participating in them. The exchange of dress, the male with the female, "excited concupiscence, and gave occasion to whoredom" and worse, if the prophets are to be believed.

The softening by Jesus of the Mosaic law, and his recognition of emasculation "for the kingdom of heaven's sake" didn't make much of a hit with Saint Paul. By the time he assumed command, the inevitable result of the gallus system, in religion or out, was working, and Paul entered a drastic protest against "men with men working that which is unseemly." But still later, the blessed Origen, who failed of sainthood because of his act, "reduced himself to the same condition as did the priests of Cybele," and his example was followed to an extent that became alarming.

"I may also notice as a remarkable fact," Dr. Inman proceeds, "that the church of Rome, whose worship resembles in so many particulars that offered in various places to Ishtar, Astarte, Venus, or Cybele, still retains the use of eunuchs in her church in the eternal city. The idea seems to be that the Almighty delights in what men call fine music, and that it is better that the treble notes shall be chanted

39

by mutilated men than by ordinary women. For ourselves, we see no reason why female voices now may not be raised in St. Peter's at Rome, just as Miriam sang of old."

This was written in 1868. The same idea seems to have occurred to the very liberal Pope Leo XIII, for in 1880 he forbade the further making of "soprani" or "castrati" for the choirs in the Sistine chapel —a practice amply justified, it would seem, in the minds of former Popes by the words of Jesus and the example of Origen.

Even if the days of the "castrati" are over, however, the Church of Rome has not liberated itself from all suggestion of the effeminacy of the pagan priesthood.

"Although the Papal priests do not actually wear feminine apparel," observes Dr. Inman—and his observation still stands after sixty years—"They do so under a figment, inasmuch as their lace, painted garments, embroidered and other robes all indicate female, rather than male attire."

He goes into detail. "Having satisfied ourselves that the ancients adopted female garments for their priests when worshipping Astarte, Venus or the moon, let us cast a hasty glance over the attire of those who appear before the modern Virgin and Child, the analogue of the ancient Ashtoreth.

"In the first place, we find the stole, originally a woman's garment, and as characteristic of the female as the toga was of the man of Rome. "In addition to this, we see an emblem of the Yoni, and called, I believe, the 'pallium,' borne across the shoulder, and sometimes prolonged both down the back and front.

40

"To this we must add a garment closely resembling a woman's chemise; long and shapeless in the body, short in the arm, and reaching from the neck to the ankles. To this the name of 'albe' is given.

"There is, moreover, another, even more conspicuously feminine, inasmuch as it resembles too closely the *vesica piscis* to be mistaken for anything else. To this the name of 'chasuble' is given.

"In ancient missals, moreover, it is to be remarked that the 'pallium' resembles more closely the *crux ansata*, or emblem of life, of the ancient Egyptians, than the sistrum of Yoni."

To the uninitiated, it may be pointed out that *vesica piscis, Crux ansata* and Yoni are all distinctively feminine, and are sublimations, in the old graphic arts, of the "Mound of Venus."

Thus the Papal priests, continues Dr. Inman, "like the hierophants of pagan goddesses, show that they worship the feminine, rather than the masculine Creator or Preserver of the universe, and that they have drawn their inspiration from heathen sources."

And, since Protestantism is a dilution of Catholicism, Christianity, however practiced, measures up—or down—to Nietzsche's specifications. Judaism, from which Christianity derives, forgot too soon Jah of Sinai.

The Jews, surrounded on all sides, succumbed often and humanly to the temptations of the hot-blooded Oriental "heathen." But even Northern priesthoods did not escape the taint of female impersonation. Again the gods were to blame—the sternly masculine Thor, of all the hierarchy, set the example.

The giant Thrym stole Thor's hammer, and refused to give it back

41

unless the lovely Freya should be given him for wife. Thor promised, but instead of sending to him Freya, he went himself disguised as the goddess to the cave of Thrym. There, after some blandishments befitting his disguise, Thor secured his hammer, beat the giant to death and returned triumphantly to the awaiting Freya—awaiting and expectant, in view of the phallic significance of the hammer Thor had recovered.

The priests of ancient Germany presided at certain of their sacrificial rites clothed as women. In Tacitus we find a suggestive passage.

"In point of dress," says he, discussing the peoples of the Rhine borders, "there is no distinction between the sexes, except that the garment of the women is frequently made of linen, adorned with purple stains, but without sleeves, leaving the arms and part of the bosom uncovered."

The people in general, he had previously pointed out, clothed themselves in the skins of beasts. The women, then, sometimes chose finer and daintier material.

Here may be a hint as to the origin of feminine garb for the priesthood, not only in ancient German, but in the entire primitive world —unless you are satisfied with our former theory that the androgynous gods themselves are to blame—or to be congratulated.

The priesthood, in general—ancient and modern—has always been the more indolent and effeminate of the male community. While the warriors were away fighting in the barbarous days, the priests were at home with the women tending the altars; or, if not at home, were with the armies in the same capacity as the women.

Another passage from Tacitus will illustrate. The Roman legions are preparing for battle.

"On the opposite shore stood the Britons, close embodied and prepared for action. Women were seen rushing through the ranks in wild disorder; their apparel funereal; their hair loose in the wind, in their hands flaming torches, and their whole appearance resembling the frantic rage of the Furies. The Druids were arranged in order, with hands uplifted, invoking the gods, and pouring forth horrible imprecations."

Though awed, the Romans "felt the disgrace of yielding to a troop of women and a band of fanatic priests." In modern warfare, the women and the priests no longer pose as blustering furies, but they are still together—associated as ministers of mercy.

The leisure of the ancient priesthood—leisure as compared with the ardors of the warriors—gave them time to cultivate the arts; and their comparative wealth from donations in the form of offerings for sacrifice gave them the means. They, like the women, would choose the finer stuffs for their garments. In that day, it was the quality and not the cut of the clothing that distinguished the sexes.

As the art of dress developed, it is probable the women chose the more tasty patterns just as they had been choosing the better materials, and the priests kept pace with them. When, finally, there came to be recognized a distinction for the sake of sex, the clothing of the priests was identified with that of the women. The priests would raise no objections—their gentler natures would incline them to associate with the women rather than with the warriors.

The theory is offered for what it is worth. Alternatives are: first, the gods; second, a wide-spread inversion; third, an equally wide-spread transvestism. General self-mutilation of virile males can scarcely account for the phenomenon of pagan priesthood—the virile male usually treasures his masculinity as highly as his life. The emoluments of the altar would not lead to a general sacrifice.

IV. LOVES OF THE PHILOSOPHERS

REVISION toward scandal of the stern old classic tales of heroic comradeship between Achilles and Patroclus, Hercules and Hylas, belongs
to a period in Greek culture when every man of fashion attached to
himself a rosy-cheeked catamite, and in the general overhauling of the
legends not even the highest gods were spared.

Zeus, scanning the world with the lascivious eye that caused him
so often to break, with bona fide females, the Seventh Commandment
of his Jewish friend, Jehovah, was so struck one day with the effeminate beauty of the boy Ganymede that he translated him to the
heavens and made him cupbearer-in-chief to the gods. Ganymede,
decked in all the finery of the youthful nymphs, was soon preferred by
the Thunderer above Danæ, Io, Leda and Semele. He set the fashion
for Grecian youths of the cult Oscar Wilde sought so tragically to revive in Victorian England. Catamitus, his pet name, degenerated into
a term of reproach among the Romans. Associated with Catamitus in
the affections of Zeus was the youth Chrysippus.

45

Phœbus Apollo, not to be outdone by his chief, took unto himself a youth named Hyacinthus. This youth seems to have had in his maidenly make-up a goodly portion of feminine fickleness, for he also fell for the blandishments of the windy Zephyrus. Zephyrus seems to have been pretty hard hit, for when the lovely boy went back to the Sun God, he blustered and blew until he blew out the brains of the faithless flirt. Apollo, it may be observed, was not above suspicion as to complete virility, most of his sculptured portraits of the classic period being decidedly effeminate.

The god Pan became crazy about the boy Cyparissus, whose reciprocal devotion was blind in view of the cut of Pan's features.

The beautiful Endymion, kissed to perpetual sleep by the chaste old maid Selene, was no less beloved by Hypnos, god of slumbers.

Tithonus, the effeminately handsome brother of King Priam of Troy, inspired so great a passion in the heart of Eos, god of the dawn, that he was granted immortality by the gods in council, at the feverish prayers of Eos. However, Aurora's co-star forgot to pray for eternal youth, too, for his catamite, and Tithonus so shrank and shrivelled as the centuries rolled over his head that finally he became lost to sight. It is not recorded whether he continued to demand of Eos: "Do you still love me, Daddy?"

Orpheus, famous for a devotion to the nymph Eurydice that even the waters of the Styx could not wash out, was nevertheless so versatile in his affections as to be overly fond of pretty youths, and was then credited with introducing Socratic love into Greece. It is not impossible that his devotion to boys as much as his constant memory of the "half-regained Eurydice" fostered his coldness toward the Thracian women, who in revengeful jealousy for the slighting of their charms tore him to pieces.

Most frankly effeminate of the gods in both mental and physical characteristics was the soft and rounded Dionysus, god of the grape, a constant wanderer up and down Greece and Asia. His best-loved companions were nymphs and the lesser female deities, as harum-scarum and boisterously playful as himself, but even the stern Amazons were among his conquests. In the Bacchic festivals in his honor, women, recognizing in him a kindred spirit, took the lead, and their frenzied orgies were both the envy and the scandal of the ancients. Men in female attire mingled with the worshippers. The wild boy would have been the despair of his protector, the senile Silenus, had not the fat, jovial old satyr been as wicked and full of mischief as himself. In classic sculpture, Dionysus, like Phœbus, is almost invariably obtrusively effeminate.

This degeneration of the fine old gods of Homer and Hesiod came about with the establishment of "Platonic love"—that "love" sanctioned and all but sanctified by the philosophers. We have so warped the term in later days, in an effort to read a holier meaning into Plato's dialogues, that "Platonic love" has come to signify non-sensual affection between persons of opposite sex. "Socratic love" has been substituted sometimes to express the idealized affection of man for boy that appealed so strongly to the esthetic sensibilities of Plato, but in its practical workings-out was anything but ideal.

The petulant Alcibiades, favorite of Socrates, may be taken as the

47

most perfect flowering on earth of the ideal represented by the tales of Ganymede and Hyacinthus on Olympus. His effeminacy of dress was as notorious as his debauchery and insolence.

"He wore a purple robe with a long train when he appeared in public," says Plutarch. "He caused the planks of his galley to be cut away, that he might lie the softer, his bed not being placed upon the boards, but hanging upon girths. And in the wars he bore a shield of gold, which had none of the usual ensigns of his country, but in their stead a Cupid bearing a thunderbolt."

Not only was his robe of rich Milesian purple held against him by the warriors and statesmen as a reproach, but they were equally scandalized at his visits to a perfumer and by the fact he kept in his house a private cook, skilled in making dainties. On the battlefield he often astonished both friends and enemies by his prowess and valor, but these exhibitions were only spurts, and, says Plutarch, "if you looked more nearly into his disposition and his actions, you would exclaim with Electra in the poet, 'The same weak woman still!' "

Alcibiades, because of his great beauty and lively disposition as well as his social importance, had many admirers, of whom the most long-suffering was the wealthy Anytus, treating him with the same patient forbearance a modern millionaire does a chorus girl.

Of all his admirers, the capricious youth was docile only to the satyr-faced Socrates, who "kept possession of Alcibiades' heart by the excellence of his genius and the pathetic turn of his conversation, which often drew tears from his young companion"—by no means a bad method to use with sentimental chorus girls.

But, like a chorus girl, the pretty youth "sometimes gave Socrates the slip, and was drawn away by his flatterers, who exhausted all the art of pleasure for that purpose," yet Socrates "took care to hunt out his fugitive, who feared and respected none but him: the rest he held in great contempt."

It was on an occasion of such a slip that Alcibiades perpetrated the prank that came near costing him his life and that was the starting point of his fame as well as his misfortunes. With several wild companions, he counterfeited and burlesqued the mysteries of Eleusis, thereby "sacrilegiously offending the goddess Ceres and Proserpine." Alcibiades was accused specifically of "wearing such a robe as the high priest does while he shows the holy things"—female impersonator he, on the stage as well as off.

He was condemned to death, but, as he was out of reach of his Athenian judges at the moment engaged in foreign wars, they confiscated his goods and excommunicated him. Instead of returning to Athens, he went to live in Sparta, and thence drifted to Persia, where, it is recorded, "he outvied the Persians themselves in pomp and splendor."

This was no mean feat in effeminate luxuriousness, even the warriors of Persia preferring soft silks to suits of steel and leather, and an incident in this connection serves to introduce a "female impersonator" more important historically than Alcibiades—namely, Alexander the Great.

Like Sardanapalus, who has become typical of the voluptuous, effeminate despots of the Orient, King Darius of Persia "slept on a

49

splendid couch, overspread by a vine of branching gold, with clusters of rubies representing grapes. He wore a dress of purple and white, with scarlet trousers, a girdle like that of a woman, and a high tiara encircled by a sky-blue turban."

After Alexander defeated Darius, his soldiers "were disgusted and alarmed when they saw him put on the tiara of the Great King, and the woman's girdle, and the white and purple robe."

Alexander, apt pupil of his father Philip, who died at the hand of a catamite, was brought up to despise women and to seek passionate friendships with boys. Taking Homer as his guide in all things military (he carried Homeric manuscripts edited by his teacher Aristotle on his marches in a superb gold casket, among his spoils from the Persians) he took likewise the legend of Achilles and Patroclus, edited down to date, as his guide in conduct, and sought, as did Oscar Wilde long afterward, to re-establish a waning custom in its full Socratic luxuriousness.

He had for his particular favorite the beautiful Macedonian Hephæstion, who became accomplished in the soft fashions of the East, and who not only himself affected the effeminate dress of the Persians, but encouraged Alexander to do so.

Hephæstion had a rival for the love of Alexander in the person of Craterus, perhaps equally pretty, but a bit more manly and more loyal to the customs of the Greeks. These youths detested each other and frequently clashed, after the manner of rival mistresses, using their fists. But, on one occasion in India, they actually drew swords—there were no long hat pins in those days.

Alexander himself stepped between them, sharply calling Hephæstion, who provoked the quarrel, a fool, and walking off with the exultant Craterus. Exultation was short-lived, however, for Alexander gave his young catamite a severe calling down in private. He then brought the youths together, and swore by Jupiter Ammon that if they quarreled again he'd cut off both their heads, in spite of the fact that he loved them above all other youths. They tearfully embraced and "made up."

Hephæstion died of a fever during a season of festivity in Media, having overeaten of roast fowl washed down by cold wine when the physician Glaucus, assigned by Alexander to look after his tender favorite, was gone to the theater.

Alexander was inconsolable. The physician he immediately ordered crucified. Music was tabooed in camp. The period of grief was unduly prolonged, and was brought to an end only by a happy thought —ascribed to an oracle of Jupiter Ammon, Alexander's favorite god and reputed father (not wholly complimentary to his mother)—to make Hephæstion a demi-god and erect to him altars.

The oracle was carried out with the utmost magnificence. Alexander built for his favorite a tomb exceeding in richness anything of the time, full worthy of holding the precious, perfumed body.

Memorial extravagance threatened to overtop even the pyramids of Egypt when the architect Stosicrates submitted a plan to carve rocky Mount Athos of Thrace into a gigantic statue of Hephæstion so huge that a city of ten thousand inhabitants should rest in the palm of the left hand, while the right should pour the torrents of a mountain river into the sea. The project pleased Alexander mightily, but he did not live to execute it.

Though he married for dynastic purposes, Alexander was indifferent through life to feminine charms. Dryden's "Alexander's Feast" would be more to the point psychologically, if less poetic, had he placed by the conqueror's side beautiful Hephæstion instead of "lovely Thais."

In the "golden days" of the Greek Ganymedes, these handsome boys cultivated all the coquettish arts and wiles of charming femininity. The youth walked with eyes downcast, and good breeding forbade him to try to catch the eye of a passerby. This rule of good breeding, of course, had the same effect it has today on girls—the boy shot many a quick, covert glance from under long lashes.

In public places he had to go chaperoned. His voice was never to be raised on the streets or in places of general assembly. When he sat in company, it was necessary that his clothing be decently and perfectly adjusted. "He avoided the shops, the baths, the Agora, the houses of the Hetairai," and all places where assembled idle chatterers, retailers of scandal, panders and "tough characters" in general. He wore the modest chlamys, the garb of youth so strongly resembling the robe of the Greek women. John Addington Symonds collected and compiled these rules of conduct.

Charmides, a model of the proprieties, the most beautiful youth in Athens when the Ganymedes were the rage, produced a sensation when he burst upon the Socratic circle—"amazement and confusion reigned when he entered, and a troop of lovers followed him."

52

Autolycus was another such model youth, who dazzled by his beauty and modest bearing. When he ventured to open his lips in one of the public gatherings, it is recorded his face was suffused with blushes, and the words he uttered, "Not I, by gad!" created a fluttering sensation. The names of these charmers were carved by their admirers on the oaks and pines of Athens and scribbled on the walls, with tender epithets, in such manner as the mistresses of knights-errant were honored later.

Not all the youths were so proper as Charmides and Autolycus. There were "tomboys" in those days as now, who looked upon the proprieties as old-fashioned. Alcibiades is typical.

These youths became the scandal of the gymnasia and the baths. Socrates on his return from the war camp went into the palæstra to see "whether a new beauty had appeared among the youths." On his visit to another such establishment, the youth Lysis was too bashful to approach the satyr-philosopher until he had gathered some of his youthful companions about him.

In the gymnasia and the baths were erected statues of Eros, god of love. "Eros, in fact, was as much at home in the gymnasia of Athens as Aphrodite in the temples of Corinth. Thus Meleager writes: 'The Cyprian queen, a woman, hurls the fire that maddens men for females; but Eros himself sways the love of males for males!" The citation, again, is from Symonds.

"It was a statue of Love which fell from its pedestal in the swimming-bath upon the cruel boy who had insulted his self-slain friend," mourns Theocritus.

It was not unusual for a statue of Eros to be erected in a gymnasium or a bath by some admirer in honor of some particular boy, and it is certain that some of the effeminate marbles of that god still extant reproduce the charms of models who posed living for the sculptors.

So notorious became the gymnasia and the baths that political reformers, from time to time, agitated their destruction. Such a reformer was Polycrates of Samos. The sins of Greece were duplicated in Rome, and the early Christian fathers proceeded against the baths with such fervor that they inaugurated an epoch when vermin infested the holy, and when filthiness was next to godliness. As a matter of philosophical speculation, what effect will the intensive revival of the public bath by such organizations as the Y.M.C.A., simultaneously with the suppression of houses of prostitution, have on contemporary male youth—nay, what already has been the effect?

Of the handsome effeminate boys in the dialogues of Plato, Phædrus inspired the outburst of passion by Lysias, that led to one of the most famous of Socrates' discourses. Another member of the Socratic circle was the boy Phædo, whose luxuriant flowing hair the philosopher fondly stroked before drinking the fatal hemlock. This boy Phædo was frankly a male courtezan, attired in all the feminine luxury of the calling, and was bought, because of his beauty, in the slave market by Cebes, an elderly friend of Socrates. But the most famous of all the catamites of the most famous of all philosophers was Alcibiades. Agathocles, tyrant of Syracuse, in his youth frequented brothels after the manner of Phædo.

Demosthenes penned a beautiful panegyric in honor of the youth, Epicrates. Demosthenes' renowned rival, Æschines, on the other hand, excoriated a similar youth, afterwards famous as Timarchus, accusing him of infamous practices to obtain money for gratification of gluttony and gaming. Æschines, none the less, had his own boy favorite.

Still another orator, Lysias, was fascinated by a pretty boy, and his oration against Simon is an outpouring of jealousy. Both were in love with the same youth, the marvelously handsome Theodotus of Platæa. Lysias had possession of the boy, but Simon claimed that Theodotus had signed an agreement with him to leave Lysias, in consideration of a big sum of money, and devote his talents to said Simon exclusively. Simon had attempted to kidnap the boy and a fight had ensued, in which friends of both men participated. The fight grew into a feud, characterized by street brawls, throwing of stones and housebreaking. Lysias brought suit against Simon, charging assault, and it was in the trial of the case he pronounced his famous oration, still extant.

A similar brawl, resulting in the death of the beautiful Actæon of Corinth, torn to pieces by his jealous rivals, led to the exile of Archias, descendant of Hercules, who thereupon founded the city of Syracuse.

Autolycus, whom we have already mentioned, was favorite of the wealthy Athenian Callias. He was so handsome that his appearance at a gathering of philosophers caused the same sort of breathless sensation that a dazzling queen of beauty registered when she swept in upon an Eighteenth century social gathering. He was eclipsed only by Charmides, the reigning "beauty" of Athens, of whom "all the world seemed to be enamoured," and whose very garments were objects of fetishistic veneration.

The philosopher Zeno in his youth was the favorite of his teacher Parmenides.

The sculptor Phidias was passionately fond of the youth Pantarkes, and used him for a model. It is to such associations we owe so many Greek androgynous statues—feministic Apollos and Dionysii, especially. Ages later, Michelangelo, indifferent to women, likewise chiselled from marble effeminate youths, or, if he attempted a woman's figure, usually narrowed her hips, made fuller her waist line and shrunk her breasts.

Plato, who both praised and blamed the Socratic circle for partiality to male lights-o'-love, and in whose dialogues is preserved so much of the Athenian scandal, had as his own particular favorites the youths Aster and Agathon.

The Spartan Pausanias set his affections on the lovely youth Agilus, who repaid him, like many a female mistress, by betraying him to his enemies.

Another Pausanias, a handsome Macedonian boy of distinguished family, resented the advances of Attalus, a soldier and friend of King Philip. He reported the outrage to Philip, but that king, tainted with the same sort of passion that distinguished Attalus, took the complaint lightly. At the feast in celebration of the nuptials of Philip's daughter, Pausanias assassinated the king. Historians doubt that the crime was inspired wholly by resentment, and have involved Queen Olympias and her son Alexander in a conspiracy with Pausanias.

The Spartan Lysander had for favorite the boy Agesilaus, who was anything but handsome, being lame, small, mean-looking, and deformed. So great was Lysander's interest, however—not unmatched in annals of liaisons between royalty and female favorites no better favored than the Spartan youth—that he exerted his power successfully to put Agesilaus on the throne.

Archidamus, son of Agesilaus, showed a greater love for the beautiful than Lysander by taking as favorite the handsome Cleonymus.

Epaminondas of Thebes was fickle in his affections, annexing to his retinue a host of effeminate boys. Two of them, Asopichus and Cephisodorus, were at his command buried in the tomb with him at Mantinea.

The Theban lawgivers, Diocles and Philolaus, were as famous for their affections as Damon and Pythias and David and Jonathan. Out of their example and the laws they inaugurated grew the immortal Sacred Band of Lovers slaughtered by Philip's more rugged phalanxes at Chæronea, and mourned by Philip in the command that damned them with the attempted exoneration: "Perish any man who suspects that these men either did or suffered anything that was base." Xenephon tells of a similar corps of beautiful boy soldiers gathered together by the artistic Episthenes of Olynthus, himself the object of the historian's affections. When Diocles and Philolaus died they were buried in the same grave.

Tragic in its outcome was the love of the noble Athenian Aristogiton for the young and beautiful Harmodius, an Athenian of equal rank, who returned his affection. The reigning tyrant Hipparchus be came infatuated with Harmodius, and sought to divert his love from Aristogiton. Harmodius turned a cold shoulder to him. The tyrant, infuriated, sought revenge by laying upon the sister of the youth a public insult.

He invited her to participate in a religious festival and then scornfully dismissed her in the presence of the other girls who were to make up a procession of basket carriers. This insult stung Harmodius to the quick and his friend Aristogiton no less. They awaited an opportunity and assassinated him, despite the fact the tyrant had been warned of his doom in a dream, through the lips of a beautiful boy. Harmodius was cut down by the guards. Aristogiton escaped, but was captured and tortured to death. When Hippias, brother of the tyrant and his successor was expelled from Athens, Harmodius and Aristogiton were venerated as deliverers and martyrs, and so rank through the subsequent history of Greece.

Chariton and Melanippus, who attempted to assassinate the Sicilian tyrant Phalaris, were a pair of lovers similar to the Athenian martyrs. Phalaris introduced them to his brazen bull, in whose red hot belly were burned alive the victims of his wrath. It may be recorded, as a matter of poetic justice, that the inventor of the bull, an Edisonian sort of person named Perillus, was the first person upon whom the tyrant tried the merits of his highly artistic furnace.

A Platonic pair who sacrificed themselves for the public weal were Cratinus and Aristodemus of Athens. Epimenides, poet and prophet of Crete, the Rip Van Winkle of antiquity, had won a great reputation for holiness by the easy expedient of sleeping for 57 years—our modern Fundamentalists have been asleep for an entire century and have hard work convincing us they are anything but boobs. The Athenians sent for Epimenides to purify their city after a violation of sanctuary in the murder of the rebel Cylon. In order to stay the plague sent by Athena, whose altar had been outraged, Epimenides called for human sacrifices. Cratinus and Aristodemus responded, and the goddess was appeased. Epimenides has the honor accorded to few "heathen" of being quoted by the Apostle Paul. Writing to his friend Titus, the holy go-getter remarks: "One of themselves, even a prophet of their own, said, The Cretans are always liars, evil beasts, slow bellies." That being the case, Epimenides' own story of sleeping fifty-seven years may be taken with a grain of salt—and perhaps a pair of Socratic lovers were sacrificed on the word of a liar that Athena had demanded their death.

Tales of sacrifices of lover for beloved are numerous. Damon's rescue of his friend Pythias from the tyrant Dionysius is typical. Antileon of Metapontum similarly braved a tyrant for the boy he loved. Diocles, an Athenian exile—not the Diocles of Thebes—died fighting for a youth, as did the Thessalian Cleomachus, whose valor in the boy's interest was so effective that he was nobly buried and ever afterward accounted a hero of first rank.

Sometimes one of these effeminate boys avenged the sullying of his honor after the manner of an outraged girl. The boy Crates killed the tyrant Archelaus for assaulting him; Pytholaus likewise punished Alexander of Pheræ, and another boy slew the tyrant Periander. Damocles, a gentler youth and of morbid disposition, killed himself

59

by leaping into a cauldron of boiling water after being outraged by Demetrius Poliorketes.

Though unable to save the life of his beloved Cleostratus, Menestratus of the city of Thespia in the legendary days, cunningly avenged the death of the youth. Each year, the city was visited by a dragon which could be appeased only by one of these lovely boys—a degenerate dragon, it would seem, for more normal dragons were satisfied with maidens or manly young men. The dragon, however, may have been a reformer, for it succeeded in ridding Thespia of all youths of the type of Cleostratus, except only the beloved of Menestratus, and he was the most beautiful of them all. Reluctantly Menestratus surrendered his boy, but first he clothed him with a coat of brass, set with sharp hooks hinged and lying close to the surface, turned toward the boy's head. The dragon swallowed his victim feet first. In the process of digestion, the hooks rose erect, and tore the monster's stomach to pieces. Cleostratus, not having the lungs of Jonah, was dead when the autopsy was performed on the dragon.

It was from a Socratic love romance that sprang originally the woes of the house of Œdipus Rex. Laius, father of the unfortunate royal Theban whose incestuous adventure brought the fury of the gods to a climax, first defiled the honor of the family by a lustful attack on Chrysippus, son of Pelops. For this crime his posterity was made to suffer.

A tragedy based on this liaison was composed by Euripides, who, like his fellow dramatists Sophocles and Æschylus, was not unmindful of the charms of effeminate boys. The name of Sophocles' favorite

60

Demophon has been preserved. Both Sophocles and Æschylus produced tragedies relating to the non-Homeric affections of Achilles and Patroclus—Plato took Æschylus severely to task for tampering with the tale of the epic master. Sophocles, too, modified in the same direction the story of Zeus and Ganymede.

Aristophanes and his fellow writers of comedy, with the license of buffoons, satirized mercilessly the practice the serious writers treated so tragically, and did not trouble to veil darkly their allusions to contemporary delinquents. The dramatist Empolis, for example, held up to ridicule Alcibiades and his crowd—much as later, W. S. Gilbert in "Patience" lampooned Oscar Wilde and the lily-decked æsthetes, though with far broader and coarser allusions.

Even more frank than the dramatists were the lyric poets, and their outbursts of rapture addressed to boys were not merely rhetorical.

Anacreon's favorites, Cleobulus, Smerdies and Leucaspis, existed in the flesh and blood, and were more closely associated with the poet than were Petrarch's Laura and Dante's Beatrice. Anacreon and the scarcely less famous Ibycus were attached to the courts of Polycrates and Hippias, and the pretty boys they celebrated were court favorites. One of them, Smerdies, a Thracian, was extraordinarily beautiful, and was a present to Polycrates from one of his nobles.

Theognis, prolific writer of elegies sung at banquets, celebrated many "fair young men," but his particular personal favorite was Kurnus, a youthful nobleman in the poet's own station of life. This Kurnus seems to have been as petulant and changeable as a woman, and often aroused the poet's bitter and jealous wrath.

The most popular of all the lyricists, Pindar, was likewise the frankest in proclaiming that superior artistic delights were to be found in the affection of boys rather than in that of women. It was in the arms of his favorite, Theoxenos, celebrated in the most famous of his poems, that he suddenly died in the theater at Argos.

The poet Alcæus had for his particular favorite "the black-eyed Lycus."

It is from the Greek lyricists primarily, though possibly through their Latin translators and imitators, that Shakespeare drew the literary inspiration for his sonnets, so frankly revelatory. Nothing except a reluctance to think so great a genius a "degenerate" can blind us to their obvious meaning. The objection is urged that the love passages in his plays are normal—but then the Greek sculptors, unquestionable addicts to Platonic love and carvers of androgynous figures, likewise did some of the most noble normal statues, male and female, of all time.

From the same source, too, as the sonnets, sprang "Venus and Adonis," which may be the connecting link between the sonnets and the plays. "Venus and Adonis" treats outwardly of the love of woman for man. But nowhere in the poem is there a glowing picture of the charms of Venus. It is the boy Adonis that excites the raptures of the poet. It is his lips and eyes that glow—not the eyes and lips of Venus. A passionate woman might have written "Venus and Adonis"—or a passionate lover of boys!

Shakespeare here is surely akin in genius to the Theognis who wrote: "O boy, so long as thy chin remains smooth, never will I cease

62

from fawning, no, not if it is doomed for me to die"; or the Anacreon of: "O boy, with the maiden's eyes, I seek and follow thee, but thou heedest not, nor knowest that thou art my soul's charioteer"; or the Pindar who celebrated "the young-limbed bloom of boys" and, speaking of Theoxenos, "the flashing rays of his forehead." And, what about Walt Whitman and his "Vigil for boy of responding kisses . . . vigil for comrade swiftly slain?"

Of Shakespeare more—much more—anon.

V. ORGY OF THE CÆSARS

ONE morning, B.C., Rome woke up long before breakfast to the
juiciest scandal that ever was rolled luxuriously on the tongue of a
wicked city. Young matrons, who had been up all night, hurried home
excitedly to tell their husbands all about it.

They had been at the house of Julius Cæsar celebrating, with his
wife Pompeia as hostess, the mysteries of the Bona Dea—aristocratic
mysteries that had not yet degenerated into the wild orgies scourged
later by Juvenal; but solemn and sacred secrets that only matrons in
the upper crust of society knew; secrets that had not been defiled by
masculine gaze.

But on this night, when the pious frenzy was at its highest, suddenly there was discovered in the midst of the mothers of Rome a man
disguised as one of themselves!

Panic ensued! In the buzz and confusion of hundreds of excited
female voices, the scantily clad women hastened into their garments,
and scattered each for her home and her husband.

Within a couple of hours there were as many versions of the affair extant in buzzing Rome as there were matrons present at the sacrifice to Bona Dea. But the young man, a gay and gallant patrician about town, had been recognized, and before long the various versions consolidated into a truth as sensational as the most vivid of the products of imagination.

More than one of the young matrons trembled when it was known for sure that the intruder was Publius Clodius. For this handsome blade, darling of patrician circles, was vaguely reputed to have a long list of conquests to his credit. And the beauties who had been too fond of him naturally feared an investigation, the extent and limits of which they couldn't guess.

Foremost of them was Pompeia herself, newly-made wife of Cæsar, whom she did not love and who did not love her. Naturally, as the mysteries were being celebrated in her house, the strongest suspicion would be directed toward her—and not without cause, for her affair with Clodius was already a semi-scandal in the smart set.

Whether Cæsar himself knew of the infatuation of his wife for the handsome patrician does not appear, but his mother Aurelia knew it —and imagine what a mother-in-law, who didn't like her son's wife anyhow, could do with a secret like that. Aurelia ran true to form, and it was her vigilance, indeed, that resulted in the profanation of Bona Dea.

Seldom was it possible for the lovers to snatch a secret moment together, so persistent was Aurelia and her spies. It was for that reason they hit upon the bold scheme of smuggling Clodius into the house during the ceremonies, when there was little danger of detection providing he could look reasonably well a woman.

For men at that period of Rome, before the celebration degenerated into a saturnalia of vice, refrained as gentlemen from going near the house set aside for the ceremonies. Nothing savoring of the male was permitted—all male animals and birds had to be taken from the place, and the women were even forbidden to wear the trinkets designed to catch the masculine eye. So universally respected were the customs surrounding the Bona Dea that it did not enter the heads of men to intrude, or of women to expect such intrusion, and little more than perfunctory care was exercised to see that they did not.

Pompeia and Clodius, therefore, laid their plans with reasonable safety if with no exemplary honor, and Abra, the most trusted of her women, was the go-between. When the high-born matrons flocked to Cæsar's house late in the evening, as the first stars were coming out, boldly in their midst walked one of the prettiest of them all, Publius Clodius, powdered and rouged, daintily clad, chatting in treble tone, and treading with mincing step, not a little proud of his disguise.

Abra, sharply on the lookout, spied him, and, at the first opportunity, smuggled him into Pompeia's private chamber, where Cæsar would not visit her that night, and then ran off to tell Pompeia that her lover awaited her.

Aurelia, not that she suspected anything, but by one of those unlucky chances of the blundering gods, espied Abra; and, as it was a busy night in Cæsar's house, had something for her to do. One task was followed by another, and Abra, though fearful and impatient, dared not show the least unwillingness. Consequently, she did not get a chance to carry her message to the equally fearful and impatient Pompeia.

Clodius, becoming vaguely alarmed as the minutes sped by with nothing transpiring, took another look in the mirror to see that his beauty was on straight, and sallied forth to investigate. He had walked into Cæsar's house with a crowd of the women, many of whom knew him, without being detected. Why couldn't he mingle safely with them now?

But he had tarried too long. By this time, the women had divested themselves of most of their garments in honor of the Good Goddess— all, if some of the reports of the mysteries are to be believed—and the ceremonies had started.

Clodius had stumbled into the court where the statue of Bona Dea was being bathed with wine, when a servant maid of the house, seeing a fully dressed woman, asked her sharply who she was and what she was doing there clothed. Clodius, discomfited by the sharp, abrupt question, replied he wanted to see Abra. But he forgot his treble tones. The maid screamed "A man!"

Clodius turned and fled, making for the chamber he had so indiscreetly quitted, but whose exact direction and location he had lost. Abra, knowing instantly what was up, slipped away in the confusion, found the flustered gallant, and succeeded in smuggling him again into the chamber, hiding him behind the draperies.

But Aurelia, with an uncanny suspicion of the truth, and with a grim satisfaction that was strong enough to overcome her sense of indignant humiliation at the profanation of her son's house, led a search party of half-clothed women direct to Pompeia's room. There they found the luckless Clodius, laid violent hands on him, and beat and dragged him out of the house. Then they all dressed and hurried home to tell their husbands about it.

Cæsar, upon learning of the scandal, doesn't seem to have been greatly disturbed, and took little trouble to investigate the guilt or innocence of Pompeia. He promptly put her away with that immortal bit of oratory: "Cæsar's wife must be above suspicion."

But if Cæsar wasn't interested, others in Rome were, and the affair became a cause célèbre. Clodius had a sister Claudia, who was as dangerous a heart-breaker as he. Among the victims of her charms was no less a notable than the orator Cicero.

As luck would have it, Tertentia, Cicero's wife, knew of Claudia's conquest and was furiously jealous. Here was her chance for revenge. Cicero and Clodius were great friends. It was Clodius who had shielded Cicero from the wrath of Catiline in the early stages of the denunciation of that conspiracy, when the life of the orator wasn't worth two straws. Consequently, any testimony of Cicero against his benefactor and friend would have great weight.

Clodius, in due time, at the formal instigation of one of the tribunes, was cited before the Senate to answer a charge of sacrilege— a capital charge in those stern days. He denied the affair in toto, declaring he was absent from Rome at the time.

But on that very day he had been in Cicero's house to consult his friend, and Tertentia knew it. She had assumed imperious sway over the orator since discovering a plot of Claudia's to have him divorce her, and now she compelled Cicero to go to the Senate chamber and testify to the presence of Clodius in town.

This testimony went a long way toward convicting the young patrician. He was declared guilty, but escaped severe punishment, owing not only to his personal influence in upper circles, but to the fact that the commons of Rome unexpectedly declared for him—they hated the Bona Dea celebration, it developed, because it was an aristocratic affair, and got huge joy out of the scandal Clodius had brought upon it.

But Clodius did not forget Cicero. He used his new popularity with the commons to get chosen tribune for the express purpose of revenging himself on the orator. Immediately after assuming office, he caused his old friend to be banished, set fire to both his country home and his house in town, and ordered all his personal property to be sold at auction.

Cicero remained in exile until Milo was chosen tribune. Milo, who had been a friend of Clodius, found fault with him for his cruelty to Cicero, and recalled the orator. This occasioned a violent quarrel between Clodius and Milo, which extended to their partisans.

For a time it looked as though a civil war was imminent, but fortunately for Rome the tribunes, each with a retinue of servants, met one day on the Appian Way. An exchange of Roman profanity was followed by blows, and in the fracas Clodius was killed.

Thus it was that a clever bit of female impersonation, in the interest of light gallantry, all but created a new Sulla-Marius epoch of massacre and rapine.

Cæsar's conduct in this affair—a cold indifference to the insult offered him as a husband and as a patrician of Rome—grew logically out of his own temperament, for the conqueror of the world, virile as a warrior, statesman, orator and historian, was, nevertheless, pathologically effeminate.

The evidence is too clear and explicit to admit of question, and at no time was Cæsar's effeminacy a secret in Rome. Even when he became dictator, poets nightly scribbled ribald verses on the walls of Rome lampooning this trait, and no efforts seem to have been made to detect and punish them. Indeed, some of the cleverer of these verses were set to music and sung by Cæsar's own soldiers, whose loyalty was above suspicion.

As a youth, Cæsar brazenly prostituted himself to Nicomedes, King of Bithynia, openly living with him as a girl, "the Queen's rival," as Dolabella bitingly expressed it later in the Roman Senate in a savage attack on Cæsar, "and the inner side of the royal couch." Curio, another Senator, supplemented the ugly remark with an uglier "the brothel of Nicomedes and the Bithynian stew." In his edicts, the tribune Bibulus proclaims his colleague under the name "the Queen of Bithynia," adding that "he had formerly been in love with a King," and now sought a kingdom. At a public function a half-crazed "natural," Octavius by name, saluted Pompey as "the king" and Cæsar as "the queen," and nothing was done about it.

During his affair with Nicomedes, Cæsar arrayed himself as a girl on occasions—and not only that, but as a painted prostitute, brazenly flaunting her profession.

Even in his early maturity, when he was becoming a man of consequence in Rome, the young patrician was extreme and gaudy in his dress, the broad purple stripe of his toga, especially, being of extra width and fringed. The young dandy, too, was proud of his soft, white skin, of which he took care with all the vanity of a girl. Not only was he extremely fastidious with his face and hands, but he had the hair plucked by the roots from all parts of his soft, lithe body.

Tales of his Bithynian adventures, not only did not annoy him, but seemed on occasions even to have amused him, after the fashion of the pathologically effeminate. One typical incident is a smart retort he gave an enemy in the Senate, when he had finished outlining his plans for the conquest of Gaul—a mission that had just been intrusted him, and which he so brilliantly executed later.

"That will not be very easy for a woman to accomplish," sarcastically observed the Senator, after listening to the details of his plan.

"Semiramis formerly ruled in Syria," retorted Cæsar good-naturedly, "and the Amazons conquered a great part of Asia."

Nor did Cæsar, at the height of his power, when his word was law, seek to punish the writer of the couplet:

> "—Whate'er Bithynia and her lord possessed,
> Her lord, who Cæsar in his lust caressed!"

Cicero, who had little love for Cæsar, supplies the information that the young Roman, in his Bithynian days, "was conducted by the

71

royal attendants into the king's bed-chamber, and lay upon a bed of gold with a covering of purple" and adds contemptuously that "the youthful bloom of this scion of Venus was tainted in Bithynia." And once in the Senate, when Cæsar was eloquently pleading the cause of Nysa, daughter of Nicomedes, and referred incidentally to kindnesses he had received himself from the king, Cicero interrupted with a mock eager interest: "Pray tell us more of that; for it is well known what he gave you, and you gave him."

The affair of Nicomedes, which suddenly ended with a violent lovers' quarrel, was not the last of the sort Cæsar indulged in, but as he grew older he became more masculine in his loves. "He was every woman's man, and every man's woman," declared the elder Curio in the Senate.

There seems to have been no depth to his love as a man, however. He was not enough interested in Pompeia to investigate her share of the guilt in the Bona Dea scandal, and there is no evidence he cared any more warmly for her successor, Calphurnia. His dalliance with Cleopatra resembles more the intimate friendship of one woman for another than that of lover for mistress, and there were openly expressed doubts that her son Cæsarion was also his. Cleopatra certainly had no worshipful affection for her effeminate conqueror.

The one woman Cæsar seems to have admired genuinely and to have loved with what little of normal affection there was in him—say in the measure Michelangelo loved Vittoria Colonna—was the handsome and somewhat senatorial mother of Marcus Brutus, the magnificent Servilia. When Brutus, as leader of the conspirators, stabbed

72

Cæsar, the dictator is reported by Suetonius to have said, not the famous *"Et tu, Brute?"* but, "What! Art thou, too, one of them? Thou, my son!"

Many of the succeeding Cæsars and the later Roman Emperors were not behind the divine Julius in their fondness for playing the woman, and while some of them assumed female guise in public spectacles in the apparent innocence of stage players, the motive must be sought in pathological bias. For it was beneath the dignity of a Cæsar to appear as an actor in any rôle whatsoever. Augustus, Tiberius, Caligula, Claudius, Nero, Galba, Titus, Domitian, Nerva, Trajan, Hadrian, Commodus, Heliogabalus, Caracalla—all displayed markedly the bias.

Augustus, Julius Cæsar's nephew, owed his inheritance of the wealth, prestige and name of Cæsar to a compliance, when a boy, to such wishes of his uncle as King Nicomedes had expressed for Julius.

As a youth, too, Augustus seems to have been as effeminate in appearance and manner as was Julius Cæsar himself, and the statues extant of him, even into full maturity, confirm the written tradition.

Like his uncle, he was annoyed by hair on his body, and had the female barbers of Rome pluck it out sometimes, and sometimes soften and refine it by singeing with burnt nut shells.

He not only prostituted himself to Julius Cæsar, but sold his favors like a common whore to at least one noble, Aulus Hirtus, in Spain, for a consideration of 300,000 sesterces—not so common, at that.

The stigma clung to the divine Cæsar Augustus throughout his life, and while he was not pursued so brazenly with it as was his uncle Julius, the irrepressible Roman populace did not let him forget it. On one occasion, in the theater, there was recited this sentence, alluding to the Gallic priest of the mother of the gods beating a drum with his thumb:

"See with his orb the wanton's finger play!"

Somebody in the audience instantly applied the speech to the Emperor, with a vulgar implication of a female physique, and the crowd applauded and shouted with laughter.

In the infamous, insane Caligula we encounter the first of the "play actors" among the Cæsars.

"Ideal portraits" of Caligula, sketched by posthumous artists, taking the mad monster's soul as the model for his face, depict him as a rough, shaggy brute, with a cruel, barbarous, heavy face. Nero, kindred in soul and as criminally insane as Caligula, is not quite so shaggy in the "ideal" sketches, but he, too, is given a stern eye and firm masculine features.

As a matter of fact, authentic sculptured heads by contemporary artists, reveal both these insane Cæsars small of features, and strikingly effeminate, which, to the psychologist, comport with their cruel, cowardly souls more nearly than do the imaginative ogerish portraits.

Pictures of Caligula that reveal him as a hairy monster are no more monstrously overdrawn than are theories of his responsibility for heinous crimes. Caligula was a madman, pure and simple. His marriage to his sister was scarcely the crime Harriet Beecher Stowe attributed to Lord Byron. It was just an aberration of the crazed egoist.

74

Did not Jupiter and Juno, imperial brother and sister of the Roman hierarchy, wed and co-habit—why not then Caligula and Drusilla? Besides, Caligula had been strongly influenced by the luxury of Alexandria, where he spent a great deal of his youth—and was it not perfectly proper, according to Egyptian standards, for brother and sister to marry? Even so late an example was pointed out, as Cleopatra and her brother. By these close unions from time immemorial, the blood of the Ptolemies had been kept royally blue. Cleopatra had not been faithful in her marriage relations, but the transgressions of the Serpent of the Nile did not invalidate the theory.

Drusilla was in no special danger physically, for Caligula was pathologically effeminate to an advanced degree, and he developed an irresistible love for masquerading in female attire, even in public. On occasions he appeared before his courtiers "all in silks and habited like a woman."

Though he derived his name from Caliga, a heavy boot studded thickly with nails, which he wore when a boy with the army—the pet and mascot of the Roman legions in Germany, commanded by his idolized father, Germanicus—Caligula after coming to the dignity of the toga affected the sock worn by women. Even when he donned the tunic, it was delicately and richly embroidered and fairly encrusted with jewels. He wore bracelets wrought for Roman maidens.

He was inordinately proud of his neck and legs, slender and graceful as a woman's. Like Julius Cæsar and Augustus, he was annoyed that hair should grow on his body. He kept his chest carefully covered to conceal the hairs he tried in vain to eradicate permanently, and even went so far as to make it a capital crime for anyone to look down upon him from above. The word "goat" was likewise capitally tabooed in his presence.

Imitating the Roman Jupiter and strange Egyptian gods in his marriage with Drusilla, Caligula took it into his crazy brain that he was himself a god, the peer of any of them. He caused statues of Roman and Egyptian deities to be collected in his palace, their heads struck off, and his own done in finest marble substituted. It is to this order we owe the preservation until today of so many excellent likenesses of him.

Not only were the male gods decapitated, but the female as well. The substitution of his head for the head of Venus gave him a new idea—he was Venus herself incarnate. Accordingly, he arrayed himself as the goddess in thin, flowing robes, appeared in her temple, and caused the sacrifices that were her meed to be offered to himself.

But the gods were aroused, and had their revenge. On the morning of his assassination, a few minutes before the event, "the statue of Jupiter at Olympia, which he had ordered to be taken down and brought to Rome, suddenly burst out into such a violent fit of laughter, that, the machinery employed in the work giving way, the workmen took to their heels."

An irony appeared in the person of the assassin. Cassius Chærea, tribune of the prætorian guard, had often been taunted for his effeminacy by the effeminate Caligula. When the tribune would come to the Emperor for the watchword, Caligula would reply "Priapus" or "Venus" or some such name, and would offer him his fist, doubled in the obscene fashion still practiced in Spain and Italy (*fare la fica*), to kiss. When the conspiracy to kill the Emperor was hatched, Chærea claimed the privilege of striking first.

In still further keeping with retributive justice, Caligula that very evening was to have made his début frankly as a stage player with some boys of noble birth from Asia whom he had brought to Rome for that purpose. Doubtless on this occasion he would have played his favorite rôle of a woman. It was while talking to these boys in a corridor of the palace that Chærea came up carelessly behind him, and with lightning suddenness gave him a heavy blow on the neck with his sword. The Emperor fell, crying out in terror that he was still alive. The other conspirators rushed in and soon despatched the tyrant, giving him thirty wounds in all.

Even more strongly swayed by the feminine side to his nature was Nero, more popularly execrated than any of the Roman Emperors, for the reason that a genuinely artistic temperament impelled him to make spectacular and refined a series of cruelties, which were no more brutal than those of the sullen Tiberius and the grandiloquent Caligula, both of whom Nero took for models.

A particular bit of this refined art in torture, which has kept his memory green, was the making of human torches of Christians to light a garden fête—"a race of men" these Christians, according to Tacitus, who is no friend of Nero but not hard on him in this instance, "detested for their evil practices," holding "a dangerous superstition" and practicing, with "their sullen hatred of the whole human race," their rites in underground Rome, "the common sink into which every-

thing abominable flows like a torrent from all quarters of the world."
It was these detestable wretches, however, who became the dominating
element of the Roman Empire and of Europe, and who have never
forgotten Nero.

Applied in other direction than the dramatization of cruelty,
Nero's artistic talents might have made him equally immortal in some
more laudable sphere. Had he not had the misfortune to be Emperor,
he might, for example, have become the greatest actor of his time.

He was a musician of genuine taste and accomplishment, although
he probably overrated himself in this field. He caused musical settings
to be made for many of the classic deeds of heroes and heroines, con-
tributing some himself, and sang them in the public theaters to his
own accompaniment on the harp.

For the singing and impersonating of Niobe, he bestowed upon
himself a crown, accepting the gift with bashful modesty. His singing
of "Canace in Labour" gave rise to a bon mot long a savory classic in
Rome. Canace, through guilty love of her brother, gave birth to a
baby. Upon hearing its cries, she was so overcome by shame and
remorse that she killed herself. The theme was a favorite with Nero,
and he included it frequently in his programs, impersonating the
conscious-stricken girl, writhing exquisitely in her prolonged agony.
Upon one occasion, when he was in the midst of his "Canace" master-
piece, a stranger in Rome asked what it was all about.

"The Emperor is labouring in child-birth," replied solemnly a
wag, sitting beside him.

In his impersonations of Niobe, Canace and the other heroines of

mythology, Nero wore masks modelled to resemble faces of Roman maids or matrons he happened to admire at the moment.

But the height of Nero's extravagance as an impersonator of women was reached in his relations with his freedman, Pythagoras, as Tacitus caught the name, or Doryphorus, as Suetonius has it.

"He personated a woman," says Tacitus, "and in that character was given in marriage to one of his infamous herd, a pathic named Pythagoras. The Emperor of Rome, with the affected airs of female delicacy, put on the nuptial veil. The Augurs assisted at the ceremony; the portion of the bride was openly paid; the genial bed was displayed to view; nuptial torches were lighted up; the whole was public, not even excepting the endearments which, in natural marriage, decency reserves for the shades of night."

Suetonius adds that on this auspicious occasion Nero "imitated the cries and shrieks of young virgins when they are ravished," and records that, after particularly obscene games in the arena, in which the Emperor was "let out of a den covered with the skin of a wild beast to assault men and women bound to stakes, he finished the play in the embraces of his freedman Doryphorus."

Like Julius Cæsar, however, Nero had an element of the masculine in his make-up, and a child of his was about to be born to his wife Poppæa, when he became violently angry with her, and kicked her so brutally in the abdomen that, in her delicate condition, he killed her.

Upon her death, and the consequent death of his anticipated heir, Nero filled Rome with his lamentations. He sought for a successor to his "beloved goddess," who should resemble her as closely as possible.

79

His choice fell, however, not upon a woman, but upon his young freedman Sporus, whose face chanced to be strikingly like Poppæa's. This unfortunate boy, the Emperor ordered his surgeons to transform into a woman. They did the best they could, and when Sporus had recovered from the operation, Nero formally married him, with all the pomp of the rose-colored veil and the most extravagant wedding festivities.

Sporus was attired in the regal splendor of an Oriental Queen, and Nero took him with him on all his tours, reclining with him in the royal litter, and treating him in every way as his wife. "It would have been well for mankind," remarked grimly a Roman, "had such a wife fallen to the lot of Nero's father Domitius."

With Nero's death the race of the Emperors with the tainted blood of the Cæsars, became extinct though the succeeding rulers of Rome continued to use a name so formidable in the city and fraught with so much terror to the barbarians. Not one of the blooded Cæsars was free from the quality of effeminacy so conspicuous in Julius, Augustus, Caligula and Nero, though the sullen Tiberius and the clownish Claudius did not flaunt their vice in the face of Rome.

Tiberius, insanely and morbidly fond of unnatural practices, doubtless indulged in many a secret revel on the isle of Capri in the guise of a woman, but neither Suetonius nor Tacitus, hardiest of historians, ever dared lift more than an edge of the veil that shrouds the obscenities of this fouled pearl of the Mediterranean, that has been the Mecca of strange æsthetes from that day to the days of Oscar Wilde and F. A. Krupp.

The evidence in the case of Claudius is still more negative. That he was weak appears from his general record as an administrator, and from the fact that he clung to his wife Messalina, most notorious nymphomaniac of all time. The fires of her lusts could not be quenched by the gentlemen of the court, and she was forced to seek relief in the lowest houses of prostitution in Rome, giving herself to all comers, taking the miserably small fee to conceal her identity. A dullard of the tainted blood of the Cæsars, content with such an Empress, could hardly have been aggressively masculine.

The Emperor Otho, Cæsar in name only, redeemed by his heroic suicide, worthy the best days of the Roman republic, many stains on his fame.

His act created all the more astonishment among his contemporaries from the fact that he was conspicuously a dandy. Like the early Cæsars, he kept the hair plucked from his body—a custom, by the way, imported from the Orient, and still practiced by Japanese female prostitutes, and demanded still in many Occidental studios of female artists' models—and sought to prevent the beard growing on his face by rubbing with soaked bread.

He was nice with his clothing, which was cut and trimmed as effeminately as he dared. On at least one occasion, he celebrated publicly the sacred rites of the Egyptian goddess Isis clad as a priestess.

In the reign of Domitian the satirist Juvenal flourished, scourge of the vices that encrusted Rome like the leprosy—vices festering even now in these United States, and not abated by the criminal ignorance of rampant "reformers" sitting on the lid of the age-old safety valve, the house of prostitution.

Juvenal had in the Emperor himself a text for his satire, for Domitian in his youth bore to the Senator Nerva the same relationship that Julius Cæsar bore to King Nicomedes. Domitian was girlishly pretty, and all through life was petulantly vain. As a young man he escaped the fury of Vitellius in one of those petty civil wars that kept the Roman Empire in a perpetual seething and ferment by assuming the female disguise of a devotee of Isis.

This Emperor, however, was more notorious in the masculine Platonic rôle, and it was his open devotion to the pretty play-actor Paris that excited the wrath of Juvenal and spurred his genius to the Satires.

The Emperor bestowed upon the girl-like pantomimist all the royal favor the French Kings of the Golden Age heaped upon their mistresses, and it wasn't long before Paris was ruling Rome as surely as Du Barry ruled France. Romans who sought political advancement paid their suit to the actor and not to the Emperor or his queen.

It was here that Juvenal slipped in with his biting regrets that Roman genius was compelled to do homage to an upstart pantomimist. Paris, stung to the quick, secured from Domitian the banishment of Juvenal.

Not long after this, however, Domitian discovered an intrigue between Paris and the Empress, Domitia, and in a violent rage, he ordered the actor executed publicly.

Following up his passionate anger, he put also to death another actor, a pupil of Paris, for no other reason than that he resembled his master in person and in his art.

Paris was highly popular on the Roman stage, as both panto-mimist and ballet dancer, expert in the impersonation of nymphs and goddesses. Juvenal records among his masterpieces Pelopea and Philomela.

Juvenal's satire did not stop with Paris. Some other renowned female impersonators of the day came under his scorpion lash, and it is from his verses we gather that the women of Rome became as mad about the pretty stage boys masquerading as girls as did the Senators —as did the women of England about the beautiful Edward Kynaston, heroine of the Restoration stage.

"While the effeminate Bathyllus is acting Leda in the ballet," observes the poet, "Tuscia cannot contain herself, Appula whines as in the feat of love, Thymele is all attention to the quick, the gentler and the slow; and so Thymele, rustic as she was before, becomes a proficient in the art."

In addition to the serious boy-actresses, Paris and Bathyllus, there was a comic female impersonator, Ubicus, whose burlesques were the delight of Rome.

In his immortally immoral Sixth Satire, Juvenal gives his famous description of the wild rites of the Bona Dea, which in his time had sadly degenerated from the mysteries that had been spied upon by the indiscreet Clodius in the house of Julius Cæsar. It was, indeed, the intrusion of Clodius that suggested the profanation which had now become a recognized part of the mysteries, lamentably transformed

83

into a wild orgy. Genuine women still started the ceremonies, but when they had worked themselves into a frenzy of excitement, there were now introduced youths wrapped in the filmiest of female garments and wearing female hoods.

"What altars are there now," exclaims Juvenal, "that a Clodius does not assail!"

Notorius even among the notorius effeminates of Rome was the exquisitely lovely Antinous, favorite catamite of the Emperor Hadrian.

Hadrian treated this young man as a veritable Empress, heaping upon him the most extravagant luxuries. Handsome of face and form, the youth was converted into a woman as nearly as it was possible for art to do.

The boy mistress of the Emperor fully and femininely reciprocated the love heaped upon him. For, when in Egypt Hadrian was told by magicians that unless he could meet a man who should voluntarily be put to death as a sacrifice to the Egyptian gods, the Emperor of Rome must himself take the cold, silent journey into the realm of the dead beyond the Nile, Antinous offered himself as the sacrifice. Hadrian, accordingly, took the lad to the bank of the Sacred River, and, with his own hands, threw him into the water, where he was drowned. The Emperor then sat down on the bank and wept convulsively.

On his return to Rome, Hadrian caused a magnificent temple to be built to Antinous, and had the Senate enroll him among the gods.

Another of Hadrian's favorites was Verus, the brother of the infamous Faustina—immortalized anew by Swinburne—wife of the gentle timid, philosopher-Emperor, Marcus Aurelius Antoninus.

Marcus Aurelius, himself, has not escaped the suspicion of being a catamite of Hadrian's, along with his brother-in-law Varus and the enshrined Antinous—a suspicion which the very gentleness of the philosopher's nature has borne out when coupled with the fact that he was advanced politically so strenuously as to become Emperor himself. But if such a relationship existed, it was not flaunted publicly.

Of the later Roman Emperors who assumed the dress and manner of women, wildest in their extravagance were Commodus and Heliogabulus.

Commodus sought to shine as a gladiator with the same mad intensity of desire Nero displayed in his ambitions as a musician. At first he impersonated Hercules, carrying a club and wearing a lion's skin. But this guise, even though it led to the Omphale interlude, did not quite satisfy the perversity of his nature, and so he combined his desire to be a hero and a woman by adopting the dress of an Amazon. He was so tickled with this solution of the difficulty that he gave himself the surname of Amazonian—Commodus Amazonian!

"This base and unworthy behavior furnished ample matter for laughter and ridicule to the Romans, when they beheld their Emperor in the circus, dressed like a woman, and degrading his dignity by such a scandalous and shameful metamorphosis," it is recorded, but the Romans dared not give vent to their true feelings.

Nor was it a laughing matter for the poor combatants, his opponents, in the arena. For the gladiators were all but disarmed, and legions stood by to offer assistance to the noble Amazon in case somebody tried to hurt him. Commodus, thus protected, slaughtered his

85

opponents with lusty valor, and the servile spectators would then shout excitedly:

"Thou overcomest the world! Thou art the conqueror, O brave Amazonian!"

It was through the innocent agency of a gentle boy, to whom Commodus, in the masculine phase of his aberration, was attached, that the monster came to his death.

This youth, scarcely more than a child, had a pretty, girl-like body, that the Emperor decked with diamonds and jewels and only the scantiest clothing—just enough to conceal his sex. He was called Philo-Commodus—the favorite of Commodus.

The boy had freer access to the Emperor's chamber than even the Amazonian Marcia, favorite concubine of Commodus, although Commodus strove to appear her twin when he wore his own Amazonian disguise. Philo-Commodus must have been a sweet boy, for Marcia wasn't jealous, and loved him as much as did the Emperor himself.

One day, the youth discovered in the Emperor's chamber a bit of folded paper, which he took promptly to Marcia, for they had their little confidences. On this paper, the terrified concubine found the names of a number of Roman nobles who were shortly to fall to the vengeance of Commodus for slights fancied and real—among them herself.

Without sharing with the lad this secret, she took the paper to some of the other proscribed persons she knew intimately, and together they plotted the Emperor's death.

Marcia, who willingly undertook the commission, since fear and indignation had transformed the little love she bore the Emperor into hate, was assigned the task of poisoning him. This she did with a cup of wine, which he received from her with a passionate kiss.

But the dose was too large, and Commodus, who had felt a great heaviness in his head immediately after drinking, fell to vomiting violently. The wrestler Narcissus, strongest man in Rome, had been brought into the conspiracy for hire in case of emergency. He sprang upon him and choked the life out of Commodus Amazonian.

The gentle Philo-Commodus wept when Marcia told him about it.

Heliogabalus ranks not a degree below Nero and Caligula for fertility in fantastic cruelty and mad aberration. He scorned the virile Roman habit of the Emperors, which even Nero, Caligula and Commodus felt obliged to wear on state occasions, and adopted the dress and the manner of the Phoenicians and Medians, "which indeed was very graceful and magnificent, but at the same time savored of the luxury and effeminacy of those nations."

It was from the Phœnician Phallic god Elagabalus, whose obscene rites he introduced into Rome, that the Emperor took his surname. The phallic image of this god he had brought to the capital from Emesa, and he himself mingled with the devotees in the temple where the image was placed, going through the effeminate rites with them.

So intense was the interest of this Emperor in the dress and affairs of women that he created a Senate of Ladies, with his mother, the companion of his debaucheries, as president. Here, with the assistance and advice of the expert Heliogabalus, the styles and fashions in women's apparel were sagely and importantly decreed. This Senate was convoked frequently and regularly, and its authority was just as weighty as the Senate of the statesmen, where the Emperor's mother, to the scandal of Rome, had also a seat.

But this Orientally luxurious madman reached the climax of extravagance when he paralleled Nero in being formally married to a powerful slave Hieracles, whom he raised from miserable poverty to immense wealth. He even went beyond Nero, by prolonging the farce and taking up the tasks, of a wife after his "marriage."

"He was delighted to be called the mistress, the wife, the queen of Hieracles, and, that he might look the more like a woman, he had himself close shaved, took a distaff, and employed his time in spinning and other feminine occupations, to the great dishonor of the sex he intended to imitate."

The Emperor's mad design to give this emancipated slave the title of Cæsar and make him his successor to the throne, led to his own downfall and murder. That he had a sincere affection in his crazy brain for Hieracles, is demonstrated by the fact that, upon noting the hostile temper of Rome, he decided to go through with his project at the cost of his own life.

He determined that his end should be noble and by his own hand, but even the proposed instrument of his suicide indicated the streak of woman in his nature. He caused to be woven for him an exquisitely beautiful silken cord, rich in colors, and this he carried around with him for the purpose of hanging himself in a desperate emergency. As further precaution, he had wrought for him a little silver poniard of delicate design, such as ladies of the Latin countries still carry in the stocking, and he also provided himself with a deadly poison, enclosed in a golden box, beautifully ornamented.

But the assassins, when they sprang upon him unexpectedly, used more brutally masculine weapons upon the royal dandy, running him through with Roman swords to their steel hilts, mingling his æsthetic blood with sordid mud.

For the marriage festivities of Caracalla, another of the late Emperors of Rome, whose name is synonymous with execration, a band of soprano singers was manufactured by a process long practiced in the East, but hitherto unadopted in the West.

Plautianius, father of the prospective bride, an African by birth and a powerful general in the Roman army, used his influence with the Emperor to have seized for his purpose many male children of well-to-do Roman families, just a grade below the nobility.

These children were transformed by his orders into eunuchs, so that their soprano voices might be preserved, and during the many months that were to elapse before the wedding they were carefully trained in the art of choristers.

Thus, in the face of high indignation on the part of the populace, a custom was introduced into Rome that persisted later under the authority of the church, when castratos were required for soprano parts in the magnificent choirs. It led some fifteen centuries later to the development of the eviratos, those marvelous secular male sopranos whose voices never were equalled by women in the entire history of the world.

They are worth a whole chapter—later.

89

VI. VERSATILITY OF SATAN

THE Dark Ages, whatever else they failed to do, produced the ideal female impersonator—no less a distinguished personage than the Devil himself!

Satan not only could paint his cheeks, rouge his lips, pencil his eyebrows, and don delicate silks and laces, but he possessed a power the catamites through all the ages must envy—he could transform his pelvic apparatus at will.

At the Witches' Sabbath, which he attended with eager regularity, the Devil chose his dancing partners with an exquisite Epicureanism. Sometimes it was a young girl he wanted—a lusty, healthy wench from the country, on her first fearful visit to this woodland citadel of whirling sin, her eyes sparkling with passion, her lips parched with the dread of damnation; sometimes, a delicate young lady of the nobility, innocent of sin herself, but shaken by the recent discovery that she was a bastard, the daughter of a Cardinal when he was a humble priest, father confessor to her maiden mother. To these, Satan

appeared as a handsome, gallant young knight, gentlemanly, of good breeding, but fairly electrical with "sex appeal."

At other times it was some vigorous young man who attracted his fancy—a secular knight, maybe; a Galahad, "stepping out" for the first time, or a warrior priest like St. Anthony, there to test the strength of his continence. Then it was the Devil transformed himself into a sprightly maiden, who allowed herself coyly to be wooed and won. That he performed the entire act of copulation in this aspect of his enviable versatility there is no question, from the records of servants of Holy Church too pious to lie, too learned to permit of their being misinformed. But, while Satan was father of a rather extensive progeny through virgins he had ravished during the wild orgies of the Sabbath, there is no record that he ever became a mother. He can scarcely be blamed for that—but the holy fathers must be blamed for their neglect, in the interest of science, to learn his method of birth control.

Witchcraft, with its lascivious orgies of the Sabbath, was the outgrowth of the Roman and pagan mysteries, a sample of which has already come to our attention in the celebration in honor of Bona Dea in the house of Cæsar. The Church of the Christians helped itself to what it wanted from these mysteries, in its gradual evolution, and then what was left over was consecrated to the Devil.

The early Christians, in the catacombs of Rome, had their own mysteries, largely of Jewish and Asiatic origin—mysteries as secret as those of the Græco-Romans. Reports of their practices, true or false, assumed such monstrous shapes that the early Emperors hunted them down and burned them at the stake. Treasonable utterances against the secular powers in authority may account for much of this persecution, but it is difficult to understand, on that ground alone, the opinion of such a liberal as Tacitus, who minced no words when he spoke even of the Emperor.

It is certain that the catacombs were populated at least as thickly by the scum of the earth—murderers, robbers, prostitutes, criminals of every variety as by devout and holy saints, and it is scarcely possible that these early Christians succeeded in keeping themselves free from the taint.

Consider how even in far later times the holy rites were profaned in communities free from the fetid breath of the catacombs. One example, from hundreds possible to cite, will illustrate. Take the celebration by Abbé Guibourg of the Black Mass, with Madame de Montespan, mistress of the King of France, stretched out in a state of perfect nudity on the altar, lying on a pall of rich, black velvet, with the holy vessels of the mass placed either on her naked abdomen or set beside her. The Host was consecrated blasphemously, and then, at the signal for the Precious Blood, a child was brought forward, its throat cut, and its warm blood allowed to stream over la Montespan. At the trial of the infamous la Voisin, procurer of children for these unholy rites, regularly celebrated not only for the King's mistress but for other ladies of the Court, this woman confessed she had procured as many as twenty-five hundred infants for the purpose, buying them from beggar women, from prostitutes and from foundling hospitals where even girls of the nobility resorted in distress. This case is a matter of documentary record in the criminal archives of Paris, and not merely a scandalous report, like the doings, for example, of the versatile Devil at the Witches' Sabbath.

Just how far the reports of Christian abominations in the catacombs that filled Rome and dammed up the founts of pity in Romans watching the massacres by Nero and the other Emperors were justified can never be determined, but there is enough to indicate that considerable sublimation was necessary before the early Christian "mysteries," celebrated behind locked doors, evolved into the rites of Rome now witnessed in our resplendent cathedrals.

These Christians in the catacombs were not a unit, but were broken up into many secret societies, each with its "mysteries." There was much jealousy, of course—much bickering—much grasping after the leadership always coveted even in a band of thieves or a community of prostitutes—much telling of scandalous tales about each other. The Christians themselves were the most industrious spreaders of rumors of abomination about rival sects, and in an age when Emperors and Senators had their catamites, when priests of all the gods and goddesses were eunuchs, either physically or mentally, it is no wonder that charges of perversion frequently appear.

St. Paul took cognizance in his letter to the Romans—"men with men working that which is unseemly," and he was considerably worried, moreover, on the score of circumcision, which the Christians of Jewish blood were not ready yet to reject for baptism.

Circumcision has been the subject of much puzzled speculation— even being put on a basis of expert scientific realization by the early

93

Jews that it was a highly sanitary measure in tropical countries, and so advised by the priests in the interest of health, but cloaked with the sanctity of a divine command. The rejection of pork by the Jews has been similarly explained—pork being unduly heavy for tropical stomachs. But neither the early Jews nor the early Christians discovered the sanitary qualities of the bath.

More expert examination of the history of the rite of circumcision, however, seems to indicate it is a substitute for castration—for effemination, that is, in the interest of the gods, who seem to have had queer tastes as to the manner of men who should serve them. The practice is far older than the Jewish institution—it was prevalent throughout Ethiopia, Egypt and Asia from prehistoric times.

Since all these peoples—as later the Jews—had a very healthy instinct of race preservation, they developed the system of castrating only a few of their males to serve the gods direct. The others, however, gave as generously as they could of the organ of creation to the creator, and still preserve unimpaired its function.

(When we speak, by the way, of God creating Adam in his own image, the Hebrew words have been alleged by certain of the savants to signify primitively that "Adam" was not the entire man but only the generative organ in a state of excitement. Adam, therefore, if we are to believe this theory, which we rejected a while back, may have looked a whole lot like God, but Eve bore not the remotest resemblance—rather a tough blow to the feminists who bob their hair and wear trousers so Jehovah won't have so much trouble spotting them.)

The practice of circumcision was adopted by the Jews and became

94

a rite as sacred as the Christian baptism. The upper class Egyptians, however, seem to have let it languish, and by the time Christ—or rather St. Paul, the real militant founder of Christianity appeared—it had been relegated to the priests, astrologers and prophets—indicating its identity, as a rite, with castration, still practiced by the priests of Cybele. Another curious custom still further fixes its status. The Hottentots, as late as the eighteenth century, deprived their male children of one testicle as an offering to the gods, reserving the other for its natural function at maturity.

St. Paul, possessor of a lot of animal vigor, and impatient, as frequently shown in his biography and his letters of the effeminate rites of the pagans, opened war on circumcision—but cautiously, for he was in an uncertain position in his ambition for leadership, with Peter, who had actually seen and talked with Christ, as a formidable rival.

There was much mud-slinging between the two. Peter, according to Paul, was not only a glutton, but he gorged himself with forbidden things—pork, even, and blood pudding, and hares, and eels. Peter or, at any rate, his comrades, regarded Paul as an upstart, who took up Christianity only to get even with the Pharisee, Gamaliel, for refusing to give him his daughter in marriage. The wishes of the girl may have had something to do with her father's refusal, for Paul was "fat, short and broad shouldered; his dark eyebrows were united across his aquiline nose; his legs were crooked, his head bald," and by some accounts he was hunchbacked.

In his fight against circumcision—sublimated effemination, Paul couldn't go the length he did in other matters, for he couldn't afford to alienate his Jews. "If they circumcised, Jesus would not avail them," he declared, but shortly afterward, bending probably to an unrecorded storm, he caused his disciple Timothy to be circumcised. His final pronouncement straddles the fence:

"For circumcision verily profiteth, if thou keepest the law; but if thou be a breaker of the law, thy circumcision is made uncircumcision"—take it or leave it.

Origen, decades later, did not stop at circumcision, as has already been related, but made himself a eunuch "for the kingdom of heaven's sake."

It was also a following up of the effemination of the pagan priesthood that celibacy was fastened upon the servants of the Church of Rome. Such priests as were not made eunuchs among the heathen were generally required to take vows of chastity. The priests of Cybele, accepting the hard decree, elected to be castrated rather than fight their passions. In the evolution of the Roman church out of the pagan mysteries, both circumcision and castration—except in the case of sopranos for the choirs—were abolished, but the vow of chastity was retained.

In Paul's immediate entourage was a personage whose sex has been disputed—at least the books attributed to St. Thecla are declared by Tertullian to have been written by a man. The tradition is that St. Thecla, a woman, filled with holy zeal, disguised herself as a man, sought out St. Paul and became his friend. She passed for a man, but was reputed a woman—a later generation transforms her into the

96

man she pretended to be, and attaches this effeminate creature, man or woman, to a confidential place with the militant apostle.

In the centuries to come, the "mysteries" of the various warring sects of the Christians gradually separated themselves from the "mysteries" of the pagans around them, and by the time Constantine the Great came into power and adopted as the state religion the system of St. Paul, now completely triumphant over that of St. Peter—though St. Peter claimed, curiously enough, and still retains the nominal victory—the Church of Rome was ready to throw out its secrets and appear before the world with its ritual—substantially the ritual of today.

Not quite all its secrets, however. There was still enough left of the old pagan rites undigested to furnish material for the Templars—and there came a time when the Temple developed into the scandal of all Europe, rivaling even the Witches' Sabbath itself for wickedness.

The proceedings against the Templars, instituted by King Philippe IV of France in 1307, with the seizing and imprisoning of Jacques de Molay, developed into the most sensational court trial of all time, and the merits of the opposing litigants and the conflicting testimony are still discussed with considerable heat by partisans, after six hundred years. The French king is alleged, by his opponents, to have been actuated by jealousy of the power and wealth of the order, and there are even stories that he sought admission to membership, but was blackballed—hardly credible, seeing that the order was aristocratic and there were few aristocrats to match in degree a king of the French.

By his friends, Philippe is credited with a genuine reform movement —an attempt to lance a suppurating sore that stank to heaven.

In scores of the charges against the Templars we are not interested, in the present inquiry. But reams of testimony indicated the Templars had adopted the vices and habits of the Emperors and aristocrats of Rome in the days of the Imperial decadence, and had kept them alive in the international aristocratic circles of Medieval Europe.

"The kiss of the Templar" is still preserved as a by-word, and is said to be commonly understood in English schools by boys, who had no difficulty in following the press reports of Oscar Wilde's trial. The kiss was a relic of ancient phallic rites, which seem to have come into the Temple without the sublimation they underwent in the costuming of the priests of the orthodox church. With the kiss, the novice in the Temple foreswore women—or, if a Templar so far forgot himself thereafter as to have sexual commerce with a virgin and a child resulted, the child was to be roasted, and an unguent made of the fat, with which their idol was to be anointed. That bit of testimony, of course, has been bitterly assailed.

Much curiosity has attached to this idol, to which numerous references were made in the testimony, and of which numerous vague, conflicting descriptions were given. Many of the witnesses testified as to a beard, others declared it the face of a woman, some combined the two descriptions—a bearded woman—all agreed it was uncanny, some were terror-stricken at the sight of it. It was curiously life-like, according to much of the testimony, with the feline feeling of a cat—some of the witnesses, indeed, testified that it was a huge cat, and no human at all. One initiate, whose observation may be significant, says the cat-like creature must have been the devil in female form—a connecting link with the Witches' Sabbath—and likewise a suggestion that the idol may have been actually alive—a female impersonator with a strong sense of melodrama. The idol was seldom shown, and only in the most secret recesses of the Temple.

In the Temple, then, where the aristocrats assembled, and in wooded recesses of the forest, where young men congregated for wild orgies, with a few women and a sprinkling of their elders and occasionally even a priest—were preserved the ancient rites of Greece and Rome. The masquerade of the male as female was the chief interest —the chief necessity for the secrecy; positively dangerous, but risked for the adventure.

Many names are preserved in the volcanic lava of the Temple scandal and in the various trials of participants in the forest orgies with Satan and his adorers, but they would have little meaning for the reader. Important personages of the French and German courts frequently went to the Sabbaths incognito—the ladies with their faces veiled—usually as spectators, sometimes to participate in the saturnalia. After long centuries the Sabbath became merely a myth—there are still stories of these orgies, with the devil present, in the fastnesses of the Hartz mountains, and the peasants of Bohemia still tell fearful tales of doings on Walpurgis night.

Witchcraft itself "degenerated" as the Sabbath lost meaning, and our zealots of New England, who persecuted old women for unlawfully exerting the influence of the "evil eye" had quite lost sight of the original cardinal sin persisting from the days of the old gods.

Even before the Templar scandal broke, the wiles of the catamite had become so offensive in many parts of Medieval Europe that severe penalties were imposed. In Paris in 1212 the penalty for sodomy was fixed at death, and Havelock Ellis cites the curious case of a man who fell under suspicion of the police for rejecting the advances of a female prostitute. He also quotes from a book, "De Planctu Naturæ" by Alain de Lille:

"Man is made woman; he blackens the honor of his sex, the craft of magic Venus makes him of double gender"; nobly beautiful youths have "turned their hammers of love to the office of anvils," and "many kisses lie untouched on maiden lips." The result is that "the natural anvils," that is to say the neglected maidens, "bewail the absence of their hammers and are seen sadly to demand them."

The Temple was not alone the repository of the "Scythian Sin" —not the only establishment whose "pious love-feasts and heroic fraternizations covered filthy, monkish amours," as Michelet savagely expresses it.

"In most monasteries," if Niccolini is to be believed, "and more particularly in those of the Capuchins and Reformati, there begins at Christmas a series of feasts, which continues till Lent. All sorts of games are played, the most splendid banquets are given, and in the small towns, above all, the refectory of the convent is the best place of amusement for the greater number of the inhabitants. At carnivals, two or three very magnificent entertainments take place; the board

100

so profusely spread that one might imagine that Copia had here poured the whole contents of her horn. It must be remembered that these two orders live by alms.

"The somber silence of the cloister is replaced by a confused sound of merrymaking, and its gloomy vaults now echo with other songs than those of the psalmist. A ball enlivens and terminates the feast; and, to render it still more animated, and perhaps to show how completely their vow of chastity has eradicated all carnal appetite, some of the young monks appear coquettishly dressed in the garb of the fair sex, and begin the dance, along with others, transformed into gay cavaliers. To describe the scandalous scene which ensues would be but to disgust my readers."

Popes Paul II, Sixtus IV and Julius II are credited with the purple sins of the Cæsars that found refuge in the Temple and in the monasteries. Henry III of France, and Edward II, William II and James I of England continued the imperial traditions in Northern courts.

Excuse was made that the Templars had acquired any effeminacy of which they might legitimately be held guilty in the East, where they long sojourned in their attempts to wrest the Holy Land from the Turks. The excuse is idle—Rome in the days of the Cæsars and after could have given lessons to Babylon. Besides, the East has enough sins of its own to answer for—including Sultan Baber.

But the Middle Ages, it is pleasant to record, were not given over entirely to Satan and the Templars and the Witches and the other powers of Darkness. A silvery interlude is the German knight and minnesinger Ulrich of Lichtenstein.

"As a page he commenced his glorious career by drinking the water in which his lady had washed her hands," Emil Lucka sums up. "Later on he caused his upper lip to be amputated because it displeased his mistress, for 'whatever she dislikes in me, I, too, hate.' On another occasion he cut off one of his fingers and used it, set in gold, as a clasp for a volume of his poems which he sent to her. One of his famous exploits was a journey through nearly the whole of Austria, disguised as Venus, jousting, dressed in women's clothes, with every knight he met."

Lucka assigns to Ulrich and not to Don Quixote the honor of provoking the great guffaw that eventually laughed chivalry out of existence.

VII. THE EVIRATI

As Europe awoke slowly from the nightmare of the Dark Ages, with the frightful shriek of the Inquisition ringing in its ears, the arts gradually were liberated from the atmosphere of the Church. Painters began doing portraits of their mistresses without the necessity of labeling them Madonnas, as Raphael had done. Drama emerged from the miracle plays. Sculptors and architects began to look beyond the somber walls of the great cathedrals.

Music, too, emerged—and with a curious result. The Church, as we have seen, had started early in its career manufacturing in Rome artificial sopranos, under dispensation from the Founder of the Faith himself, it was contended—"eunuchs for the kingdom of heaven's sake." The industry had continued all through the fearful night when men's minds lay under the heels of the priests.

So that now, early in the seventeenth century, when music began to take on a secular phase, the art of making and training these soprano castrates was so highly developed that the golden age of the

Evirati dawned—musical eunuchs with voices such as the world never heard before nor since.

These artificial "prima donnas," taken from the church choirs and trained for the concert stage and the opera, became possessed of voices combining the sweetness of the female voice with the strength and superior artistry of the male—a combination impossible to attain in nature. The most renowned of the Evirati, Farinelli, is still reckoned, by all odds, the finest singer who ever lived. He vanquished, in their own sphere, Cuzzoni and Faustina, the two greatest female soprani of their time, and two of the greatest in the history of singing.

The race of the Evirati, persisting brilliantly for a hundred years, ended with Crescentini, favorite of Napoleon, around whom buzzed a tempest of more than teapot proportions.

The Evirati were as melodramatically emotional and as pettily vain as the women artists with whom they placed themselves in direct rivalry. They created mighty furores in court and social circles. They were sought eagerly by female admirers, to whom they displayed something of the same sort of gallantry Mlle. de Maupin showed her feminine adorers. The most gossipy of all the centuries since the world began, the Eighteenth, preserves many little choice bits of scandal of the Evirati, showing the feminine trend of their minds as well as their voices.

Napoleon's favorite, for example, ready to go on one night in Venice in the opera "Gli Orazii e Curiazii" as Horatius, discovered that the leading tenor, in the rôle of Curiatius, was dressed more elegantly than he. Crescentini insisted on exchanging costumes. The

104

manager interposed, but the Evirato was obstinate. Finally, when the audience was getting impatient for the curtain to rise, the exchange was arranged, and "throughout the evening a Curiatius, six feet high, was seen wearing a little Roman costume, which looked as if it would burst any moment, while a diminutive Horatius was attired in a long Alban tunic, with its skirt trailing to the ground."

Gizziello, another of these "sublime eunuchs," on first hearing Farinelli, "burst into tears and fainted away with despondency." Later this same gentle Gizziello played the opposite rôle in a similar outburst of feministic temperament.

Caffarelli, haughtiest of all the Evirati, journeyed one afternoon from Naples, where he himself was appearing in opera, to Rome, where Gizziello, a fresh sensation, was the idol of the hour, on purpose to hear the new singer so as to be able to tear his art to bits. Caffarelli took a seat far back in the pit. He sat gloomily silent while the vast audience applauded the star's entry. But, during the course of the opening aria, Caffarelli gradually warmed to his rival, and at its close was so carried away by his emotion that he sprang to his feet and cried: "Bravo, bravissimo, Gizziello! 'Tis Caffarelli who shouts it!" and he rushed, blind with tears, from the theater.

Farinelli once excited an Evirato of tougher fiber than Gizziello to an outburst of emotion more characteristic of a woman than a man. This was the veteran Senesino, dean of the tribe, whose soprano, while clear and penetrating, was certainly heavy enough to be classed as mezzo—some critics even rate him a contralto. At their first meeting on the stage, "Senesino had the part of a furious tyrant to represent, and Farinelli that of an unfortunate hero in chains; but, in the course of the first song, he so softened the obdurate heart of the enraged tyrant that Senesino, forgetting his stage character, ran to Farinelli and embraced him in his arms."

Senesino may, perhaps, be forgiven this outburst, in view of the emotional influence Farinelli's marvelous singing is credited with having had on normal men and women alike.

Farinelli was brought from Italy to London by Senesino to co-star with himself and the female soprano, Cuzzoni, already a London sensation. Senesino had become established in the British metropolis as an operatic producer, backed by Lord Cooper and the composer Porpora, in opposition to the great Handel, for whom Senesino had sung until they quarreled.

At the first private rehearsal, in Cuzzoni's apartment, after Farinelli's arrival, "Lord Cooper, observing that the band did not accompany the singer, but were all gaping with wonder, desired them to be more attentive, when they confessed that they had been so overpowered with admiration and astonishment as to be unable to follow him—an incident vouched for to Dr. Burney by one of the band."

Then, on the opening night in London, in Lincoln's Inn Fields, in the opera "Artaserse," Farinelli created a furore such as had never been seen in the English metropolis. At the close of a song, interpolated and especially composed for him by Porpora to show the wonderful brilliance of his voice, and in which he ran away from the violins, the audience sprang to its feet and shouted and applauded for five full minutes. Above the din was heard a female voice from a box.

excitedly exclaiming, "One God and one Farinelli!" an expression Hogarth has immortalized in "The Rake's Progress."

Senesino's display of feminine emotionalism is not confined to the incident of the tyrant and the hero in chains. One night in London, in the most popular of his operas, "Giulio Cesare," he was chanting the words, "Cæsar never knew fear," when a piece of heavy scenery crashed from the roof onto the stage, barely missing him. "The poor hero was so frightened that he trembled, lost his voice, and fell crying."

Besides being effeminately emotional, the Evirati were, with scarcely an exception, almost pathologically vain. Perhaps the one least afflicted in this respect was the greatest genius of them all, Farinelli, while the vainest of them was his nearest rival, Caffarelli.

It may have been that Caffarelli's vanity, which became monstrous and odious, served to keep a tendency in Farinelli in check. Their stations in life were at the opposite ends of the social scale.

Farinelli was of noble birth, as is proven incontestably by the fact that the King of Spain admitted him into the orders of Calatrava and St. Igoe, whose candidates must submit letters of nobility to the most rigid scrutiny. It was quite by accident that he became an Evirato. As a young boy he sustained an injury in riding that made necessary the operation by which he retained his treble.

Caffarelli was of mean origin. He was the son of a peasant, who opposed the boy's musical inclination, because it interfered with his chores. He was taken from his peasant tasks almost by violence by Caffaro, mæstro of the Chapel Royal, Naples, who heard him sing and

107

recognized his genius. Caffaro sent him to Norcia, "to be prepared for the career of an Evirato, according to the barbarous custom of those days; and on his return gave him elementary instruction in his own house in reading, and writing and music."

But neither Caffaro—from whom the peasant boy, Gætano Majorano, took the name he was to render immortal—nor, after him, Porpora, best of all the instructors of the Evirati, who also trained Farinelli, could educate the boorishness out of Caffarelli. To his latest days he retained a peasant coarseness and insolence that made him intolerable in polite society. His natural vanity was heightened at the outset of his public career by the parting observation of his master, Porpora. "Go, my son," said he, who was also Farinelli's instructor. "I have nothing more to teach you. You are the greatest singer in Europe."

Farinelli and Caffarelli became naturally intense rivals. The aristocrat was as popular personally as the peasant's son was unpopular. But the genius of the latter could not be denied, and he had his critics who ranked him, despite his personality, above the nobleman.

Caffarelli's opinion of his own genius may be gathered from an incident that happened at Turin on his first visit. Farinelli had just preceded him. The Prince of Savoy, after hearing him sing, praised him warmly, and in course of conversation remarked that the Princess was coming to the next concert, though she thought it scarcely possible any one could wholly please her after Farinelli.

"Tell her," replied Caffarelli, "she shall hear two Farinellis."

The Evirati, though later often cast for males, nearly always made their débuts in family rôles, although women by this time had come pretty well into their own on the Continental stage. Sometimes they put their voices, in challenge, against the voices of their women co-stars.

Senesino, thus, created a remarkable sensation in London in 1728 on the production of the opera "Tolomeo" in an echo song "Dite che fa" sung by the female Cuzzoni. The male mezzo, standing behind the scene, repeated Cuzzoni's song passage for passage and tone for tone, giving the effect of an echo miraculously true. It was this same Cuzzoni, matched by Senesino, who was vanquished in a contest with Farinelli.

Guadagni, rated the best actor among the male sopranists, was chosen by Handel to sing the parts in the "Messiah" and "Samson" which he had composed for Mrs. Cibber.

In acting, Guadagni was a pupil of Garrick, who had been delighted with his playing of young girl parts. Garrick trained him personally for a rôle in "The Fairies" (a name of baleful foreshadowing) and took as much delight in teaching him to act as Gizziello did in cultivating his singing voice.

"As an actor," remarks Dr. Burney of this talented eunuch, "he seems to have had no equal on any operatic stage in Europe; his figure was uncommonly elegant and noble; his countenance replete with beauty, intelligence and dignity; and his attitude and gestures were so full of grace and propriety, that they would have been excellent studies for a statuary."

Caffarelli, it is recorded, "made his début in Rome in a female character, as was usual for sopranists, when his beautiful voice, perfect method and handsome face procured him his first triumph."

Bernacchi, one of the first of the Evirati, styled "the king of singers," sang for Handel in his "Rinaldo" a rôle that had previously been sung by Boschi and Galerati, two female contraltos.

It was when a young singer, making his mark in female attire, that Farinelli achieved the astonishing vocal feat that made him famous over Europe. He was singing in Rome, a boy of seventeen, under the direction of his master, Porpora.

"There was a German trumpet player at the time in the capital, who excited the admiration of the Romans by his marvelous powers. For this artist, Porpora wrote an obbligato part to a song in which his pupil vied with the instrument in holding and swelling a note of extraordinary length, purity and volume. Although the virtuoso performed this in a wonderful manner, Farinelli excelled him in the brilliance and gradual crescendo and diminuendo of the note, while he carried the enthusiasm of the audience to the highest pitch by the novelty and spontaneity of the shakes and difficult variations which he introduced into the air."

Carestini, who, at a late date, headed Handel's opera company in London, and "was able to hold his own" against even the great Farinelli in the rival opera, and who possessed "the fullest, finest, deepest contralto ever, perhaps, heard," made his first appearance in Rome at sixteen in the female part of Costanza in "Griselda."

In spite of their direct rivalry with female artists in voice, appearance and manner, the Evirati were not without gallantry, and their

love affairs with adoring matinée idol worshippers, serious at least as those of Mlle. de Maupin, sometimes created a furore.

The irrepressible Caffarelli was the hero of more than one scandal. In Rome, "he was courted by the highest society, and in one of his numerous *bonnes fortunes* nearly lost his life. Owing to a sudden alarm, he had to escape by passing the night in an empty cistern in a garden, where he caught a severe cold, which kept him in bed for a month. After this he went about everywhere protected by four bravos from the vengeance of the husband." In another similar adventure in Vienna he was saved from a duel only by the interposition of the female singer, Tesi.

One of these soprano eunuchs, Tenducci, carried an affair of the heart so far as to marry the object of his pathetic passion, Dora Maunsell, a Limerick girl—thereby duplicating the marriage of La Maupin with the petite Marseillaise. Tenducci eloped with his colleen, and the escapade became a nine days wonder. There appeared a book, "A True and Genuine Narrative of Mr. and Mrs. Tenducci," written by a woman, which created a sensation similar to that aroused by Nan Britton's "The President's Daughter," and was as eagerly snapped up. The Tenduccis seem to have lived happily.

Women, generally, made much of the Evirati, and the eunuchs, rendered perhaps even more melodramatically sentimental than the average actor by the nullification of their natural virility, were intoxicated by the adoration.

Even Farinelli, most evenly balanced of them all, became, on his London début, "ridiculously popular: from the highest nobles to the

meanest citizens and their wives, all seemed to go mad about him."
The sopranist, while not entirely impervious to the obvious, bungled
compliments paid him in bad Italian, kept healthy his sense of
comedy, and on his return to his native Italy built, out of the wealth
showered upon him, "a very superb mansion in which he dwelt, choosing to dignify it with the significant appellation of 'The English
Folly.' "

Kings, from the first appearance of the Evirati, vied with nobles
and commons to do them honor, and sometimes gave their favorites
positions of high importance in the State.

Under Philip V of Spain and Philip's successor, Ferdinand VI,
Farinelli became an even more important political factor than the
actor Paris was under the Roman Emperor Domitian; while Napoleon's decoration of Crescentini with the Iron Cross had as much
significance in the affairs of state as the winning of a battle or the
signing of a treaty.

From the outset, because of his noble birth, Farinelli had entrée
into the best society, and the condescension of kings was all the easier.
On his hit in London, he was received immediately by the Royal
Family, where he became such a favorite that the Princess of Orange,
an accomplished musician, accompanied him, with her own fingers, on
the harpsichord.

It was due to the friendly, familiar interest of a still more important royal personage, shortly before his London début, that the
noble eunuch acquired a quality in his singing that contributed
immeasurably to his immortality.

The cultured Emperor Charles VI, on Farinelli's visit to Vienna in 1731, was not wholly pleased with his concert. "You have excited only astonishment and admiration," said the Emperor after the performance, "but you have never touched the heart; it would be easy for you to create emotion, if you would but be more simple and more expressive."

Farinelli, it is pleasing to record, instead of resenting his royal critic, "adopted this admirable counsel, and became the most pathetic, as he was still the most brilliant of singers."

It was only two years after his English triumph, from which he carried off, among countless souvenirs, a "fine wrought-gold snuff-box, richly set with diamonds and rubies, in which was enclosed a pair of diamond knee-buckles, as also a purse of 100 guineas," the gift of the Prince of Wales, that Farinelli went, by invitation, to the Court of Spain.

In the interim, however, he made another conquest, this time in France, where prejudice against foreign singers ran high. Farinelli not only overcame this prejudice, but was invited to the Queen's apartments to sing for Louis XV and the highest dignitaries of the court. Louis "applauded him to an extent that astonished the court" and "gave him his portrait set in diamonds and 500 Louis d'Or."

With the endorsement of the Viennese, English and French courts, Farinelli journeyed to Madrid, intending to remain there a few weeks. Instead, he stayed a quarter of a century.

King Philip V was a prey to melancholy—the same sort of an "evil spirit" that afflicted old King Saul of the Jews. He sat brooding by the hour, neglecting affairs of state and refusing to preside at council. The Queen decided to try the remedy that had worked so magical a change in Saul. The David of her choice was the newly arrived soprano, who had already conquered Madrid with the same ease he had taken Vienna, London and Paris.

Farinelli, accordingly, was brought into a room adjoining the apartment of the King, where he sang tender and pathetic airs. The listless Philip was struck, moved and finally overcome, or, like Saul, "was refreshed, and was well, and the evil spirit departed from him."

He gratefully sent for Farinelli, thanked him extravagantly, and told him to name his own reward.

"Farinelli, coached, said his best reward would be to see Philip return to the society of court and the cares of state. The King consented, and allowed himself to be shaved for the first time in weeks."

The singer lost nothing financially by his sentimental declaration of his "best reward," for the Queen engaged him at an annual salary of 50,000 francs to remain permanently at court, and Farinelli, as some critical biographer laments, "thus became lost to the art world forever."

During the remaining ten years of Philip's life, the sopranist sang, for his half million francs, four songs to the King every night, without change or variation—surely punishment enough for his forsaking of the Muse for Mammon.

In Philip's reign, Farinelli was merely a court ornament, with no political power. But Philip's successor, Ferdinand VI, bestowed upon him the highest honors, and while he was not formally designated prime minister, no minister of Europe enjoyed more real power than this eunuch.

Ferdinand, like Philip, was of melancholic temperament, and like him could find relief only in the magic of Farinelli's voice. One of the first acts of the new monarch was to bestow upon his favorite the cross of Calatrava, and from this moment Farinelli became possessed of "power unbounded—greater than any ever enjoyed by a singer." He was consulted by ministers and ambassadors and "ever showed the greatest prudence, modesty and moderation."

It is recorded that he "made no enemies, strange in those days, but conciliated those jealous of his power by gaining favor for them. Hearing one day an officer in the antechamber complain of the King's neglect of his thirty years service while riches were heaped on a 'miserable actor,' Farinelli begged a commission for the grumbler, and gave it to him, to his great surprise, observing mildly that he was wrong to tax the King with ingratitude."

Through Farinelli's influence, Ferdinand established an Italian opera in Madrid, with the favorite as manager. Thither were invited some of the first singers of Italy, including the modest Gizziello. In the conduct of his opera, Farinelli displayed a severity little short of tyrannical, knowing the iron hand is the only sure rule in the stage world.

This severity manifested itself in the case of Caterina Mingotti, a formidable female rival of Faustina, who came to Madrid with Gizziello.

"Scarcely had she settled in the Spanish capital before she found the control of the all-powerful vocalist and manager extremely irksome. He was so rigid, so intolerant, that he would not permit her even to practice in a room overlooking the street, and would not grant her leave to sing anywhere but in the opera or at court. The Spanish nobility, eager to hear the charming cantatrice, overwhelmed her with pressing invitations to sing at private concerts and balls, but she was compelled to decline all such offers.

"Once Farinelli was forced to yield. A lady, in a very delicate state of health, felt a particular desire to hear Signora Mingotti, but was unable to gratify it by a visit to the theater, fearing the excitement of the scene. Her husband urgently pressed on Farinelli the request that Mingotti should visit the invalid, but received a decided refusal; the Señora persisted, and her lord, wishing to indulge her, went at length to the King, and laid a complaint before him. His Majesty immediately issued a royal mandate that Mingotti was to receive the lady at her house, and to sing for her; to which behest Farinelli, much against his will, was obliged to bow."

It was not often that Ferdinand opposed the wishes of his favorite. He enjoyed almost royal power during the fifteen years of the King's reign, and seems more seldom to have abused it than normal ministers.

A party, however, was formed in court against him, but with political rather than personal enmity; and shortly after the ascent of Charles III Farinelli, clashing with this group which was favored by the new King, on a political matter involving France and Naples, was given orders to leave Spain. His salary was guaranteed, because of past services, on condition that he should retire to Bologna and live there instead of at Naples.

Farinelli consented, and passed the last twenty years of his life in luxury in a splendid palace a mile out of Bologna. He was courteous to visitors, loved to dwell on his political rather than his artistic honors, played the viol and harpsichord, and composed a little. He made a fine collection of musical instruments, which was the delight of his palace, and an equally fine collection of paintings by Murillo and others, including a portrait of himself with Faustina, the work of Amiconti. He died July 15, 1782, in his seventy-eighth year, and the royalty of all Europe did him honor.

In his behavior in the sunlight of royal patronage, the peasant Caffarelli again furnishes a striking contrast to his more renowned rival. Louis XV, on the Evirato's conquest of Paris in 1750, "sent him a present of a snuff-box; but Caffarelli, observing that it was plain, showed the messenger, one of the gentlemen of the court, a drawer full of snuff-boxes, and remarked that the worst of them was finer than the gift of the King of France.

" 'If,' said he, 'he had sent me his portrait in it!'

" 'That,' replied the gentleman, 'is only given to ambassadors.'

" 'Well,' was the retort, 'and all the ambassadors of the world would not make one Caffarelli!'

"This, when repeated, made the King laugh heartily; but the Dauphine sent for the singer, and, giving him a passport, said:

" 'It is signed by the King himself—for you a great honor; but lose no time in using it, for it is only good for ten days.'

117

"Caffarelli left France in high dudgeon."

With the enormous fortune he accumulated, Caffarelli "purchased a dukedom and built at Santo Dorato a palace, over the gate of which he inscribed with characteristic modesty, *'Amphion Thebas, ego domum.'* A commentator added, *'Ille cum, sine tu!'* "

He blustered a lot, quarreled a little—the female singer, Tesi, saved him from a duel with a gentleman who expressed himself as anxious to operate further on the Evirato's anatomy.

He died Nov. 30, 1783, leaving his wealth and dukedom to a nephew.

Guadagni won the favor of the Electress of Saxe, who heard him at Verona and brought him home with her to Munich. The Elector, also, was highly pleased, and Guadagni remained at the court of Munich until the death of the Prince. Going then to Potsdam, he sang for Frederick II, who was so charmed that he made him a present of a gold snuff-box encrusted with diamonds—"the finest he had ever given."

Gizziello enjoyed the patronage of Charles III, King of Naples. Bernacchi won the friendship of the Elector of Bavaria, and later was taken into the service of the Emperor. Pistacchi, one of the earliest of the Eviratos, and the founder of the famous school for teaching the artificial sopranos at Bologna, was renowned as the court singer of Parma.

Senesino, in 1739, then living in Florence, sang a duet with the Archduchess Maria Theresa. Nicolini, praised by Addison as "the greatest performer in dramatic music that is now living, or that per-

118

haps ever appeared on the stage," was decorated in Venice with the Order of St. Mark.

Napoleon's experience in conferring the Order of the Iron Crown on Crescentini was little less sensational than his divorce from Josephine.

The Emperor first heard this marvelous eunuch, the last of a brilliant school, at Vienna in 1805, and was so charmed with his voice that, on his return to France, he sent for Crescentini, offering him a permanent position in Paris at a handsome salary. The Evirato accepted, and the following year left his position as professor of singing to the Austrian Imperial family to come to the French court.

One night in 1808, "Romeo e Giulietta" was staged at the Tuileries with Crescentini and Madame Grassini in the star rôles. "Never was the sublimity of song combined with dramatic art more powerfully exhibited than then!" The climax came in the exquisite third act, with Romeo's prayer, his cry of anguish and his air "ombra adorata, aspetta."

"The audience were bathed in tears. The Emperor, carried away and forgetting the rules of etiquette, clapped his hands and shouted like a schoolboy; and Talma, seated on a bench near the orchestra, did not attempt to conceal his emotion: the great tragedian confessed he had never been so deeply touched by anything in his life before."

After the performance, Napoleon sent to Grassini twenty thousand francs, and on Crescentini he bestowed the Order of the Iron Crown, of which he was Chevalier.

Immediately there arose a storm of criticism—nothing unusual, except for its violent intensity, since everything Napoleon did had to undergo the baptism of fire not only from the old nobility, who resented the upstart Emperor, but from the better grade of the commons, who, despite the Revolution, still retained a sense of the proprieties of the old France.

In Crescentini's case, he was not only a "play actor"—a reproach that has scarcely lost its connotation of the contemptuous, even to this day—but he was a eunuch as well, and since the day when Jehovah commanded, through the mouth of Moses, that no man "who hath his stones broken" should be allowed to come into the holy presence, eunuchs have been pretty generally barred from admission into choice groups of men. Witness the secret societies that prevail currently.

Napoleon was assailed from all sides, choice remarks as to his real emotions for Crescentini were made, but the fact that the names of the two were not linked in a dirty scandal that has persisted in history, is pretty good evidence that Napoleon, whatever his passionate admiration for the military genius of Alexander and Cæsar may have been, had no inclination to follow their habits in private life.

Such a scandal, could there have been found the flimsiest excuse, would have been easy to fix—easier, indeed, than the one that has come down, that his love for his worshipped sister Pauline was more than brotherly—for the Emperor was cold in his desire for women—abnormally so in his youth. His many mistresses were thrust upon him and influenced him not at all.

This pathological coldness, for a Corsican, seems not to have savored at all of inversion, for the Emperor was just as cold to men. It may have affected, however, the Bonaparte blood. Hector Fleischmann cites the case of a woman, in love with Napoleon III, nephew of the great Napoleon, who "admitted that he produced upon her the effect of a woman." Napoleon III, moreover, in youth disguised himself as a flower girl to get to a sweetheart. But he was discovered by the girl's husband and beaten.

"One morning at St. Helena," long after the Crescentini incident, "Napoleon was speaking of the tenacity with which the French clung to slight matters of decorum.

" 'In conformity with my system,' observed he, 'of amalgamating all kinds of merit, and of rendering one and the same reward universal, I had an idea of presenting the Cross of the Legion of Honor to Talma; but I refrained from doing this, in consideration of our capricious manners and absurd prejudices. I wished to make a first experiment in an affair that was out of date and unimportant, and I accordingly gave the Iron Crown to Crescentini. The decoration was foreign, and so was the individual on whom it was conferred. This circumstance was less likely to attract public notice or to render my conduct the subject of discussion; at worst it could only give rise to a few malicious jokes. Such,' continued the Emperor, 'is the influence of public opinion. I distributed sceptres at will, and thousands readily bowed beneath their sway; and yet I could not give away a ribbon without the chance of incurring disapprobation, for I believe my experiment with regard to Crescentini proved unsuccessful.'

" 'It did, Sire,' observed some one present. 'The circumstance occasioned a great outcry in Paris; it drew forth a general anathema

121

in all the drawing-rooms of the metropolis, and afforded ample scope for the expression of malignant feeling.

" 'However, at one of the evening parties at the Faubourg Saint Germain, a bon-mot had the effect of completely stemming the torrent of indignation. A pompous orator was holding forth, in an eloquent strain, on the subject of the honor that had been conferred on Crescentini. He declared it to be a disgrace, a horror, a perfect profanation, and inquired what right Crescentini could have to such a distinction. On hearing this, the beautiful Madame Grassini, who was present, rose majestically from her chair, and, with a truly theatrical tone and gesture, exclaimed: "His wound, Monsieur! Do you make no allowance for that?"' This produced a general burst of laughter and applause, and poor Madame Grassini was very much embarrassed by her success!'

"The Emperor, who now heard this anecdote for the first time," continues Las Cases, "was highly amused by it. He often afterward alluded to it, and occasionally related it himself."

Though artificial in their creation, the Evirati must not be regarded as mere "freaks" in their accomplishments—not nearly to the degree of our female impersonators on the stage of today. Serious artists they were—geniuses some of them—unmistakable and genuine. They profoundly moved persons of the highest culture, as has already been pointed out. Critics who lavished praise upon them, like Addison, Steele, Dr. Burney and Lord Mount-Edgcombe were not given to idle laudation and were not easily imposed upon.

No artists since the world began were ever more carefully, more

122

severely trained than the boy eunuchs. Porpora, reputed the profoundest master of singing who ever lived, kept the youthful Caffarelli for five years on a single page of exercises.

The sort of art discipline imposed by Porpora on his still more brilliant pupil, Farinelli, can be gathered from an anecdote related of this young singer shortly after he left his master's guidance.

When twenty-two, Farinelli, already famous and apparently a "finished product" of instructor skill, went to Bologna to meet Bernacchi, then styled "the king of singers." They were matched as rivals in a grand duo.

"Farinelli poured forth all the beauties of his voice and style without reserve, and executed a number of most difficult passages, which were rewarded with tumultuous applause. Nothing daunted, Bernacchi replied in the same air, repeating every trill, roulade and cadenza which had been sung by Farinelli. The latter, owning his defeat, entreated his conqueror to give him some instruction, which Bernacchi, with equal generosity, willingly consented to bestow; thus was perfected the talent of the most remarkable singer, perhaps, who has ever lived."

Handel thought so highly of the Evirati that he composed special airs for Senesino, Bernacchi, Gizziello and Carestini. For Guadagni, Gluck wrote the opera of "Telemacco." Mozart composed for Tenducci a song that has been lost.

The quality of their voices was distinctly feminine, and, because of their greater lung power, the best of them quite easily excelled their female rivals in many direct contests.

An exception may be noted. The Evirati attained long, flexible ranges of sky-rocket brillance, but none ever equalled in this respect Lucrezia Agujari, known better as La Bastardina or Bastardella, the bastard daughter of a nobleman of Ferrara, born in 1743. La Bastardella's soprano range is the longest on record, extending from Middle C through three octaves up—"a lovely voice," says Mozart, "flexible throat, and incredibly high range." She could shake on F''''. In addition, her lung power was little inferior to that of her semi-male rivals.

This female quality of the voices of the Evirati, together with the marvelous culture and finish attained, is attested in floods of contemporary criticism.

Farinelli's voice was pronounced a marvel because so perfect, so powerful, so sonorous and so rich in its extent, both in the high and the low parts of the register "its equal has never been heard in our time. He possessed a creative genius which inspired embellishments new and so astonishing that no one could imitate them." His breathing was perfect—so soft and easy no one could detect it—"art died with him." His voice, in quality, was a rich soprano, "the most beautiful ever heard."

Guadagni, a contralto, changed his voice later to soprano, "perfectly delicate, polished and refined," extending its compass from six or seven notes to fourteen or fifteen. He produced his most spectacular effects by singing unaccompanied and "fining off his notes to a thread."

Gizziello "gained a round, full, sweet voice of great extent and penetrating quality, which was united to a strong natural taste and feeling in music."

Bernacchi, one of the first of the Evirati, born at Bologna about 1690, won his title, "the king of singers," as a sopranist in his teens. He developed a few years later a contralto voice, and it was as a contralto that he appeared in England and at first disappointed his hearers in Handel's operas, who expected much of "the king." Only the musicianly could appreciate the perfection of a technique without soul. On his return to Italy, Bernacchi proceeded to alter his style. He introduced a veritable "embroidery of roulades." So sensational was the success of this innovation, that the other singers immediately took it up. The purists—as ever in art and literature—raised a great outcry, accusing Bernacchi of sacrificing expression to execution and "opening the door to all the innovations which have debased the art." His old master Pistocchi, venerable patriarch of the Evirati (born at Palermo, 1659) exclaimed on hearing him in his new style:

"Ah! Woe is me! I taught thee to sing, and now thou wilt 'play'!"

Senesino's mezzo-soprano was considered by some good judges superior in quality to Farinelli's, although greatly limited in compass. It was "clear, penetrating, flexible and faultless in intonation." The shake was considered perfect and the style "pure, simple and expressive."

Partisans of Caffarelli who regarded his voice, too, as superior to Farinelli's, declared their favorite to excel in slow, pathetic airs.

But in all such cases of comparison, it is noticeable that Farinelli is taken as the standard, in itself a confession of superiority.

Carestini's voice, at first a "powerful, clear soprano," developed into "the fullest, finest, deepest contralto ever, perhaps, heard." Nicolini, so lavishly praised for his acting by Addison—with whose opinion Steele agreed—was also a soprano who sank into a "fine contralto."

Crescentini was "the last great singer Italy has produced; and he finished the series of sublime infant virtuosi of that classic land of melody. Nothing could exceed the suavity of his tones, the force of his expression, the perfect taste of his ornaments, or the large style of his phrasing."

But the chorus of praise is not without its strident discord. Listen to Voltaire—it is the blasé Senator Pococurante speaking to Candide:

"Let who will go to see bad tragedies set to music, where the scenes are contrived for no other end than to introduce two or three songs ridiculously out of place, to show off an actress' voice. Let who will, or who can, die away with pleasure at the sight of an eunuch quavering the rôle of Cæsar, or of Cato, and strutting awkwardly upon the stage. For my part I have long since renounced those paltry entertainments which constitute the glory of modern Italy, and are purchased so dearly by sovereigns."

And in the garrulous old Princess' account of her mating, in maidenhood days, with the soulful eunuch, Voltaire takes a direct rap at Farinelli, in his character of minister.

"He carried me to a neighboring house," the Princess tells Candide and his pretty Cunegonde, speaking of the eunuch who had rescued her from a massacre, "put me to bed, gave me food, waited upon

126

me, consoled me, flattered me; he told me that he never so much regretted the loss of what it was impossible to recover.

" 'I was born at Naples,' said he, 'there they geld two or three thousand children every year; some die of the operation, others acquire a voice more beautiful than that of women, and others are raised to offices of state. This operation was performed on me with great success, and I was chapel musician to Madame, the Princess of Palestrina.' "

Though with Crescentini the male sopranists passed as a school, there have not been lacking instances since of youths with high voices assuming female rôles.

Among them may be mentioned the renowned Rubini, to whose brilliant execution both Bellini and Donizetti owed much of their popularity as composers. Rubini, boy member of a church choir, showed so little talent that the choir leader would have nothing to do with his training. The elder Rubini, a music master himself, was determined, however, to make a singer of the lad. He gave him intensive instruction, and, at the age of twelve, presented him in an opera at his native Romano in the rôle of heroine. The boy rose to the part, and from that time his career was assured. Liszt was interested in the career of this boy.

Of Antonio Tamburini, a contemporary of Rubini, an amusing instance of the assumption of a female rôle has passed into the volume of immortal classic stories of genius.

It was during the carnival at Palermo in 1822, Tamburini, a basso, was matched with Madame Lipparini, a high soprano, in Mer-

127

cadante's opera "Elisa e Claudio." The boisterous carnival crowd assembled in the theater, armed with drums, trumpets, tin pans, shovels, and anything else that would make a noise.

When the curtain arose, the clatter began, the audience drowning out even the orchestra. Nothing daunted, Tamburini started off in a manner of the utmost unconcern, apparently oblivious of the deafening disturbance. But his basso could not be heard across the footlights. Madame Lipparini, too, tried to carry through her opening number, but became so frightened that she rushed off the stage, amid the cheers and good-natured jeer of the noisy audience.

Then an inspiration struck Tamburini. Retiring for a moment from the scene—to the joy of the crowd, which believed it had conquered his nerve—he soon reappeared dressed in Lipparini's clothing and began to sing Lipparini's song, imitating admirably her voice and tones, though, dressed as he was in her badly fitting bonnet and gown, burlesqueing her actions and walking with her affected mincing step.

The audience was so delighted with Tamburini's audacity that tin pans, drums and shovels were soon silenced. Tamburini, now complete master of the situation, decided to go through with the opera, singing the heroine's part as well as the hero's. He did not shun even the duets, impersonating Elisa with high falsetto and Claudio in his own basso. At the finish he even executed Lipparini's dance.

The astonishing performance was a huge success, the theater rang at the finish with "Bravos!" from the conquered crowd. Nor was it wholly a burlesque—there are on record enthusiastic opinions that Tamburini's falsetto eclipsed seriously Lipparini's high soprano.

A few cases are on record of boys whose voices did not change in the normal course of natural growth, and who continued to sing soprano well on into maturity. One of these was Willibald von Sadler-Grun, who toured Germany in the early days of this century, and sang his songs dressed as a woman. His stage name was Urany Verde. He was a baritone by preference, but could sing soprano with equal ease. Dr. Iwan Bloch, the eminent author of "The Sexual Life of Our Time," heard him. He describes the singer as a "typical effeminate" with breasts of a "completely feminine character." His primary sex organs, however, were male.

"My voice has never cracked in a definite way," the singer is quoted. "At twenty-three years of age I could sing soprano, and can still do so today, at the age of thirty. The deeper tones for speech and singing I acquired only by instruction and practice."

VIII. THE BOY FRIENDS OF SHAKESPEARE

"ALL hope abandon, ye who enter here!"

Dante's legend might appropriately be blazed in letters of fire above the threshold of the Shakespearean labyrinth. For few there are who tread these mazes and return mentally normal.

However, may we not invoke some kindly Ariadne—the Muse of Persiflage, perhaps—to lend us her silken thread, by whose grace we may return from our search for the boy actress whom Shakespeare adored—to whom he wrote the Sonnets—for whom he wrote Ophelia, and Desdemona, and Juliet, and Rosalind?

"Oh Calumny!" booms Victor Hugo.

Yet, the evidence of the Sonnets is strong, and presumptive evidence is corroborative.

Oscar Wilde, who wandered only a little way into the labyrinthine fog, making no such extensive excursion as we propose, laid his hands upon the shadowy "Willie Hughes" as Shakespeare's Platonic boy. But he never positively identified "Mr. W. H."—unless in that manuscript announced for publication just before his disaster which disappeared on the day of the sale of his effects following his arrest. We hope for better luck.

The commentators who have plunged into the London fog that hangs heavily over the Elizabethan stage have bothered themselves little about the boy actresses. And yet they were an active scandal of the times, as will be abundantly shown, and Shakespeare, who knew what was going on around him, was keenly aware of their presence, as passages presently to be cited will demonstrate.

Shakespeare was a practical dramatist, however visionary his poetic imagination. He wrote for his audience, just as do our successful dramatists of today, and he designed parts for his actors. He knew before setting pen to paper that Burbage could project across the footlights a Macbeth, an Othello or a King Lear. He was not writing for posterity—proof positive is furnished by his fools. The remarks of his court jesters—poor, dull and witless as they seem to us now—were lively chaff in the mouths of Richard Tarleton (Hamlet's "poor Yorick") and his successor William Kemp. Queen Elizabeth and her court rocked with laughter—and the Queen was not stupid, neither was Raleigh nor Essex. The lines had topical intimations, which are lost, but even more they were written to be spoken by Tarleton or Kemp with their peculiar mannerisms—Jesse Dandy's pronunciation of "Cincinnati," and Jack Pearl's roll of the "R" in "Roses" are contemporary analogies.

May not Shakespeare have taken an even greater delight in designing Desdemona for the pretty "Dickie" Robinson, or Ophelia for

131

"Nat" Field, or Lady Macbeth for "Alex" Cooke, or Cleopatra for "Bobbie" Goffe, or Rosalind for "Willie" Ostler?

The learned, unimaginative commentators are content to dismiss the boy actresses with a curt paragraph to the effect that they must have been a detriment rather than a help to the play—a necessary makeshift in deference to the morals of the times that forbade women to appear on the stage—and even if they could be identified, what would be gained? The playwright's idiosyncracies they ignore—these same commentators who seek for the minutest scrap of information about Petrarch's Laura or Dante's Beatrice.

Let the German Schelling speak for them: "More destructive of dramatic illusion than want or crudity of scene must it have been to hear—as Egypt's queen prophetically laments:

> Some squeaking Cleopatra boy my greatness,

and doubly difficult must have been the task of 'the quick comedian' personating Rosalind in the Forest of Arden, who was compelled at once to seem to be that which he was not and to avoid appearing that which he was. And hence, although Field is reputed to have been famed for female rôles, and Kynaston renowned in later times for his beautiful woman's face, no name has been handed down to fame for the creative part of Ophelia, Abigail or Cordelia, to stand beside Alleyn's Faustus and his Jew of Malta or beside the Hamlet or King Lear of Burbage."

The citation is a little unfortunate, in that Taylor probably was the first Hamlet instead of Burbage—but let that pass—and let

132

George Moore, gifted with imagination whatever his shortcomings, answer in a language strange to commentators' ears.

In his "Confessions," Moore relates how, upon his return from his beloved Paris to his hated London, he went one night to the theater.

"I had never seen Shakespeare acted, and I went to the Lyceum and there I saw that exquisite love song—for 'Romeo and Juliet' is no more than a love song in dialogue—tricked out in silks and carpets and illuminated building, a vulgar bawd suited to the gross passion of an ignorant public. I hated all that with the hatred of a passionate heart, and I longed for a simple stage, a few simple indications, and the simple recitation of that story of the sacrifice of the two white souls for the reconciliation of two great families. My hatred did not reach to the age of the man who played the boy-lover, but to the offensiveness with which he thrust his individuality upon me, longing to realize the poet's divine imagination: and the woman, too, I wished with my whole soul away, subtle and strange though she was, and I yearned for her part to be played by a youth as in old time: a youth cunningly disguised would be a symbol, and my mind would be free to imagine the divine Juliet of the poet, whereas I could but dream of the bright eyes and delicate mien and motion of the woman who had thrust herself between me and it."

Whatever may have been Shakespeare's personal idealism—and Victor Hugo and Frank Harris are in angry opposition to Oscar Wilde's theory, and probably impatient of George Moore's musings—it was not through choice that he wrote his heroines for boy actresses instead of women. Even if it be granted that he was not a victim of the aberration his Sonnets to "Mr. W. H." would seem to indicate, he would still have been compelled to worry along with the smooth-faced youths.

France and Italy had recently conquered the prejudice of the Dark Ages against women appearing on the stage, but it was not until the Restoration, when the gay and profligate young Charles II returned to London from Paris, chockfull of French liberalism, that Puritanic England was ready to follow suit. Stout, bitter, narrow-foreheaded guardians of public morals like Brand, Prynne and Field (Field, by the irony of fate, the father of Nat Field, later one of the most renowned of boy actresses) had seen to it that the stage of London was not corrupted by the French scandal.

When, a little after Shakespeare's death, a theatrical company with female players came over from Paris, with the secret approbation of their fellow countrywoman, Queen Henrietta Maria, consort of Charles I, "Glad am I to say," wrote Brand to his fellow reformer Laud, "they were hissed, hooted and pippin-pelted from the stage, so that I do not think they will soon be ready to try the same again." Brand nasally continues that "all virtuous and well-disposed persons in this town" were "justly offended." "Monsters," Prynne calls the actresses, "unwomanish and graceless."

Queen Henrietta Maria was too discreet to try to brave the storm, and though there is evidence that women of her court participated in amateur theatricals, these were kept profoundly secret from Brand, Prynne and Laud.

There have been conjectures that women were smuggled occasionally into the professional companies, such as Shakespeare's, but, if so, the tenure of none of them could have been long, so watchful were the self-appointed Puritan censors, and they could have accomplished nothing in the way of "art." At most such an appearance could have been only a "lark" in Elizabeth's time—she was a stickler for public propriety, whatever her private and court morals; James was more liberally inclined, and Charles I, as broad-minded as his Queen, would have thrown down the barrier, except for the thunders of the preachers.

These same thunderers, incidentally, not strong enough to abolish the stage entirely, but strong enough to keep the women off, consigned the boys to hell fire: "The woman shall not wear that which pertaineth unto a man, neither shall a man put on a woman's garment: for all that do so are abomination unto the Lord thy God." There were light-hearted lads, however, who braved the Hebrew and the Puritanic "abomination," and the plays of Shakespeare became a possibility.

The guess of Schelling and his fellow commentators that there was no "actress" of sufficient talent among the boy players to stamp his name definitely and authentically on Desdemona or Cordelia need not worry us too much.

In the curious mists that hang over the Elizabethan stage all images are blurred when not lost completely. Burbage's own record is preserved by the merest chance in an epitaph of bombastic doggerel, indefinite and incomplete. King Lear and Othello are his pretty positively, and as leader of the Shakespearean company he would scarcely have passed up such a chance as Hamlet—yet there is a tradition that

135

Taylor played the Dane originally, and under Shakespeare's own instruction. Shakespeare is credited with the Ghost, and with Old Adam —what other parts did he play? Who was the first Falstaff, who so delighted Queen Elizabeth? Or the first Romeo? Or the first Iago?

Then why marvel so much that the first Ophelia is lost, or the first Juliet, or the first Desdemona?

The traveler Coryat, on a visit to Venice in 1611, was astonished to find that the female rôles in the Italian theaters were played as well by women as they were in England by men!

There is fairly explicit evidence that at least two of the boy actresses of the Elizabethan period were quite able to perform creditably any of the difficult rôles of Shakespeare—Nathan Field and Richard Robinson. These young men, from meager current reference, most certainly had little difficulty "looking the part," and there is evidence both were highly trained players of talent approaching genius.

The commentators who have bothered about the matter at all, have given up in despair the job of positively identifying either with any particular one of Shakespeare's heroines. But their results are negative and not positive, and they have not proven that Field was not Ophelia—that Robinson was not Desdemona. Their evidence is the same flimsy cobweb that is spun any time it is sought to prove anything about the personnel of the Elizabethan stage—to prove Shakespeare wrote the plays, to prove he didn't; to prove Burbage was the first Hamlet, to prove he wasn't.

In the present impossibility of definitely fixing upon any one of the boy actresses the honor of creating Juliet, the next best thing we can do is piece the scraps of evidence together that there were young men in those days with "special qualifications of age, voice and build necessary for taking the part of young girls," as W. Creizenach is ready to admit, and for taking the part with the most brilliant success.

Besides Field and Robinson, then, there were Robert Goughe, Alexander Cooke, William Ostler and possibly John Underwood, all contemporary with Shakespeare, who gained more or less renown as players of female rôles.

Of them all, "Dicky" Robinson was the most popular fellow about town, while Nat Field seems to have been the most talented.

Robinson is spoken of in terms of fondest comradeship by Ben Jonson, and he seems to have been a whole-souled, agreeable, hearty and healthy sort of a personage—the Elizabethan Julian Eltinge. Like Eltinge, Robinson "understood the art of dress better than many a fine lady." This is borne out by an amusing incident related by Ben Jonson in "The Devil is an Ass." Engine speaks:

There's Dickey Robinson

A very pretty fellow, and comes often
To a gentleman's chamber, a friend of mine. We had
The Merriest supper of it there, one night
The gentleman's landlady invited him
To a gossip's feast: now he, sir, brought Dick Robinson,
Drest like a lawyer's wife, amongst them all:
I lent him clothes—But to see him behave it,
And lay the law, and carve and drink unto them,

137

And then talk bawdy, and send frolics! O,
It would have burst your buttons, or not left you a seam.
Meercroft: They say he's an ingenious youth.
Engine:　　O Sir! and dresses himself the best, beyond
　　　　　　Forty of your very ladies!

The first trace of Robinson the commentators can find is in the list of actors who presented Ben Jonson's "Catiline" in 1611. The negative conjecture is made that he must have been very young at this time, and, since he appears among "the names of the principal actors in all these plays" prefixed to Heminge and Condell's folio of "Mr. William Shakespeare's Comedies, Histories and Tragedies," he "may have been an original actor in some of Shakespeare's later dramas."

However, by 1616, Robinson was so well known about town and so excellent an actor that Jonson did not hesitate to incorporate him into the text of his comedy.

And Cowley, addressing Sir Kenelm Digby, in verses prefixed to "Love's Riddle," remarks:

Nor has't a part for Robinson, whom they
At school account essential to a play.

If the guess, based on nothing, that Robinson in 1611 was a very young, inexperienced actor, playing a minor rôle in "Catiline" is good, then a guess, a little better, is that Robinson, proverbial in 1616, may have taken an important rôle in "Catiline" in 1611, and may have had both enough age and experience to have played important females in some of Shakespeare's earlier mature plays, as well as in his later ones—Juliet, possibly, or Ophelia, or Desdemona, or Lady Macbeth.

The only female part in which Robinson is known positively to have appeared is that of the Lady of Govianus in "The Second Maiden's Tragedy." In 1621, he played an elderly man in "Wild Goose Chase" by Beaumont and Fletcher; and in 1622 in Webster's "Duchess of Malfi" he followed the experienced Condell as the Cardinal. It is presumed, but with little authority, that Robinson was, by this time, disqualified for female rôles. He became a power among the players, and when the dramas of Beaumont and Fletcher were published, it was Richard Robinson who subscribed the dedication.

The last scene in light-hearted Dicky Robinson's life is one of the most pathetically tragic in stage history.

"When the stage was put down," records Wright in "Historia Histrionica" (1699), "and the rebellion raised, most of the players except Lowin, Taylor and Pollard (who were superannuated) went into the King's army, and, like good men and true, served their old masters, though in a different yet more honorable capacity. Robinson was killed at the taking of a place (I think Basing House) by Harrison, he that was hanged at Charing Cross, who refused him quarter, and shot him in the head when he laid down his arms, abusing Scripture at the same time in saying: 'Cursed is he that doth the work of the Lord negligently!' "

Harrison's brutal deed, self-judged by his quotation of Scripture —"the blasphemous cant of those ferocious times"—was piously commended the day after the taking of Basing House in an official report made by Hugh Peters to the Puritan Parliament: "There lay upon the ground, slain by the hands of Major Harrison (that godly and gallant gentleman) Major Cuffe, a man of great account among them, and a notorious Papist, and Robinson, the player, who, a little before the storm, was known to be mocking and scorning the Parliament."

While Dicky Robinson arouses more than any player of his time our human sympathies, the palm of perfection as a female impersonator in Shakespeare's day must be awarded to Nathaniel Field.

Field retired from the stage when he was only thirty-six, ranking second only to Richard Burbage as the greatest actor of a great epoch. As his face and general physique were naturally feministic, he could not, even at the time of his retirement, have been much above the age for the effective playing of female rôles. The genius that enabled him to overcome physical difficulties so as to present a very masculine Othello, equal if not superior to Burbage's, undoubtedly stood him in splendid stead in the playing of women parts to which his appearance and manner were peculiarly adapted and in which he had been trained from childhood.

It is Field, perhaps, who makes it no matter of marvel that the traveler Coryat was astonished to find in Italy actresses who could play women quite as well as English men.

Field, like Robinson, appears in the list of "the names of the principal actors in all these plays" (of Shakespeare); but, as in Robinson's case, it has been impossible to identify him with any particular rôle.

Field was the son of John Field, a Puritanical preacher and one of the bitterest enemies the stage could boast. Writing to the liberal Earl of Leicester in 1581, John Field reviled him for having interfered "in behalf of evil men, as late you did for the players, to the great grief of all the godly," and adjured him not to encourage "those wickednesses and abuses that are wont to be nourished by those impure interludes and plays." Not long afterward, an accident occurred that delighted the heart of the Rev. Mr. Field. At a theatrical performance on a Sunday in a public garden, a grand-stand collapsed, killing or injuring nearly a thousand people. The preacher used the accident as a text for a virulent tirade against the theater, pointing to the "late judgment of God" for a violation of the Sabbath.

Fortunately for the feelings of this pious Puritan, he died long before his son disgraced him. This blessed riddance took place when Nathaniel was less than a year old.

Field's stage career was the result of one of the most sensational kidnaping episodes in the history of the world. Queen Elizabeth, fond of music and theatricals, took what turned out to be a drastic and dangerous measure to secure talent for her chapel. She issued this proclamation:

"Elizabeth by the grace of God, etc., to all mayors, sheriffs, bailiffs, constables, and all other our officers, greeting. For that it is meet that our Chapel Royal should be furnished with well-singing children from time to time, we have, and by these presents do authorize our well-beloved servant, Nathaniel Giles, Master of our children of our said Chapel, or his deputy, being by this bill subscribed and

141

sealed, so authorized, and having this our present commission with him, to take such and so many children as he, or his sufficient deputy, shall think meet, in all cathedral, collegiate, parish churches, chapels, or any other place or places, as well within liberty as without, within this our realm of England, whatsoever they be."

The "well-beloved Giles" was exactly the sort to execute this commission. Like Nicholas Udall, operator of a boys' school, whose name was still as lively a memory in England for his scandalous devotion to his pupils as for the authorship of "Ralph Roister Doister" (1541), the first English comedy, Giles took a quivering delight in the developing of very young male talent that came under his care. Before the ink was scarcely dry on the paper that made him the happiest legal hunter of catamites in the history of the world, Giles set about rounding up talented boys "whatsoever they be." Among those forcibly kidnaped was "Nathaniel Field, a scholar of a grammar school in London, kept by one Mr. Monkaster."

Another little fellow, who has no immediate concern with our story, but who merits the passing tribute of a tear, was Salathiel Pavy, "apprentice to one Peerce," as Giles' record shows, who became a wonderful child actor of old men's parts and whose death at thirteen brought forth this exquisite tribute from Ben Jonson:

Weep with me, all you that read
This little story
And know, for whom a tear you shed
Death's self is sorry.

142

'Twas a child that so did thrive
        In grace and feature
As heaven and nature seem'd to strive
        Which own'd the creature.
Years he number'd scarce thirteen
        When fates turn'd cruel,
Yet three fill'd zodiacs had he been
        The stage's jewel;
And did act, what now we moan,
        Old men so duly,
As, sooth, the Parcæ thought him one
        He play'd so truly.
So, by error, to his fate
        They all consented
But, viewing him since, alas, too late!
        They have repented:
And have sought, to give new birth,
        In baths to steep him.
But being so much too good for earth,
        Heaven vows to keep him.

The Queen desired the children of her chapel not only to sing but also to act in plays for royal entertainment, and this put an idea into the head of Giles. Why not use a regular theater for their training, and, incidentally, why not earn a little honest money for Giles?

It is not recorded whether it was Giles who took the first steps toward carrying out the idea, but on Sept. 2, 1600, one Henry Evans secured a lease on Blackfriars for twenty-one years and installed a children's company culled from Giles' flock.

Giles, whatever his morals and general excellences as a citizen, was a marvelous stage director, and his "little eyases" became the sensation of London. So great, indeed, was their sudden bid for popularity, that Shakespeare and his company were forced to close the Globe and go on tour for a time, their playhouse being deserted.

An echo is preserved in "Hamlet." Rosencrantz announces the coming of the players.

"What players are they?" asks Hamlet.

"Even those you were wont to take delight in—the tragedians of the city," replies Rosencrantz.

"How chances it they travel?" again queries Hamlet, who adds, with the true instinct of the actor bred on Broadway, "their residence, both in reputation and profit, was better both ways."

"I think," replies Rosencrantz, "their inhibition comes by the means of the late innovation."

"Do they hold the same estimation they did when I was in the city? Are they so followed?"

"No, indeed, they are not."

"How comes it?" then asks Hamlet, and still with Broadway perception hazards, "do they grow rusty?" Note, too, the up-to-date colloquialisms.

"Nay, their endeavour keeps in the wonted pace," answers Rosencrantz, whose very name smacks of the East Side, and then it comes out: "But there is, sir, an aery of children, little eyases, that cry out on top of question, and are most tyrannically clapped for't: these are now the fashion; and so berattle the common stages—so they call them—that many wearing rapiers are afraid of goosequills, and dare scarce come thither!"

There were Broadway critics in those days, too!

Then, after a satirical fling at the children, wondering how they'll feel when they grow up and become "common players" themselves, Hamlet asks as to their ability: "Do the boys carry it away?"

"Ay, that they do, my lord, Hercules and his load too."

The popularity of his company at Blackfriars, combined with the Queen's favor and his own natural arrogance, caused Giles to throw all discretion to the winds in his kidnaping sallies.

One morning Giles and his agents waylaid and captured, on his way to school, the little son of Henry Clifton, a well-to-do gentleman of Norfolk. The child, crazed with terror, fought his captors, but was easily subdued, and after a brutal beating to tame him, he was carried off to Blackfrairs.

Clifton, upon learning of the kidnaping, went angrily to Giles and demanded his son. Giles, coolly and tauntingly, exhibited the Queen's commission, and he and Evans, who was also present, told Clifton they had "authority to take any nobleman's son in the land." And, to further infuriate Clifton, whom they deemed powerless, they handed the child a "part" and ordered him, in his father's presence, to learn it quickly on penalty of a sound beating.

Clifton, seeing he was temporarily whipped, withdrew, but went

145

to the Privy Council, before whom he told his story. It was not long before young Clifton was mysteriously ordered back to his home and his studies.

Clifton, however, was not satisfied. He started an investigation of the practices of Giles and Evans, and on Dec. 15, 1601, laid his findings before the Star Chamber. A few weeks later, the Chamber censured Evans and ordered him to give up all rights to the theater and the plays he had acquired. Giles, too, they censured, and warned him to engage no further in theatrical activities. The Queen, bending to the storm of indignation the whole unsavory affair was creating in London, gave orders that the children of her chapel should take no further part in theatrical activities, even for the amusement of the Court.

Giles, however, she seems to have shielded, and he carried on his occupation, though without effrontery and with stealth, of collecting the chapel children and training them not only as singers but for the stage, through the remainder of her reign and the reign of James. The Parliament of Charles I, however, took sharp notice of Giles about 1626, and bade him flatly to desist from his double activity, remarking of the little stage children brought back for chapel service, "it is not fit or decent that such should sing the praises of God Almighty."

Through the action of Elizabeth's Star Chamber, Blackfriars was closed, but Evans held his lease. On the death of the Queen, two years later, he reopened the house with a company of children "bootlegged" to him by Giles, but new scandals developed. The venture continued a hazardous and uncertain course until 1608, when public

146

indignation finally forced Evans out for good. Burbage took the lease, and with it the more talented of the child actors, who were annexed to his and Shakespeare's company for female rôles.

It was when Field was one of the "Children of the Queen's Chapel," twelve or thirteen years old, that Ben Jonson saw him and took a great fancy to him. Field became the dramatist's pet protégé, and from him learned the arts both of fine technical acting and of playwriting. In 1600, Jonson cast the boy for the star part in his "Cynthia's Revels."

The new Queen Anne, consort of James I, was, like Queen Elizabeth, a lover of amateur theatricals, and by 1609 when Jonson's "Epiocene" was ready, we find the piece brought out by the "Children of Her Majesty's Revels," with Field as the star comedian.

It was in the following year that Field, just turned from boyhood to man's estate, but still one of "Her Majesty's Children," wrote his own first play, "A Woman Is a Weathercock," which was presented by himself and his companions under the Queen's patronage. On this presentation, Field, then in his twenty-third year, is described as having "a peculiarly smooth and feminine look, with no whiskers," and accordingly not "disqualified as soon as many of the others for acting with his juniors." A portrait of Field at this period is extant.

Field, according to Malone, "performed female parts at the Globe and Blackfriars," as well as with the children's companies. It is argued by some commentators that this actor switched as early as 1607 to masculine rôles, because in this year he played the leading male part in "Bussy d'Ambois." But this performance was with a children's company—when our school girls of today stage "The Merchant of Venice" it is quite the custom for some fair miss to play Shylock.

Field is known to have played early opposite Burbage in a Beaumont and Fletcher drama, and it is not overstraining probabilities to assign him Juliet to Burbage's Romeo and Desdemona to Burbage's Othello. More or less meager evidence has been found that he was a member of the Shakespeare-Burbage aggregation in 1613; and that in 1614 he joined Henslowe in the rejuvenated Paris Garden, where the collapse of the grand-stand thirty years before had furnished his father with so excellent a text for a vituperative sermon against the stage; and that in 1619, following the death of Burbage, he became principal actor with the King's Players.

The excellence of Field as an actor is attested by semi-proverbial references in contemporary writers. Thus, his old friend and patron, Ben Jonson, in "Bartholomew Fair," records this conversation:

> Cokes: Which is your Burbage now?
> Leatherhead: What mean you by that, Sir?
> Cokes: Your best actor, your Field?

And in Flecknoe's "Short Discourse of the English Stage" (1664) Burbage and Field once again are coupled: "In this time, were poets and actors in their greatest flourish; Jonson and Shakespeare, with Beaumont and Fletcher, their poets, and Field and Burbage their actors."

Before he died, Burbage, who had garnered all the laurels the stage of the time could afford and who seems to have grown more or less weary of plaudits in a quarter of a century of occupancy of the highest dramatic pinnacle, contracted the habit of permitting younger actors in his company to assume from time to time his rôles. It was probably on such an occasion that Field first played Othello, in which he scored a mighty triumph—astounding for an expert in rôles like Desdemona. An epigram of the times preserves the general opinion, gathered, too, from other sources, of Field's interpretation of the Moor, though the doggerel is aimed at one of the two besetting sins in the actor's character:

> Field is, in sooth, an actor—all men know it,
> And is the true Othello of the poet.
> I wonder if 'tis true, as people tell us,
> That, like the character, he is most jealous.
> If it be so, and many living swear it,
> It takes not little from the actor's merit,
> Since, as the Moor is jealous of his wife,
> Field can display the passion to the life.

Jealousy, the one sin, was matched by extravagance, the other, and though his earnings from his acting and his plays were large for the times, he was in constant poverty.

Field was a mighty favorite with the ladies, who regarded him as an exceedingly "pretty fellow." That at least one of them lavished upon him, for a time, both fortune and favors, is gathered from a punning epigram, entitled "Field, the Player, to His Mistress, the Lady May":

149

It is the fair and merry month of May,
That clothes the Field in all his rich array,
Adorning him with colors better dyed
Than any king can wear, or any bride.
But May is almost spent, the Field grows dun
With too much gazing on that May's hot sun;
And if mild Zephirous, with gentle wind,
Vouchsafe not his calm breath, and the clouds kind
Distil their honey-drops, his heat to 'lay
Poor Field will burn e'en in the midst of May.

What Mrs. Field thought of the epigram and its heroine is not recorded—maybe adventures like that inspired her to give her pretty lord cause for his raging jealousy. She bore Field five children, however, removing from the fair actor suspicion of effeminacy off stage.

Massinger, like Jonson, was Field's warm friend. Whether Shakespeare is to be added to the list cannot be determined in that uncanny fog that hangs around the central genius of the times, without so completely obscuring his contemporaries.

Field retired from the stage at thirty-six and died at forty-six, renowned as actor, dramatist and poet.

Alexander Cooke is Boswell's guess as the creator of Shakespeare's heroines. "From the plot of 'The Seven Deadly Sins!' " observes the biographer of Samuel Johnson, "it appears that this actor was on the stage before 1588, and was the stage-heroine. He acted some woman's part in Jonson's 'Sejanus' and in 'The Fox'; and, we may presume,

150

performed all the principal female characters in our author's (Shakespeare) plays."

Payne Collier finds difficulty in Cooke playing woman's parts in 1588 so well as to be "heroine of the stage" and continuing to play them in 1605. But Cooke may have been a precocious boy and may have retained his youth for a long time, as did Nat Field and the marvelous Kynaston of the Restoration.

It appears from the order of names of the actors that Cooke was the Agrippina of "Sejanus" and the "Fine-Madame Would-Be" of "The Fox." Both parts require a certain maturity in the player—a maturity that would sit well on a male actress of Lady Macbeth. Cooke's name is listed again in the casts for "The Alchemist" (1610) and "Catiline" (1611) but in such position as to indicate that by that time he was playing important male rôles.

Nothing seems to be preserved of the characteristics of this actor on the stage or off. He died in 1614, fairly wealthy, leaving to a son and a daughter and to an unborn child fifty pounds each, besides considerable property to his wife. Guessing from the 1588 date of his youthful renown, he must have been about Shakespeare's own age.

The fourth and last prominent claimant to consideration as a possible creator of the immortal women of Shakespeare is Robert Goughe or Goffe, who is known to have played "Aspasia" in Tarlton's "Second Part of the Seven Deadly Sins" prior to 1588, and to have joined the Shakespeare-Burbage outfit at the start, and to have been a constant member of the King's Players, both at the Globe and the Blackfriars. Though tradition has preserved no other character creation of his than Aspasia, there is a persistence of vague opinion that female rôles were his forte.

The opinion may be strengthened by the fact that he was father of the more famous Alexander Goffe, renowned as "the woman-actor of Blackfriars." Alexander, youngest child of Robert, who was married in 1603, was born in the summer of 1614, two years before the death of Shakespeare. When only twelve years old, and two years after the death of his father, Alexander played "Cænis, Vespasian's concubine" in Massinger's "Roman Actor," and three years later he was Acanthe in the same dramatist's "Picture."

Alexander was still playing women when the theaters were closed by the Puritan fanaticism of the Civil War. A last romantic picture is preserved by an old stage historian. When the wars were over, it is related, the actors gathered in private to revive their old trade. They made up a company and acted with great caution and privacy, fearful of Cromwell's spies, at the Cockpit, or, journeying out of London, in the houses behind curtained windows of liberal noblemen. Few, necessarily, were in the audiences—they played for the love of the profession, and defrayed expenses by passing the hat. "Alexander Goffe, the woman actor of Blackfrairs (who had made himself known to persons of quality) used to be the Jackal, and give notice of the time and place."

Some of the picturesque glory of Alexander may be reflected back over his less illustrious father, Robert.

Coupled in tradition with the names of the boy actresses is that of John Underwood, though nothing is known as to the parts he played.

He was one of the "chapel boys" who went to Blackfriars about the time Nat Field did. He never became prominent. From various and miscellaneous mention of his name, it may be surmised he was a trusty "utility," and in that capacity may have played minor female parts.

Another of the "Children of the Queen's Chapel," who may turn out to be the girl-boy we have been seeking in the Elizabethan fog, was William Ostler.

In 1601, Ostler played with Field, Pavy and Underwood in Ben Jonson's "Poetaster." His name does not appear with those of Field and his companions the previous year in "Cynthia's Revels," so that Ostler is presumed to have been a new acquisition for the "Poetaster." Not long after 1601 and certainly before 1604, he was drafted into His Majesty's Players, "possibly as a young man to sustain female rôles," as a commentator guesses. By 1611, he seems to have discarded female parts, for the position of his name in "Catiline" seems to indicate a male rôle—though it may be observed, and this applies throughout our discussion, position is not an absolute criterion. Names in those days were not placed after the characters assumed, as in our programs, but were arranged rather in the order of prominence of the actors. In a "cast of characters," it was the general custom to print all the males first in order of their importance in the play, followed then by the females in their order, as is still done in the Shakespearean texts. An actor like Field or Robinson, might, because of his prominence in the company, appear near the top in the list of players, though his rôle would be near the bottom in the cast of characters.

Stronger evidence, however, that Ostler was playing male parts in

153

the latter days of Shakespeare, is found in an extravagant eulogy by Davies of Hereford, who, in "Scourge of Folly," applauds him as "the Roscius of these times" and "sole king of actors"—possibly, because of sustaining evidence, an elaborate press agent puff by a personal friend and admirer.

Ostler was married in 1612; became the father of a boy whom he named Beaumont for his friend, the dramatist; and was lost to the stage by 1623. The date of his death is unknown and the facts of his life obscure.

Now for a little wild speculation, permitted to every pilgrim into the Shakespearean fog. Hitherto, this adventurer has stuck closely and painfully to the facts—now for my fling! Ostler shall be my text.

In the list of "The King's Company" dated April, 1604, Ostler's name is spelt "Hostler"—William Hostler. Here then is a "Mr. W. H." presented to Oscar Wilde's hand, and without recourse to the fantastic "Willie Hews"!

Hostler joins Shakespeare's company, too, at the very time the dramatist began sketching his passionate heroines. A recent American investigator, Dr. Thorndike, has dared reconstruct the poet's psychology much more rationally than his professional predecessors.

Shakespeare, heretofore (following Dr. Thorndike along the trail) had put "little emotional stress into the lines for ladies, nymphs and goddesses." . . . "Shakespeare's women could hardly have been conceived, if the boys had not been skillful and charming in their parts" . . . by the time of the maturely passionate plays, "we may be sure that Shakespeare had found a remarkably competent boy

actor" . . . an actor who had "acquired a very large range of difficult women's parts, including prostitutes, faithless wives and tragic
queens."

William Hostler came into Shakespeare's company before Field,
and probably in time to play Ophelia—certainly in time for Desdemona and for Cressida, to the latter of whom Frank Harris assigns so
much importance in Shakespeare's emotional development—though
Harris has no patience with the theory that the dramatist was a lover
of boys. With Harris, the object of Shakespeare's passion was Mary
Fitton.

The obscure William Hostler does not fit so well Prof. Thorndike's
demand for "a remarkably competent boy actor" with "a very large
range of difficult women's parts" as the better attested Field or Robinson, but that consideration can be waived in the speculation that
Shakespeare might have thought his pretty new "W. H." marvelously
gifted—just as many a dramatist and producing manager of our own
day has fallen blindly for a chorus girl with no talent and elevated her
to stardom. Shakespeare seems to have had little executive power in
his company—he was dramatist and stage manager, not casting director, probably Burbage's job. He may have written Desdemona for
"W. H." and then seen her go, despite his protests, to Field or
Robinson.

Can "W. H." have been Willie Hostler instead of Oscar Wilde's
"Willie Hews"?

Though "The Portrait of Mr. W. H." is written in an idle, whimsical, perverse vein, it must not be presumed that Oscar Wilde re-

155

garded his theory lightly. This "theory beneath that delicate brain play," Arthur Ransome, personal friend and biographer, assures us, "had a lasting fascination for him, and, with its proofs, grew in his mind till it overbalanced Cyril Graham and doubting Erskine. He wrote it at greater length, after delays. When he was arrested, the publishers, who had already announced it as a forthcoming book, returned it to his house, whence it disappeared on the day of the enforced sale of his effects. It has never been recovered."

Oscar Wilde may be regarded as a third victim of the "W. H." theory. The first is spirituelle Cyril Graham (strongly suggestive of Lord Alfred Douglas and of Willie Hews himself), inventor of the theory, who put a bullet into his brain when the forgery of the portrait was discovered, to prove he believed so strongly in the theory that he was willing to die for it.

The second was Erskine (developed from "an awkward, weakly lad, with huge feet and horribly freckled," passionately fond of Cyril Graham—surely sketched from Wilde himself), who, by heightening the fever of consumption dies deliberately by his "own hand for Willie Hughes's sake: for his sake, and for the sake of Cyril Graham, whom I drove to his death by my shallow scepticism and ignorant lack of faith."

And then came Oscar Wilde himself, in the flesh and blood, who, with an emotional aberration, reasoned himself into the belief that the fancied passion of Shakespeare and the known kindred passion of many an artistic Greek and Roman and Persian and Egyptian was beautiful beyond the power of ordinary mortal perception, flaunted

156

his passion in the faces of ordinary mortals and suffered the consequences.

Willie Hostler fills all the requirements of Willie Hewes or Hughes, as sketched by Wilde, except the punning play on the name fancied in the Sonnets.

Willie Hostler, just as well as Willie Hews, might have been "the boy-actor for whom" Shakespeare "created Viola and Imogen, Juliet and Rosalind, Portia and Desdemona, and Cleopatra herself." The young man to whom Shakespeare addressed the strangely passionate sonnets "must have been somebody who was a really vital factor in the development of his dramatic art; and this could not be said either of Lord Pembroke or Lord Southampton. Indeed, whoever he was, he could not have been anybody of high birth."

"It is of course evident that there must have been in Shakespeare's company some wonderful boy-actor of great beauty, to whom he intrusted the presentation of his noble heroines," reasons Graham, "for Shakespeare was a practical theatrical manager as well as an imaginative poet," and William Hostler comes into the company about the time the great characters are to be created.

But, still more strangely apt is the argument that it was through Shakespeare's persuasion that the boy "W. H.," whom he passionately adored, became a player.

"The children he begs him to beget" in the Sonnets, reasons the narrator of "The Portrait of Mr. W. H.," "are no children of flesh and blood, but more immortal children of undying fame. The whole cycle of the early Sonnets is simply Shakespeare's invitation to Willie

157

Hughes to go upon the stage and become a player. How barren and profitless a thing, he says, is this beauty of yours if it be not used. . . . You must create something in art: my verse 'is thine and born of thee'; only listen to me, and I will 'bring forth eternal numbers to outlive long date' and you shall people with forms of your own image the imaginary world of the stage. These children that you beget, he continues, will not wither away, as mortal children do, but you shall live in them and in my plays."

The date of the beginning of Shakespeare's passion for this marvelous boy is conjectured by Wilde as 1594 or '95, which would fit admirably into the Willie Hostler theory. Shakespeare might have persuaded the youth to go with the children of the chapel for a little while to acquire some technical skill to fit him for the parts he was about to lavish on him—on him "whose physical beauty was such that it became the very corner-stone of Shakespeare's art; the very source of Shakespeare's inspiration; the very incarnation of Shakespeare's dreams."

In one of the Sonnets, Shakespeare is found "complimenting Willie Hughes on the versatility of his acting, on his wide range of parts, a range extending from Rosalind to Juliet, and from Beatrice to Ophelia."

After a long investigation of the Sonnets, "Willie Hughes became a kind of spiritual presence, an ever-dominant personality. I could almost fancy that I saw him standing in the shadow of my room, so well had Shakespeare drawn him, with his golden hair, his tender flower-like grace, his dreamy deep-sunken eyes, his delicate mobile limbs, and his white lily hands. His very name fascinated me. Willie Hughes! Willie Hughes! How musically it sounded! Yes; who else but he could have been the master-mistress of Shakespeare's passion, the lord of his love to whom he was bound in vassalage, the delicate minion of pleasure, the rose of the whole world, the herald of the spring decked in the proud livery of youth, the lovely boy whom it was sweet music to hear, and whose beauty was the very raiment of Shakespeare's heart, as it was the keystone of his dramatic power?"

But Willie Hews did not respond to this idolatry any better than the average stage beauty to her mad adorer. "He could act love, but could not feel it, could mimic passion without realizing it"—Oscar Wilde, penning this observation, borne out by the Sonnets, was doubtless thinking bitterly of Lord Alfred Douglas, whom he brings so severely to account in the suppressed pages of "De Profundis." The boy-actress deserts Shakespeare for a time for a rival dramatist. Cyril Graham conjectures Chapman, but Wilde, after further investigation, fixes upon Marlowe. Why not Beaumont, for whom Willie Hostler afterward named his son?

But enough of " Mr.W.H."—for "this way madness lies!"

Cyril Graham, in his college days, was an ideal Rosalind—and here Oscar Wilde's imagination quite parallels George Moore's. No actresses being allowed on the college stage, "well, of course, Cyril was always cast for the girls' parts, and when 'As You Like It' was produced he played Rosalind. It was a marvelous performance. In fact, Cyril Graham was the only perfect Rosalind I have ever seen. It would be impossible to describe to you the beauty, the delicacy, the

159

refinement of the whole thing. Even when I read the play now I can't help thinking of Cyril. It might have been written for him."

Rosalind lends herself more readily to a boy-actress than does Ophelia or Desdemona. "In one particular indeed," to quote Dr. Thorndike, "the influence of the boy actors is noticeable, the tendency of the heroines to masquerade as pages. Julia, Portia, Nerissa, Viola, Rosalind and Imogen appear on the stage as handsome youths, and in this respect found admirable portrayal."

Exciting as would be Shakespeare's particular "boy friend" could we identify him, he would still be overshadowed by one other astonishing masquerader in the Elizabethan period, if a tradition can be credited—none other than the boy cousin of Henry VIII's little dead daughter, who assumed women's clothing and mounted the throne of England as Queen Elizabeth!

Her tale anon.

IX. PETS OF THE RESTORATION

In Restoration days, there were vague rumors of a female Desdemona having appeared before the Civil Wars, possibly in the life-time of Shakespeare himself, preventing the certain assignment to Mrs. Hughes ("A mighty pretty woman," says Pepys, "and seems, but is not, modest") of the honor of being the first Desdemona of her natural sex.

The rumor is far from improbable. The age of Elizabeth and James was an age of mental and moral daring, and it would be a cause for wonder if some adventurous girl, maybe going to work in boys' clothes, did not invade the stage. The thunders of the Puritan preachers that kept the stage as "pure" as it was, were as irksome to red-blooded Londoners of both sexes as the present-day admonitions of the Anti-Saloon League and the Lord's Day Alliance, and it was the boldness of Charles I in a determination to put an end to the nuisance that cost him his head.

Whether Shakespeare ever saw a woman in any of his creations has not been determined, but in the "Court Beggar" played at the Cockpit in 1632, there is put into the mouth of one of the characters a significant speech: "The boy's a pretty actor and his mother can play her part. The women now are in great request."

Queen Henrietta Maria was known to favor the innovation—it was under her protection the actresses from Paris made their disastrous début at Blackfriars about this time. In private theatricals in the court, too, the Queen's women in attendance participated—in one such performance it was alleged as scandal that King Charles himself had played a rôle.

But as the rising tide of fanaticism grew higher and higher, the theater was compelled to exercise more and more caution, and the female actresses, if there were any, were well eliminated by the time of the catastrophe in October, 1647, when Parliament decreed the end of stage plays in England.

The theaters ostensibly were wiped out and the profession of acting abolished—but there was one little gleam in the midnight blackness. A very important Puritan did not share the fanaticism of Prynne, Laud and Harrison—the Volsteads and Wheelers and Bryans of their day—and his name was Oliver Cromwell. During the reign of the Iron Dictator, plays were sometimes performed very privately at court, just as, during the World War, certain of our high army officials are alleged to have indulged in wine and women secretly in Washington, while depriving the poor devils of soldiers on the battlefield or in training camp of such sinful luxuries.

With the Restoration, came the joyous swing of the pendulum to

162

the furthest extravagant extreme. One of the first to hear the blast of victory from the trumpet of General Monk was Rhodes, a Charing Cross bookseller, who had been prompter at Blackfriars, and who, despite the vigilance of the Puritans, ever suspicious of him, had managed to keep some sort of an eye on the scattered players, always hoping for better times.

Under the direct patronage of Monk, old Rhodes went excitedly to the task of assembling a company, with which in 1660, he reopened the Cockpit in Drury Lane. In this company were two flaming stars, Thomas Betterton, reckoned still the greatest actor the English stage has ever had, and Edward Kynaston, with little doubt the finest actor of female rôles in the history of the theater.

Rhodes, living in the memory of the brilliant past before the war, organized his company along the old lines, with boys to play the women's rôles. Besides Kynaston, there were in his company for these assignments, William Betterton, a brother of Thomas; James Nokes, who possessed genius second only to Kynaston; Angel, Floid and Mosely.

Awakened England was ready, however, for the daring French innovation, and there was no dearth of female beauties who so far forgot modesty as to flock eagerly to the stage.

Margaret Hughes was among the first, and by January 1, 1661, either she or Anne Marshall—authorities wrangle—had played Desdemona. Anne Marshall's sister, Rebecca, also was in that first invasion—and Mistress Saunderson, afterward Thomas Betterton's wife; and Mistress Moll Davies, who became for a time the King's adored favorite; and Mistress Gibbs, and Mistress Holden, and Mistress Jennings, and Mistress Long—most of them as frail as they were fair.

Had Prynne and Laud survived the wars, they would have seen their prophecies of scandal fulfilled—should women invade the stage —by not only Moll Davies, but Mistress Margaret Hughes, lovely doxy of Sir Charles Sedley, and the beautiful Marshall sisters, wayward daughters of the Rev. Stephen Marshall, learned divine who had often been called upon to preach before the Long Parliament. These creatures had adopted for stage purposes the dignified title of "Mistress" because "Miss," at the time, was equivalent to "concubine," but they brought the term "Mistress" into a reproach it has not lived down, and helped restore "Miss" to dignity.

But godless London, forgetting Prynne and Laud, made heroines of these young women, and worshipped dazzled at their shrine—and, a little later at the shrine of Nell Gwyn, just now selling oranges in a Drury Lane theater, hurling back at the fops as smart smut as they threw her.

The actresses were introduced by Davenant, whom the Duke of York had put into his theater as partner for the aged and failing Rhodes, and by Killigrew, who had obtained patents for a rival theater. Davenant moved more slowly than Killigrew, being held back by Rhodes. It was Killigrew who sprung on London Mistress Hughes and Mistress Anne Marshall, making sport of Rhodes' "boys," some of them in their forties—Rhodes having been loyal to his friends of the old days. Davenant, however, was ready with his real ladies only about six months after Killigrew, and then the war started—Davenant's Mistress Davenport against Killigrew's Mistress Hughes.

Some idea of Killigrew's enterprise may be gathered from the fact that in 1664, three years after the introduction of the actresses, he presented a comedy called "The Parson's Wedding," with women playing all the rôles—male as well as female. This play was unusually profligate, even for the days of lusty King Charles, and, in addition to its sex buffoonery, it had the bad taste to treat the plague as a comic incident. Some of the odium fell on the "all-girl cast," and Killigrew did not repeat the experiment.

With Davenant alert to keep pace with Killigrew, Rhodes fades rapidly out of the picture, but Kynaston and Nokes had come so strong into popular favor that they continued to interpret female rôles in competition with the women of the company.

But, before relating the entertaining history of Kynaston, let us dispose of another worthy old-timer, even more interesting and scarcely less important than Rhodes. He is Charles Hart, grandson of Shakespeare's sister Joan—or possibly great grandson.

The records of Hart are so confused by that strange decree of fate that muddles everything pertaining to Shakespeare, that it is not certain whether there were two Charles Harts or one. If two, they were father and son, both being definitely fixed as descendants of Joan Shakespeare, and both were actors of female rôles. The elder Hart— if there were two—participated gallantly in the wars on the King's side, where the players universally were ranged. He is identified in the traditions as a player of women. After the war, Hart became a prominent figure in the London theaters. A reference to the age of the Hart of the battlefields conflicts with the age of the Hart of the Restoration —hence the theory there may have been two, father and son.

Anyhow, the Hart of the wars "carried on" in the days of the Dictatorship much after the fashion of Goffe, his fellow actor of female rôles.

When the curtain is raised on the Restoration, Charles Hart is found along with Burt and Clun engaged for female rôles with Killigrew's company, that astute manager not fully trusting his female actresses, fearing they might prove an evanescent fad and the London stage would return to the good old days of the boy-girls. These three are all reputed pupils of Robinson, slain in battle by the fanatic Harrison.

Hart, whether or not the blood of Shakespeare had anything to do with it, became a London favorite, Killigrew's best rival of Kynaston, though he was considerably older—Kynaston being only a boy— and nearly past doing women. But he was still good enough to be lauded as the Duchess in Shirley's "Cardinal." Killigrew soon transferred him to the male side of his casts, however, and Hart's Othello was pitted against Betterton's Hamlet, with Shakespeare's nephew getting the shade.

Hart's immortal contribution to the theater, though, is his discovery of Nell Gwyn. It was he who first sensed the stage value of the saucy beauty of the little Irish orange girl, exchanging repartee so sharply with the theater's customers, always bringing a roar of laughter with her good-natured sallies. Hart started out by making

166

Nell his mistress—no difficult matter—since she had already bartered her favors to the frequenters of the gay house of one Madame Ross, and then he and his fellow player, Lacy, a comedian who sometimes assumed female rôles in broad burlesque, set out to instruct her for the stage.

She was quick to learn, and under the avowed auspices of Hart, she made her début as Cydaria in the "Indian Emperor." She was only fifteen—with a life as long as Rachel's, at the same age, behind her. Cydaria was too serious a part, and Nell was unnoticed. Hart quickly rectified his mistake, however, and little Mistress Gwyn, "stamping the smallest foot in England on the boards," saucily assuming comic parts and speaking prologues and epilogues, was soon the rage of London.

It was not long before the handsome young Lord Buckhurst dazzled Nell and made her forget Hart. She even quit the stage, and went to live in the Buckhurst mansion.

Hart didn't commit suicide, however, but entered into a new intrigue with no less a personage than Lady Castlemaine, beautiful mistress of Charles II, whose fickle attentions at that moment were diverted to Mistress Davies, the actress, an "impertinent slut," if the Castlemaine is to be believed. Rebecca Marshall is credited with having brought Hart and Lady Castlemaine together.

Buckhurst, for some reason, tired of Nell, and sent her back to the stage. She returned repentant to Hart, but that lover of the far mightier Castlemaine would have none of her. Nell tossed her Irish nose higher—so high that before many months, no less a personage than King Charles Stuart was at her feet. Thereupon, she snapped her fingers in double glee at both Hart and Castlemaine.

Nell Gwyn retired shortly afterward from the stage, this time for good—and to play a more important rôle on the stage of history, as the mistress of the King and mother of his children. But, it is of interest to note, in connection with her affair with Hart, she won distinction on the stage not only in girl rôles but as boys—as Hart had done.

Nell's last rôle before leaving the stage was Almahide in Dryden's "Conquest of Granada."

"Her old lover Hart," relates a historian, "played Almanzor; and his position with respect to King Boabdelin (Kynaston) and Almahide (Nelly) corresponds with that in which he stood toward King Charles and the actress. The passages reminding the audience of this complex circumstance threw the house into convulsions."

Charles Hart's election to play female rôles is commended to the attention of the psychologists ever busy with Shakespeare. That Hart, his grand nephew, won distinction in this class of rôles, may be significant in the analysis of the sonnets. Congenital effeminacy in Hart might be questioned on the score that in his latter years he was the best Othello of his time—but so was Nat Field, after the death of Burbage, and the record of Field is pretty clear that he was effeminate to the finish, and overcame the defect by sheer force of art. Kynaston, too, turned, in his later years to male rôles, and won applause, but some of the applause may have been polite. "His early practice, in representing female characters," relates the gossipy Dr. Doran, "affected his voice in some disagreeable way. 'What makes you feel sick?' said Kynaston to Powell—suffering from a too riotous 'last night.' 'How can I feel otherwise,' asked Powell, 'when I hear your voice?'"

Edward Kynaston rivals even the great Betterton as being the most perfect stage artist of his time. If half the laudation of the period is to be believed, he certainly played females better than any boy who ever trod the stage. "It has since been disputable among the judicious," observes the conservative Downes, "whether any woman that succeeded him, so sensibly touched the audience as he."

"Tom and I and my wife," relates Samuel Pepys, "went to the Theater, and there saw 'The Silent Woman.' Among other things here, Kynaston the boy had the good turn to appear in three shapes: first, as a poor woman in ordinary clothes, to please Morose; then in fine clothes, as a gallant; and in them was clearly the prettiest woman in the whole house: and lastly, as a man; and then likewise did appear the handsomest man in the house."

It was in a serious rôle, however, that of the Duke's sister in Beaumont and Fletcher's "The Loyal Subject," that Pepys thought Kynaston "the loveliest lady" he ever saw in his life. His Evadne in "The Maid's Tragedy" was a classic, sure to fill the theater with excited women and girls whenever repeated.

For Kynaston, after the fashion of handsome female impersonators, appealed peculiarly and particularly to the feminine mind. Campbell mentions, as a matter of scandal, "Kynaston, the most beautiful youth who figured in petticoats on the stage, having been

169

carried about in his theatrical dress by ladies of fashion in their carriages. This," he then adds piously, "was an unseemly spectacle, and we can forgive the Puritans for objecting to see 'men in women's clothing.' "

Colley Cibber records the same feminine worship a little more circumstantially and without any moralizing: "Kynaston at that time was so beautiful a youth that the ladies of quality prided themselves in taking him with them in their coaches to Hyde Park in his theatrical habit after the play; which in those days they might have sufficient time to do, because plays then were used to begin at four o'clock, the hour that people of the same rank are now going to dinner. Of this truth I had the curiosity to inquire, and had it confirmed from his own mouth, in his advanced age."

Another bright page from Cibber tells an amusing story that has become an anecdotal classic, of how a stage queen kept a live king waiting. Here it is, in Colley's words:

"Though women were not admitted to the stage till the return of King Charles, yet it could not be so suddenly supplied with them but that there was still a necessity, for some time, to put the handsome young men into petticoats—which Kynaston was then said to have worn with success, particularly in the part of Evadne in 'The King's Tragedy,' which I have heard him speak of, and which calls to my mind a ridiculous distress that arose from these sorts of shifts which the stage was then put to. The King coming a little before his usual time to a tragedy, found the actors not ready to begin, when His Majesty, not choosing to have as much patience as his good subjects,

170

sent to them to know the meaning of it, upon which the master of the company came to the box, and, rightly judging that the best excuse for their default would be the true one, fairly told His Majesty that the queen was not shaved yet; the King, whose good humor loved to laugh at a jest as well as to make one, accepted the excuse, which served to divert him till the male queen could be effeminated."

Kynaston early began to mingle handsome boy rôles with his pretty girls, as the female actresses became established in popularity; but one day he got so bright an idea in his capacity of male actor that his brilliant stage career came near being terminated abruptly and violently.

One of the best looking as well as most fashionable young men of the town was that Sir Charles Sedley, who was envied for captivating the wayward fancies of the lovely Mistress Margaret Hughes. It came semi-roguishly and semi-seriously into Kynaston's head to ape this "mirror of fashion" in dress and manner, not only on the stage but off. It wasn't long before London was making merry over the two Sir Charles's. This angered the baronet, who hired a ruffian to waylay Kynaston in a dark corner of a park, spring on him, hail him as "Sir Charles" and give him a sound thrashing in the character of the baronet, pretending he had done him an injury.

Kynaston guessed Sedley was at the bottom of the beating, and, a few nights later, in a play called "The Heiress," he varied his make-up to caricature the baronet, and gave an uproariously funny burlesque of his enemy. Sir Charles, doubly enraged, this time hired three or four ruffians, who waylaid the actor and beat and clubbed him so severely that Kynaston was "mightily bruised and forced to keep his bed."

The King was "very angry with Sir Charles Sedley for his being beaten," says Pepys. The baronet, alarmed at the vigor with which his ancestors of the modern gunmen had carried out his instructions, entered a formal denial of his share of the transaction, and the matter was allowed to drop—after all it was a nobleman against only an actor. When Kynaston next appeared on the stage, this time in "The Island Princess," he was not yet quite himself and certainly not Sir Charles. "Here we find Kynaston," notes Pepys, on his visit to the King's playhouse, "to be well enough to act again; which he do very well after his beating by Sir Charles Sedley's appointment."

As a player of serious male rôles Kynaston rapidly matured, and soon became one of the two leading actors of his time, Betterton being his only rival. He is accredited with a "grace and ease that nothing ever surpassed" and with having "thrown a peculiar dignity into everything he performed." His Henry IV was so free from the rant and bombast of that age of acting as to excite special comment. His whisper to Hotspur, "Send us your prisoners, or you'll hear of it," was enthusiastically admired by Cibber as conveying "a more terrible menace in it than the loudest intemperance of voice could swell to."

"To the last of him his handsomeness was very little abated," eulogizes Colley. "Even at past sixty his teeth were sound, white and even as one could wish to see in a reigning toast of twenty. He had something of a formal gravity in his mien, which was attributed to the stately step he had been so early confined to, in a female decency.

But even that, in characters of superiority, had its proper graces; it misbecame him not in the part of Leon in Fletcher's 'Rule a Wife,' &c., which he executed with a determined manliness and honest authority well worth the best actor's imitation. He had a piercing eye, and in characters of heroic life, a quick, imperious vivacity in his tone of voice, that painted the tyrant truly terrible. There were two plays of Dryden, in which he shone with uncommon luster—in 'Aurengzebe' he played Morat, and in 'Don Sebastian' Muley Moloch; in both these parts he had a fierce lion-like majesty in his port and utterance, that gave the spectators a kind of trembling admiration."

When Cibber created the character of Syphax in Addison's "Cato," he carefully worked it out along lines he believed Kynaston would have traced had he been alive to play the part.

Kynaston, whose stage career covers the period from 1659, when Rhodes took him, an eager boy, from a London shop, to set him on the stage General Monk had authorized, to 1699, when he retired wealthy and laden with honors, lived past three score, dying in 1712. He wisely left the stage when his memory began to fail and his buoyancy to leave him, and when the disagreeable quality in his voice began to grow pronounced. He lies buried in the churchyard of St. Paul's, Covent Garden, along with such illustrious dead as Wycherley, Susanna Centlivre, Wilks, Macklin, and the Duke of Marlborough's stage friend Estcourt, reputed the most accomplished of mimics.

Kynaston was father of a boy, to whom he left his fortune. This, the young man augmented as a mercer in Covent Garden, and began an upward climb of the Kynastons to respectability—stage players

173

still were little better socially than "vagabonds," with whom they were classed legally in Elizabeth's time. The mercer had, in turn, a son, who became the Rev. Mr. Kynaston, of high standing in the Church, both because of his piety and his wealth. A pretty good evolution, any thoughtful Englishman must acknowledge, out of the youth the ladies used to carry off in their carriages in his fluffy finery to play with in the park.

James Nokes, second in importance only to Kynaston as a female impersonator when the stage was restored, was, like Kynaston, canny in money matters, and retired from the stage a prosperous gentleman. Nokes, while he played male rôles when the first blush of youth wore off, never completely abandoned petticoats, and to the finish of his career continued to play the nurse in "Romeo and Juliet" (in Otway's adaptation of Shakespeare) and that other popular nurse of the times in Nevil Payne's fiery tragedy "Fatal Jealousy."

But Nokes, while accomplished in tragedy, was more famous for his comedy.

"He scarce ever made his first entrance in a play but he was received with an involuntary applause; not of hands only, for those may be, and have often been, partially prostituted and bespoken," writes Colley Cibber, who knew, "but by a general laughter, which the very sight of him provoked, and nature could not resist; yet the louder the laugh the graver was his look upon it; and sure the ridiculous solemnity of his features were enough to have set a whole bench of bishops into a titter, could he have been honored (may it be no offence to suppose it) with such grave and right reverend auditors.

174

In the ludicrous distresses which, by the laws of comedy, folly is often involved in, he sunk into such a mixture of piteous pusillanimity, and a consternation so ruefully ridiculous and inconsolable, that when he had shook you to a fatigue of laughter, it became a moot point whether you ought not to have pitied him. When he debated any matter by himself, he would shut up his mouth with a dumb, studious pout, and roll his full eye into such a vacant amazement, such a palapable ignorance of what to think of it, that his silent perplexity (which would sometimes hold him several minutes) gave your imagination as full content as the most absurd thing he could say upon it."

Nokes appears to have been as good a comedian off stage as on, and became a great favorite with King Charles and his court. He had a grave and sober countenance, which, at the right moment in conversation as well as in the playing of a character, would light up, and a twinkle or a grimace would set his companions in a roar.

Once, however, Charles II was the instigator of a little scene that went too far. The King took him, along with the Court, to Dover to meet the aged Queen Mother, Henrietta Maria, who was arriving from France on a very formal visit of state.

"When Henrietta Maria arrived," relates the historian Doran, "with her suite of French ladies and gentlemen, the latter attired, according to the prevailing fashion, in very short blue or scarlet laced coats, with broad sword belts, the English comedians played before the royal host and his guests, the play, founded on Molière's 'Ecole des Femmes,' and called 'Sir Solomon.' Nokes acted Sir Arthur Addel, in dressing for which part he was assisted by the Duke of Monmouth.

In order that he might better aid the French mode, the Duke took off his own sword and belt, and buckled them to the actor's side. At his first entrance on the stage, King and Court broke into unextinguishable laughter, so admirably were the foreign guests caricatured; at which outrage on courtesy and hospitality, the guests, naturally enough, were much chagrined. Nokes retained the Duke's sword and belt to his dying day, which fell in the course of the year 1692."

Charles II—really an excellent judge of plays and players—is credited with the "discovery" of Nokes, and had for him all the fondness lavished by the powerful on an accomplished protégé. The fact that Nokes was pretty and a player of girl's rôles, however, is no reflection on the "morals" of Charles. That pleasantest of all English monarchs was too busy with his Nell Gwyns, his Castlemaines and his pretty Moll Davies to give any Cesarian attention to Nokes.

One of the most famous of the male rôles of Nokes was Jupiter Ammon, which, from descriptions, must have been a delicious burlesque on the pompous classic deity, Nokes augmenting the fun by endeavoring to make his short stature measure up to the dignity of Jupiter.

Of the other associates of Kynaston and Nokes whom Rhodes gathered together to play female rôles in the restoration of the stage, not much has been preserved. William Betteron, the younger brother of the great Thomas, was cut off untimely, before he could show of what Thespian stuff he was made—accidentally drowned. Angel was cast for waiting maids, and thence drifted into low comedy Frenchmen and foolish lords. Mosely and Floid became famous for

176

prostitute types—and their names are further linked by the peculiar fact that they died almost at the same time, in 1674.

The record of Charles Hart's associates in the rival Killigrew company, Burt and Clun, is as meager. Though trained by Dicky Robinson, as was Hart, they either had not the skill or the opportunity to win distinction as stage women. They seem to have played women only in their "juvenile" period, and both scored later in male rôles.

Burt was cast by Killigrew as Othello, but King Charles again showed his keen interest and good judgment by intervening, and suggested that Hart play the Moor, exchanging rôles with Burt, who became Cassio. Hart's Othello, as has already been related, gave Betterton's Hamlet at the other house a battle royal. Clun played Iago, and was reputed the best Iago of the time. When Jonson's "Catiline" was put on, Hart was cast in the title part, and Burt played Cicero. This was the climax of Burt's career, while Hart's Catiline was "so unapproachable," relates a historian, "that when he died, Jonson's tragedy died with him."

That other friend of Hart's, Lacy, the comedian who helped him train Nell Gwyn for the stage, also appeared at times in female rôles. But he seems to have made no pretense at "impersonating" women— he merely burlesqued them broadly and in a low comedy vein, much, probably, as George Munro has done in our own time.

With the advent of the women, the necessity for the serious boy actress was gone, and the custom of casting boys in feminine rôles sank rapidly and completely into oblivion. The opposite custom, introduced by Killigrew, has persisted however, even to this day, and there is

177

scarcely a Shakespearean revival without a page or a Prince in the Tower being played seriously by a girl, to say nothing of freakish ventures like Sarah Bernhardt as Hamlet. Outside of Shakespeare, a Maude Adams, too, can play Peter Pan. Our present day boy-heroines, however, are either college amateurs, when serious, or are burlesquers or satirists of female types. A later chapter will be devoted to this development.

Meanwhile, a last glimpse of the serious male heroines. In "The Rehearsal," that rich old comedy that raised the curtain on stage folks long before "Trelawney of the Wells," Sheridan makes the First Player say to the impatient director: "Sir, Mr. Ivory is not come yet, but he'll be here presently; he's but two doors off."

The sally was greeted with a laugh by the wise of London, who knew Mr. Ivory and his reputation and knew what sort of a place "two doors off" signified.

Mr. Ivory was Abraham Ivory, once quite skilled in playing female rôles in the latter, lean years of that profession—skilled enough to be known all over London. But he took heavily to drink and became notorious for neglect of duty. He descended lower and lower in the casts, and finally was given the very smallest of bits. Even these he retained only out of sentiment on the part of the manager of the theater, for he sometimes missed even his cue to come on and say, "My lord, the carriage waits," owing to tardiness in leaving the neighboring wineshop.

The last of the boy actresses thus passed from the scene to be embalmed in a playwright's jest.

X. PRINCES IN PETTICOATS

FROM the days when Achilles, at his mother's harassed behest, reluctantly "put on women's ways" and hid himself among the daughters of Lycomedes to escape draft for the Trojan War, to the days when the present Prince of Wales annoyed and scandalized the British Empire by assuming the prima donna rôle in a one-act farce comedy, "The Bathroom Door," on the battleship Repulse at sea, a prying plebeian world has frequently surprised royalty masquerading in petticoats.

The most astounding of all the procession that shall pass under our survey is the personage history knows as Queen Elizabeth of England.

Legend knows the "Virgin Queen" as the "Bisley Boy," and the late Bram Stoker, who investigated the legend thoroughly and gave it generally to the world as the exciting climax of his thrilling book, "Famous Imposters," identifies the personage who sat on the throne in the most brilliant period of British history, as the illegitimate son of Henry VIII's own natural son, the Duke of Richmond, posing first as the little dead Princess Elizabeth, his cousin, to overcome a temporary difficulty, and then compelled to keep up the imposture all the rest of his life as Princess and as Queen.

In the little village of Bisley, high up in the Cotswold Hills of Surrey, Bram Stoker, friend and biographer of the late Sir Henry Irving, stumbled onto a tradition that has persisted for three centuries, with a wealth of circumstance, that in the Manor House of the place, died, when she was scarcely twelve years old, the Princess Elizabeth, daughter of Henry VIII and Anne Boleyn. She had been sent into the hills to escape the pestilence raging in London. The death of the little Princess was sudden, and came just before her royal father was to pay her a visit.

"The governess feared to tell her father," Mr. Stoker relates. "Henry VIII had the sort of temper which did not make for the happiness of those around him."

The poor woman, in despair, hid the body of the Princess, and rushed off to the village "to find a living girl child who could be passed off for the princess.

"Throughout the little village and its surroundings was to be found no girl child of an age reasonably suitable for the purpose required. More than ever distracted, for time was flying by, she determined to take the greater risk of a boy substitute—if a boy could be found. Happily for the poor woman's safety, for her very life now hung in the balance, this venture was easy enough to begin. There was a boy available, and just such a boy as would suit the special purpose

180

for which he was required—a boy well known to the governess, for the little Princess had taken a fancy to him and had lately been accustomed to play with him. Moreover, he was a pretty boy as might have been expected from the circumstance of the little Lady Elizabeth having chosen him as her playmate. He was close at hand and available. So he was clothed in the dress of the dead child, they being of about equal stature."

The exciting suspense of the governess in her search for a proper boy for the purpose is a little gratuitous on the part of Mr. Stoker, since the tradition, as it works out, makes the little female impersonator Elizabeth's bastard cousin, strongly resembling her, despite his illegitimacy—Elizabeth herself, by the way, escaped being a bastard by only a few weeks, Anne Boleyn being a bride on whose forehead the orange blossoms already had withered.

This boy, born of the girl who afterward became the Duke of Richmond's wife, had been sent into the Cotswold Hills to conceal the indiscretion of the lively little bride-to-be, the pretty Lady Mary Howard. The waif, naturally in his mother's way, passed as a Neville, poor relations of the Howards, with whom he was left in the hills of Surrey. The legend argues the substitution could have been made with few questions asked. Also, if the boy actually was there, he must have looked like a godsend to the governess.

"The visit passed off successfully. Henry suspected nothing; as the whole thing had happened so swiftly, there had been no antecedent anxiety. Elizabeth had been brought up in such dread of her father that he had not, at the rare intervals of his seeing her, been accustomed to any affectionate effusiveness on her part; and in his hurried visit he had not time for baseless conjecture."

The imposture, of course, had to be kept up to protect the heads of all concerned. Though doubly illegitimate, this grandchild of Henry's had both mother and grandmother from the nobility, and was as high-born on the female side as the male. He was a bright, handsome boy, strongly resembling Elizabeth and Henry himself, precociously clever, and easily capable of doing his part in keeping up the deception. Thus, Mr. Stoker argues, he was capable of becoming one of the strongest monarchs of England, and the mightiest "queen" in the history of the world.

Stoker analyzes the character of the Queen Elizabeth history knows, making much of the strongly masculine trend of her mind, noted by all historians; of the fact that she, though a daughter of the passionate Henry and the daring Anne, and descended from a line of not overly moral ancestors, preferred to remain a virgin (historians, however, have refused to take her virginity as seriously as her lauding subjects, including Shakespeare); that there was a profound secret in her life which historians have sought in vain to penetrate, shared only by her old nurse, Mrs. Ashley, and Sir Thomas Parry, both protectors of her childhood. These two alone, he avers, of all who surrounded her, were never victims of her outbursts of insane temper. On this theory, too, can be explained Elizabeth's belligerent aversion to doctors, refusing their intimate attendance even on her deathbed.

A pitiful confirmation of Stoker's theory came to light a few years ago. In a little walled-in garden of the Manor is a flower bed "set in

182

an antique stone receptacle of oblong shape which presents something of the appearance of a stone coffin of the earlier ages. . . . When the governess wished to hide the secret hurriedly, she hid the body, intending it to be only temporarily, in the stone coffin which lay in the garden at Overcourt outside the Princess's window. Some ten years ago the bones of a young girl lying amidst rags of fine clothing were found in the stone coffin. The finder was a churchman—a man of the highest character and a member of a celebrated ecclesiastical family. The said finder firmly believed in the story of the Bisley Boy."

The appearance of the Queen Elizabeth of history is examined by Mr. Stoker and fitted into his theory. By the laws of heredity, this red-headed personage sitting on the British throne, would have come more naturally out of Henry in his dalliance with the "faire damsel," Elizabeth Blunt, daughter of Sir John Blunt, than with the little brunette with black hair and beautiful brown eyes, Anne Boleyn. The son of Henry and Elizabeth Blunt, first called Henry Fitzroy, and later created Duke of Richmond and Somerset, was of the color of his parents. Mary Howard, with whose co-operation Fitzroy brought into the world young Neville, the Bisley boy, was also "faire." It's an ideal ancestry for the "Queen," but then, it is not unthinkable that Henry could have stamped his complexion on his daughter Elizabeth, despite the brunette beauty of Anne. Mr. Stoker also points to the fact that Henry was bald and brings himself almost to the point of believing that, in later life, Queen Elizabeth may have been bald, too, from her anxiety about her wigs, almost as morbid as her fear of intimate examination by her doctors—the latter a well attested fact. When

183

Elizabeth traveled, Mr. Stoker points out, she carried with her not fewer than eighty wigs.

Well, if Queen Elizabeth was the "Bisley Boy," here's hoping some sharper investigator following us will identify him with the "Mr.W.H." of the Sonnets! What a romance that would be!

Anne Boleyn, mother of the Princess Elizabeth, who may or may not have grown up to be Queen, came near falling a victim to certain "female impersonators," bent on beating her to death—destroying her, in the name of Holy Church, and the baby, known to be Henry's, lying illegitimately in her womb.

It happened during the feverish excitement over Henry's contemplated break with Rome, which was refusing him a divorce from Queen Katharine in order that he might espouse the pretty, black-eyed Anne.

She had been supping with the King at a villa on the Thames. A mob of seven thousand to eight thousand women of London, "with a number of men disguised in their midst," went out to seize "Boleyn's daughter, the King's sweetheart," with the intention of killing her, but she escaped by crossing the river in a boat. Fuel was added to the flame of the wrath of the women of London—and of the men so eager to help tear her to pieces that they joined the mob in female disguise —by reports that Anne was herself the King's illegitimate daughter, so that Henry was about to flaunt incest as well as impiety in their faces.

Elizabeth's successor, James I, gentle poet coming out of Scotland and patron of letters, including the translation into English of the Bible, is reputed to have possessed the soul of a woman imprisoned in

184

none too masculine a body. But he, like William Rufus, Edward II and William III, refrained from overt public masquerade. In the dedication prefixed even yet to the King James version, James is lauded as "caring for the Church, as a most tender and loving nursing father." The word "nursing" may have no significance in this connection—but then, again, it may have arisen quite unconsciously out of the soul of the writer, familiar with the King's character. James, after the manner of men-women, may even have sensed the significance and taken it as a delicate compliment.

While English Kings were maintaining their masculine dignity out of deference to their people, across the Channel there flourished a Prince with no such scruples. He was Philip, Duke of Orléans, son of Louis XIII of France and Anne of Austria, and brother of Louis XIV.

Philip has some association with England, in that he took as first wife the Princess Henrietta, sister of Charles II. Henrietta died suddenly, and there was suspicion Philip had poisoned her for accepting attentions from his more virile brother, King Louis. Philip then married Charlotte Elizabeth, Princess Palatine, who had no high opinion of him (maybe some such opinion helped prove fatal to poor Henrietta, throwing up to Philip his charms in comparison with his brother's.)

"He had the manners of a woman rather than those of a man," the Princess Palatine recorded of Philip for the benefit of posterity. "He liked to play, chat, eat well, dance and perform his toilet—in short, everything that women love."

"He always dressed like a woman," says Saint-Simon, who knew

185

him at Court, "covered with rings and bracelets; precious stones everywhere; a long wig, black and powdered, and ribbons wherever they could be placed; also redolent of all sorts of perfumery. He was accused of putting on an imperceptible touch of rouge."

O. P. Gilbert, a Frenchman has made a recent study of Philip and of the Abbé de Choisy, another renowned man-woman of the Court of Louis XIV. His book which has been done into English as "Men in Women's Guise," examines into "the motives which induced Anne of Austria and Cardinal Mazarin to bring up the prince as though he were a princess. Possibly it was a fear that he would one day prove a thorn in the side of his brother Louis." Louis seems to have shared this fear, for Philip, "more afraid of sunburn than bullets," defeated William of Orange at Cassel. "Louis, jealous of his first success, took care that he should not gain any others by relieving him of his command."

Scandal was common at Court that Philip had Cardinal Mazarin's Italian blood in his veins, instead of Louis XIII's. The Medici blood would have needed none of the Cardinal's to taint it to produce Philip, for a sister of the next Louis, daughter of Anne's legitimate son was a prioress, and notorious for her practice of tribadism with her young nuns.

Philip was a popular favorite about court, especially with the ladies.

"He loved to be with women and young girls, and attire them and dress their hair. He knew what suited each one better than the most expert maid, and his greatest joy when he was grown up was to adorn

186

them, and to purchase jewelry to lend or give to those who were fortunate enough to be his favorites." Gilbert is quoting Madame de Motteville, who may have heaved a little sigh at this point.

"He was well made," she proceeds, "his features appeared to be perfect, his black eyes were bright and handsome, with an expression of mildness and gravity. His mouth somewhat resembled that of the Queen, his mother; his black hair, in large natural curls, suited his complexion, and his nose, which was aquiline, was well formed. If age does not diminish his beauty, he will rival the handsomest women of the day, but it does not appear that he will ever be tall."

"Monsieur was greatly attached to the Queen, his mother," testifies Madame de la Fayette. "All his inclinations were towards feminine occupations—in which he differed entirely from his brother. He was handsome and well made, but of a beauty more suitable to a princess than to a prince."

All these more delicate beauties, about which his girl friends raved, seem to have been lost on his wife. "Though he had not a mean appearance," admits the Princess Palatine, "he was very short; his hair was as black as jet, the eyebrows thick and brown, a long narrow face, a big thick nose, a very small mouth, and bad teeth." Saint-Simon is crueler still: "He was a little pot-bellied man, mounted on such high heels that they were more like stilts."

The Abbé de Choisy, whose mother was bringing him up in imitation of "Monsieur," sketches a vivid picture of Philip, on visits to the de Choisy home, when the Abbé was a youth:

"I was dressed up as a girl every time that the Duke of Orléans

187

came to our house, and he came at least two or three times a week. I had my ears pierced, diamonds, patches, and all the other little fopperies which are so easy to get accustomed to, and so difficult to get rid of. Monsieur, who liked all that, paid me a hundred little attentions as soon as he arrived. He was accompanied by the nieces of Cardinal Mazarin" (Cardinal's "nieces" in those days was a circumlocution, like Pope's "nephews," and these charming girls possibly were Monsieur's bastard sisters) "and some of the Queen's daughters"—maybe more close relations.

"He seated himself at the toilet-table, and they dressed his hair; he had on a bodice tight to the waist; this bodice was embroidered. They took off his coat and put on him a woman's mantle and petticoats. It was said all this was done by order of the Cardinal, who wished to make him effeminate for fear that he should cause trouble to the King as Gaston did to Louis XIII. When he was dressed and decked out, we played at 'primo,' which was the fashionable game then, and at seven o'clock a collation was brought, but no servants appeared. I went to the door of the room, took the dishes and put them on small tables. I poured out the drink, and was rewarded with kisses on the forehead, with which these ladies honored me. Madame de Brancas often brought her daughter, who has since become Princess d'Harcourt. She helped me to lay out the repast, but although she was extremely handsome, the Queen's daughters loved me best, no doubt because, in spite of the headdress and the petticoats, they felt that there was something masculine about me."

This talkative Abbé de Choisy is one of the most interesting of all

188

the female masqueraders of history, from the fact that he not only had a brilliant mind, but could turn his brain actively to an introspection of his own psychology. But, before going into that, we might as well dispose of "Monsieur," who, thanks to the precautions of the Cardinal and his regal mistress, that he cause no uneasiness to Louis, lived an easy life about Court, the pet of all the women except his wife, who may have been on guard lest he dispose of her as he did of her English predecessor. He died in 1701, just turned sixty, and still well preserved enough to appear a handsome dowager in his dainty finery. Let his Duchess have the last word:

"Monsieur has feminine tastes. He likes finery, and he takes care of his complexion. He is interested in needlework and ceremonies. He dances well, but he dances like a woman. Except in time of war, he could never be prevailed upon to mount a horse. The soldiers said of him that he was more afraid of the heat of the sun, or the black smoke of gunpowder, than he was of musket bullets."

The Abbé de Choisy, while not of royal birth, was closely associated with the court through both his father and his mother. His father was Chancellor of the Duke of Orléans, and his mother was a very pretty girl of the noble family of Harault, and besides "in the early days of the Regency, she so pleased Cardinal Mazarin that one day, being at Marshal d'Estrées house, he said, 'What! you are amusing yourselves here and Madame de Choisy is not present! How can there be any amusement without her?'" Knowing the way of the Cardinal even with Queen Anne of Austria, there might be a suspicion that the Abbé and "Monsieur," so much alike in taste for feminine finery, may both have been "nephews" of the commanding, irresistible churchman.

Madame de Choisy, at any rate, hung eagerly on every word of the Cardinal, and did everything she could to make her son Francois Timoléon a replica of "Monsieur." She was more than forty-three, however, when her child was born, and had escaped the breath of scandal in a scandal-mongering court, so let the coincidences be taken as accidental.

In his infancy and early youth, records Gilbert, "his mother saw in him nothing more than a pretty doll to be dressed, undressed, and have his hair done." She attired him completely as a girl, and at eighteen, "his waist was encircled with tight-fitting corsets which made his loins, hips and bust more prominent. Everything boyish about him was gradually repressed."

At this period, he took an examination at the Sorbonne, and "thanks to the recommendation of the Archbishop of Paris, he was received as an abbé without opposition." Again the fine Italian hand of the Cardinal might be suspected, but we waive the point.

The Abbe, whose racy "Memoirs of Choisy," are the source book of Mr. Gilbert's study, at about the period he became a churchman, also made a bid for honors as an actress at the Bordeaux theater.

"During five months I played in comedy at the theater of a large city, dressed as a girl," he records. "Everybody was deceived; I had lovers to whom I granted small favors, but was very discreet as to great favors, and had a reputation for prudence and virtue. I enjoyed the greatest pleasures that one can taste in this life."

In the flower of his débutante youth, apparently just before he entered upon his pretense as a churchman, which never weighed heavily on him, de Choisy gives, with maidenly modesty, this description of himself:

"I had a bodice embroidered with natural flowers on a silver ground, the skirt of the same material with a long train; the skirt was fastened up on both sides with yellow and silver ribbons, with a large bow at the back to mark the waist; the bodice was very high and padded out to make believe that I had a bust, and, as a matter of fact, I had as much as a young girl of fifteen.

"From my childhood, they had made me wear bodices that were extremely tight, and this had pushed up the flesh which was fat and plump. I also took great care of my neck, rubbing it every night with veal broth and a pomade of sheeps'-foot oil, which makes the skin soft and white.

"My black hair was done into large curls; I had big diamond earrings, a dozen patches, a necklace of false pearls that were quite as good as real ones, for no one seeing me with so much jewelry would have believed that I was wearing anything false.

"I had exchanged at Paris my diamond cross, which I did not like, for five ornamental pins that I placed in my hair, which I also decorated with yellow and silver ribbons, which went very well with my black hair. No headdress, for it was June; a large mask which covered both cheeks to prevent sunburn, white gloves and a fan. Such was my get-up, and no one would have ever guessed that I was not a woman."

191

His bedroom he describes with the same minute detail of fluffy finery, so dear to the feminine heart, winding up triumphantly with "lace-edged sheets, three large pillows, and three or four small ones, the corners tied up with flame-colored ribbons."

Becoming an abbé, it was necessary to conform to some extent with the traditional dress, but he applied his inventive genius with the result that, when he called upon the Curé of St. Medard, that excellent divine greatly praised his dress "and said it was much more graceful than that of other young abbés, whose long coats and little cloaks did not inspire respect."

In assuming his holy duties, relates Choisy, "I began by having my ears repierced for the holes had become stopped up. I put on embroidered bodices, and a black-and-gold dressing gown with trimmings of white satin, a belt with a busk and a large bow of ribbon at the back to mark the waist, a long train, a well-powdered peruke, ear-rings, patches, a little cap with a topknot of ribbon. At first, I wore only a dressing-gown of black cloth, buttoned down the front with black buttonholes down to the ground, and a train half an ell in length, which was carried by a lackey, a small peruke, slightly powdered, very simple ear-rings, and two large velvet patches on the temples."

It was in this modest attire he paid his respects to the Curé. Leaving that excellent and enthusiastic divine, "I went then to see the churchwardens, who had given me a seat right opposite the pulpit, and afterwards I paid my visits in the quarter—Marquise d'Usson, Marquise de Menières, etc.—and when I saw that I had succeeded in my

192

purpose, I undid five or six of the lowest buttons of my dress and showed underneath a robe of spotted satin, the train of which was not so long as that of my dress. I had also underneath that a petticoat of white damask which was not seen except when the train was carried. I did not wear small clothes, they did not seem to me to be feminine, and I was not afraid of being cold as it was summer time. I had a muslin cravat, the tassels of which fell over a large bow of black ribbon, which was fastened to the top of my bodice, but did not prevent my showing a portion of my shoulders, which had kept very white owing to the great care I had taken of them all my life." And, a little later he observes, "I thought myself really and truly a woman."

Despite this obsession for clothes, Mr. Gilbert is of opinion that the abbé, "though one of the prettiest women of his day in appearance, was a man of sound mind and normal condition, but his beauty and the education he received from his mother gave him a second nature which did not correspond with his sexual desires." Yet, he relates, "except for some small adventures—of no great importance—Choisy was as staid and virtuous as a holy friar. He was too much occupied by his own beauty to interest himself much in that of others."

At the age of thirty-two, "he abandoned feminine attire and became Ambassador of Louis XIV in Siam; honors rained upon him; he entered the academy. But all this did not satisfy him, and during all his life he regretted the delightful time when with his waist tightly strapped in a corset, his breast uncovered, and the long curls falling artfully on his shoulders, he felt himself envied by the women and admired by the men."

Before this gloomy "old age," however, the abbé had a fling at matrimony. Only, in the rôle of "Madame Sancy," a name he assumed in the circle of his immediate friends, he married "Monsieur de Maulny," otherwise Mademoiselle Charlotte, a pretty girl neighbor who had fallen distractedly in love with him. To humor him, Charlotte dressed herself as a young man, and, with the consent of her family, they went through the marriage ceremony, he as the bride and she as the groom.

"Monsieur de Maulny had, at my request, had his hair cut short like a man's," relates Choisy. "After I was in bed" (on the wedding night) "he appeared in a dressing-gown, with his night-cap in his hand, and his hair tied up with flame-colored ribbon. He was rather bashful about getting into bed, but at last came and lay by my side. All her relatives came and kissed us; our good aunt drew the bed curtains, and everybody went home. We then abandoned ourselves to delight, without however, passing the bounds of propriety, which may be hard to believe, but is nevertheless true."

The "marriage" continued for a time in extravagant happiness for both. Then, growing tired of each other, and their affair prompting an ever-increasing scandal, and Charlotte having a chance to marry a more masculine personage, Choisy surrendered her to his rival, still a virgin, he alleges—"I had never attacked her honor, because I was too much engrossed with my own beauty."

The abbé lived to be eighty-one, passing through numerous adventures, all tinged with his obsession of being a woman, but suffering in his later life the mortification of having to appear in men's attire since

194

he no longer looked convincingly feminine in his petticoats. However, to the last, he wore, in his study, his faded female finery, and thus bedecked wrote his learned "History of the Church," his "Imitation of Jesus Christ," his more secular "Memoirs of Choisy"—the only one of his books still worth reading—and a novel, "The New Astrae," with himself as the hero under the name of Celadon, a stilted tale of shepherds and shepherdesses, tedious despite the vagrant urge of the handsome young tender of sheep to disguise himself as a girl.

The abbé was a serious thinker, and sought to analyze his own emotions, recognizing their departure from the normal. Here is the result:

"I have tried to find out how such a strange pleasure came to me" —namely, his delight in believing himself a woman—"and I take it to be in this way. It is an attribute of God to be loved and adored, and man—so far as his weak nature will permit—has the same ambition; and as it is beauty which creates love, and beauty is generally woman's portion, when it happens that men have, or believe they have, attractions for which they may be loved, they try to increase them by putting on woman's attire, which is very advantageous for that purpose. Then they feel the inexpressible pleasure of being loved. I have had that pleasant experience many a time, and when I have been at a ball or theater, in a beautiful dress, and with patches and diamonds, and I have heard some one near me whisper, 'There is a pretty woman!' I have felt a pleasure so great that it is beyond all comparison. Ambition, riches, even love cannot equal it, because we always love ourselves more than we love others."

195

Which may be well enough to satisfy his soul—but it is a woman's soul, despite Mr. Gilbert. Not a normal male vanity could have induced the Abbé's disguise, nor could even the thorough training as a girl his mother put him through induce the delight he felt when men admired his white bosom. Rather is it to be believed he had scattered among his interstitial cells a liberal number of the female corpuscles Professor Steinach so recently has discovered in his anatomical analysis of homosexuals.

That he was not all woman, psychologically, however, despite the fact Mademoiselle Charlotte left his bed after many weeks still a virgin, is indicated by his adventure later with a pretty actress named Rosalie, whom he dressed in men's clothes, as had become his habit in numerous affairs since he "divorced" Charlotte, and called Monsieur Comtin. This affair continued for several months, "but then unhappily," he relates, "Monsieur Comtin began to have belly-aches, loss of appetite, and 'morning sickness.' I suspected the cause of her illness, and made her resume her female attire, as being more suitable to her present condition, and better adapted to hide it."

"The fruit of dishonor," as his conscience bids him call it, duly appeared in the form of a little girl. As soon as Rosalie was able to go about her business as an actress, the abbé arranged a marriage for her with an actor in her old company, and so bade her godspeed. The chances are he never saw her any more—just as he had never laid eyes again on Charlotte—"I could never bear married women."

But he kept the child, of whom he believed himself to be the father, had her "well brought up, and at the age of sixteen, I married

196

her to a gentleman who had five or six thousand livres a year: she is very happy."

In which light frame of mind, let us leave him, look in for a moment on the Abbé d'Entragues, another of Mr. Gilbert's hero-heroines, and then pass on to the Chevalier D'Eon, the most renowned "man-woman" of history, who made the female masquerade a profession in itself.

The Abbé d'Entragues was a contemporary of the Abbé de Choisy and of "Monsieur," the King's fair brother. He is reputed to have belonged to the de Balzac family and his brother married the half-sister of the King's mistress, Louise de la Vallière.

His mother wanted a daughter, but getting a son instead, sought to make a monkey of Providence by bringing up d'Entragues as a girl. The "girl" became a great wit, with a rather morbid habit, however, of keeping pretty and white by being constantly bled.

This abbé wore the regulation garb of his calling, but at night indulged in the luxury of feminine negligée—"a woman's night-cap trimmed with lace, top-knot and other finery, corset laced with ribbons, bedgown, and patches." He led a dissolute life, "became a trifle crack-brained," joined the Protestants, was exiled, and returned to Paris repentant, and to Mother Church. "His original mania for feminine attire reasserted itself, and he appeared in full ball dress whenever an opportunity occurred." Despite the fact that he slept with his arms fastened above his head in order to keep his hands white, he lived to be eighty.

While the Chevalier d'Eon had not the blood of royalty in his

197

veins—nor the suspicion of any—he makes his début into history in woman's garb as the rival of Madame de Pompadour as a pretty new "mistress" for Louis XV. It was all a joke—and not a very delicate one at that—but the King was tickled instead of being sore, took a fancy for the handsome young man purely as a male, and the Chevalier's subsequent long career is intimately involved with the highest affairs of state.

D'Eon's father was a lawyer in Paris, in prosperous circumstances, and the young man, by the time he reached twenty-one, was beginning to make some little noise on his own account. He was bright and willing, and the powerful Prince de Conti was taking an interest in his advancement. It was through this connection that he was at a masque ball, where Louis and all the court were present. The Chevalier, possessor of girlish face, wide hips, full and well-rounded bust, was masquerading quite innocently as a girl. The King saw the feminine newcomer, most dazzling of all the young beauties, and did not conceal his admiration. It was then the idea of the joke flashed into the heads of de Conti and other of d'Eon's friends.

They arranged a secret tryst, installed d'Eon in a private apartment, and then doubly endangered him by tipping off Madame de Pompadour that Louis was to meet the new beauty, before telling Louis himself. The Pompadour flew to the apartment, and had d'Eon been a genuine girl she probably would have vanished then and there from history. As it was, the Chevalier explained things quite frankly —and Madame de Pompadour went away chuckling over what was in store for the King.

Shortly afterward, Louis made his advent. The wine must have been extra good that night, or d'Eon must have been an especially winning young man for Louis, too, admitted the joke was on him, and did whatever was the royal equivalent to passing around a box of cigars.

"Are you as intelligent as a boy as you are modest as a girl?" the King is reported to have asked during what must have been an embarrassing conversation, and, being satisfied with the answer, he annexed d'Eon to his service, and before long the youth was a trusted member of that corps of Louis's secret diplomats, who kept Europe in turmoil, seriously thwarting the work of his accredited ministers.

D'Eon rose rapidly to renown, and in the interesting days that immediately preceded the French Revolution, he was as great a wonder as Cagliostro. A favorite diversion of the young sports of Paris and of London was to bet on the sex of the Chevalier, and the size of the bets was limited only by the resources of the purses. Many attempts were made to gather correct data for the settling of these wagers, but it was not until after d'Eon's death that the matter of sex was fully cleared up. An official autopsy was then held, and the medical certificate, signed in the presence of Père Elisée, first surgeon to Louis XVIII, reads:

"I certify, by these presents, I have inspected the body of Chevalier d'Eon, in presence of M. Adair, M. Wilson and Father Elisée, and have found the male organs perfectly formed." The signature is that of Dr. Copeland, intrusted with the inspection, which included dissection.

In 1755, d'Eon went to Russia on a secret mission for Louis, disguised as the niece of the King's accredited agent, the Chevalier Douglas. In his rôle of a girl, d'Eon insinuated himself into the graces of the Empress Elizabeth, and gathered some valuable information. Douglas failed in his mission, but d'Eon, going back to Russia the following year, this time in the rôle of a man and as Louis' official representative, was able, on the strength of the secrets he had gleaned, to bring the matter to a happy termination.

On his second trip, he represented himself to Elizabeth as the brother of the handsome girl who had won her heart the year previously. It is a toss-up, perhaps, in view of the Czarina's alleged versatility in the matter of love, whether she preferred him as a man or as a woman, and his long and intimate popularity with her may have been due to his letting her into the secret of his fascinating duplicity.

This impersonation of the niece of Douglas, when d'Eon was 27 years old, is the first of which there is record, after his introduction to Louis at the masked ball. It is testified by various memoir writers of the time—France was as full of them as America is today—that d'Eon in his youth was indifferent to female beauty, and that in later life, as a soldier and male diplomat, he was as cool to the most ravishing of the sex as Frederick the Great, or Sir Isaac Newton, or Charles XII of Sweden.

Upon his return to France from his second visit to Russia, the King, out of gratitude, commissioned d'Eon a captain of dragoons. As a soldier he was brilliantly successful, some of his adventures being of the most daring and virile sort. Whatever his feelings when arrayed

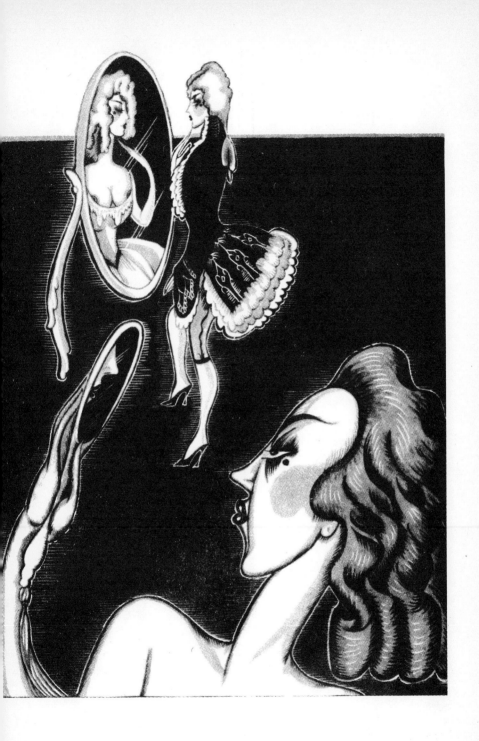

in petticoats, there was never a question of the Chevalier's courage on the battlefield or on the field of honor.

Louis, a little later, appointed d'Eon minister plenipotentiary to Russia, a place which he held with distinction. The King recalled him from Russia to go to England, ostensibly as secretary to the French Embassy, but really as a personal and secret agent of Louis, as on his first visit to Russia. Madame de Pompadour intercepted some of the private correspondence between d'Eon and the King which was not to her liking, and by her influence, d'Eon was dismissed from the embassy and publicly disgraced. But Louis rewarded him privately with a huge pension, and kept him in England, apparently as a gentleman of leisure and of fashion, but still his confidential agent.

In England, during his period with the embassy and later, the story of d'Eon's disguise on his first trip to Russia, together with his present habits, gave rise to the London doubts as to his sex. For, though d'Eon dressed in male attire, he was by nature beardless or else had learned a trick of being close shaven without any evidence of the razor. He was "fussy" to a fault about his clothing and appearance, even in an age of dandies, and indulged in none of the gallantries with young women, which were the sport of young men of fashion. The fast set of London began to speculate d'Eon was disguised now instead of on the visit to Russia when this charming creature appeared as a girl, and both London and Paris began to lay those bets as to the Chevalier's sexual equipment which were settled only many years later by the autopsy.

The reason for d'Eon's permanent assumption of female attire after the death of Louis XV is confused in the conflicting "memoirs" and "correspondences."

A caprice of Marie Antoinette, the new Queen of France, is sometimes blamed. It is alleged that the young Queen, giddy and light-minded, insisted that the Chevalier, after his return to Paris, be presented to her formally as a woman, though it had been his own wish to appear at Court in his uniform as Captain of Dragoons. The Princess Lambelle's story, however, seems more characteristic of the lively, human impulses of the likable, feather-brained Queen:

"I remember," relates this picturesque Princess, who has not escaped suspicions of being rival of the new King for this pretty Queen's affections, "a ludicrous circumstance arising from the Queen's innocent curiosity, in which, if there were anything to blame, I myself am to be censured for lending myself to it so heartily to satisfy her Majesty.

"When the Chevalier d'Eon was allowed to return to France, her Majesty expressed a particular inclination to see this extraordinary character. From prudential as well as political motives, she was at first easily persuaded to repress her desire. However, by a most ludicrous occurrence, it was revived, and nothing would do but she must have a sight of the being who had for some time been the talk of every society, and at the period to which I allude was become the mirth of all Paris.

"The Chevalier being one day in a very large party of both sexes, in which, though his appearance had more of the old soldier in it than of the character he was compelled in spite of himself to adopt, many of the guests having no idea to what sex this nondescript animal really belonged, the conversation after dinner happened to turn to the manly exercise of fencing.

"Heated by a subject to him so interesting, the Chevalier, forgetful of the respect due to his assumed garb, started from his seat, and pulling up his petticoats, threw himself on guard. Though dressed in male attire underneath, this sudden freak sent all the ladies and many of the gentlemen out of the room in double quick time. The Chevalier, however, instantly recovering from the first impulse, quietly put down his upper garment, and begged pardon in a gentlemanly manner for having for a moment deviated from the forms of his imposed situation.

"All the gossips of Paris were presently amused with the story, which, of course, reached the Court, with every droll particular of the pulling up and clapping down the cumbrous paraphernalia of a hoop petticoat.

"The King and Queen, from the manner in which they enjoyed the tale when told them (and certainly it lost nothing in the report), would not have been the least amused of the party had they been present. His Majesty shook the room with laughing, and the Queen, the Princess Elizabeth, and the other ladies were convulsed at the description.

"When we were alone, 'How I should like,' said the Queen, "to see this curious man-woman!'

" 'Indeed,' replied I, 'I have not less curiosity than yourself, and I think we may contrive to let your Majesty have a peep at him—her, I mean!—without compromising your dignity, or offending the minister who interdicted the Chevalier from appearing in your presence.

I know he has expressed the greatest mortification, and that his wish to see your Majesty is almost irrepressible.'

" 'But how will you be able to contrive this without its being known to the King, or to the Count de Vergennes, who would never forgive me?' exclaimed her Majesty.

" 'Why, on Sunday, when you go to chapel, I will cause him, by some means or other, to make his appearance, in full dress, among the group of ladies who are generally waiting there to be presented to your Majesty.'

" 'Oh, you charming creature!' said the Queen. 'But wont the minister banish or exile him for it?'

" 'No, no! He has only been forbidden an audience of your Majesty at Court,' I replied.

"In good earnest, on the Sunday following the Chevalier was dressed in the height of fashion, with a large hoop, very long train, sack, five rows of ruffles, an immensely high powdered female wig, very beautiful lappets, white gloves, an elegant fan in his hand, his beard closely shaved, his neck and ears adorned with diamond rings and necklaces, and assuming all the airs and graces of a fine lady!

"But, unluckily, his anxiety was so great, the moment the Queen made her appearance, to get a sight of her Majesty, that, on rushing before the other ladies, his wig and headdress fell off his head; and before they could be well replaced, he made so ridiculous a figure by clapping them, in confusion, hind part before, that the King, the Queen and the whole suite could scarcely refrain from laughing aloud in the church.

"This ended the longed-for sight of this famous man-woman!

"As to me, it was a great while before I could recover myself. Even now, I laugh whenever I think of this great lady deprived of her head ornaments, with her bald pate laid bare, to the derision of such a multitude of Parisians, always prompt to divert themselves at the expense of others.

"However, the affair passed off unheeded, and no one but the Queen and myself ever knew that we ourselves had been innocently the cause of this comical adventure.

"When we met after mass, we were so overpowered that neither of us could speak for laughing. The bishop who officiated said it was lucky he had no sermon to preach that day, for it would have been difficult for him to have recollected himself, or to have maintained his gravity. The ridiculous appearance of the Chevalier, he added, was so continually presenting itself before him during the service that it was as much as he could do to restrain himself from laughing, by keeping his eyes constantly riveted on the book.

"Indeed, the oddity of the affair was greatly heightened when, in the middle of the mass, some charitable hand having adjusted the wig of the Chevalier, he re-entered the chapel as if nothing had happened, and, placing himself exactly opposite the altar, with his train upon his arm, stood fanning himself coquettishly, with an inflexible self-possession which only rendered it the more difficult for those around him to maintain their composure."

A long time, indeed, had elapsed since this ridiculous old "dowager" was the belle of the ball, in the days of the present King's father, and when the Pompadour's will was law in France instead of the whims of Marie Antoinette.

"Thus ended the Queen's curiosity," continues the Princess Lambelle, whose gossipy pen, before the guillotine claimed her head as well as the Queen's, recorded so lightly and so vividly the exciting little adventures of the Court. "The result only made the Chevalier's company in greater request, for everyone became more anxious than ever to know the masculine lady who had lost her wig!"

The late Andrew Lang, in a highly controversial and combative essay on d'Eon, suggests that the Chevalier, after the death of Louis XV, and the consequent termination of his employment as a secret personal agent, adopted the female dress as a matter of self-advertisement, simply for the purpose of keeping himself prominent in the public eye.

It is also recorded that d'Eon struck a bargain with the powerful new Minister of Finance, the dramatist Beaumarchais, by which, for a large money consideration, he yielded some valuable secret papers to the minister and agreed to assume the feminine disguise in order to avoid a duel with the son of an old political enemy, which would have reeked with scandal, dangerous to the government and to French society in general.

Beaumarchais was of either the personal or diplomatic opinion that d'Eon was a woman, "a blushing spinster, a kind of Jeanne d'Arc of the eighteenth century, pining for the weapons and uniform of the martial sex, but yielding her secret and forsaking her arms in the interest of the King."

Upon which, Voltaire retorted: "Our manners are obviously softened—d'Eon is a Pucelle d'Orléans who has not been burned."

But whether d'Eon became a woman permanently out of deference to no very creditable whim on the part of Marie Antoinette, or as a matter of self-advertisement, or because a powerful minister—who may or may not have believed him feminine—thought it best as a matter of state policy he should retire into petticoats and set at rest a feud with the powerful de Guerchy family, it is certain that the Chevalier, once his mind was made up, entered into the rôle in earnest and perhaps with something of the psychology of the Abbé de Choisy.

He complained seriously to a friend that he was "the most unfortunate of unfortunate females," and expressed a desire to take the veil and become a nun. But, after living for some years in retirement, he seems to have become more cheerful, for, when the Revolution was over, he suddenly blazed upon London in silks and diamonds as a "grande dame" of the Old Order.

D'Eon lived the better part of a century—born in 1728, died in 1810. His career was singularly free from "affairs of the heart," the nearest approach to a scandal developing when he was ambassador, as a male, to the court of Russia.

One of the Czarina's maids of honor fell in love with him, and her love seems to have been mildly reciprocated. The Empress Elisabeth resented the attachment, since she herself had taken a fancy for d'Eon in his rôles of both female and male, and there has been speculation that the wrath of the Czarina may have been the real reason for d'Eon's recall to France. The speculation, however, is as mild as the affair with the maid of honor seems to have been—Louis needed his very efficient spy for more important work in England.

The late Edgar Saltus, in a general characterization of the Empress in "The Imperial Orgy," and with no special reference to d'Eon, throws a light on her character that is illuminating:

"Elisabeth objected to rivals but not to shadows, only to women. With these she was merciless. Otherwise she enjoyed herself hugely. She hunted all day and danced all night. At some of the dances she appeared as a man. On such occasions, it was etiquette for all young women to appear as men and for all young men to appear as women. Elisabeth liked that. She liked young men in women's clothes. Moreover, that they might be properly set out, she acted as dresser, selecting in the process those that pleased her most. In regard to her own masquerade, she had a reason quite as interesting. Her leg was well turned, she knew she looked well as a man—knew, too, that women generally look the reverse." ·

With such a queen, an expert in female attire like d'Eon could scarcely help shining as a star. At the same time, d'Eon's mild sexual vigor could hardly have made him completely a favorite with this "Northern Messalina," who liked to help her men friends dress and undress, and her resentment against the maid of honor may have been purely petulant, however terrible in its consequence to the girl.

Another alleged affair of gallantry involves Queen Sophia Charlotte of England, consort of King George III. The story, on vague authority, is that the Queen kept a midnight tryst with the Chevalier, wherein they were surprised by the King himself. The Queen declared vehemently that d'Eon was a woman, and George III accepted her word without searching investigation. This story alleges another motive for the Chevalier electing to remain permanently a woman—in order to save the honor of the British Queen.

D'Eon, however, despite the revelations of the autopsy, seems not to have endangered his female admirers even to the extent the Abbé de Choisy did. It took a call to battle or to a duel to arouse the virility he possessed. Psychologically, he was a brother of the warrior Condé, who so disappointed the eagerly expectant Ninon de l'Enclos, and of the warrior Prince Eugene. He was more fortunate than they in his chances to flit the fan as well as flourish the sword.

Among the many excited speculations that buzzed about Paris when Mademoiselle Jenny Savalette de Lange died at Versailles, May 6, 1858, was that Jenny might have been the long-missing Louis XVII. The excitement died down after a while, however, and Paris— and history—accepted the official certificate of the death of an "unknown man having borne the name of Henriette-Genny Savalette Delange, bachelor, of no profession, born at (place of birth cannot be stated) in the year 1790."

The most astounding fact about Jenny was that she had lived for nearly seventy years about Paris, a pensioner of the Government when the Royalists were in power for some forgotten reason (restored to the pension after the Republican interregnum, nobody knew why, least of all those who put her name on the resumed list); had had many lovers but no husbands; had mingled freely in the circles of the few who knew or cared anything about her, and finally had died, without anybody ever suspecting she was not a woman. It was only when two old women were engaged to lay her out to prepare her decently for burial that they made an amazing discovery, and then hastened to notify the police.

Every clew, no matter how vague, was run down to find out who Jenny was and why the disguise—the newspapers joining the police diligently in the search, but Mr. O. P. Gilbert, from whose account we take these facts, reports the mystery was never solved. Jenny appears to have been no beauty—"tall, thin, lopsided, and leant on an umbrella; her features were hard, her look stern, and her voice shrill and cracked. She wore a dress that dated from the Empire or the Restoration, and on her head a black cap surmounted by a broad-brimmed hat."

Returning for a moment to the Court of Russia: Catherine II, Elisabeth's successor, was her defender against scandal, and walked in her footsteps. Elisabeth introduced into her court the songs of Lesbos, but seems to have been too busy with her grenadiers to have emulated physically the disciples of Sappho. Catherine, however, is suspected of practices that need not detain us—since we are dealing with men-women and not women-men—except that, upon one occasion, she punished savagely a girl friend who had betrayed a love secret, by giving her over to six stout women—men, really, in women's garb—to be beaten. The girl was taken naked from the arms of her husband on their bridal night, and flogged almost to the point of death, Catherine looking gloatingly on. The Empress herself had arranged the marriage for the additional dramatic kick she would get out of the contrast between the girl's love encounter with her husband and the beating at the hands of the men-women.

During the Second Empire, there was, in Paris, a club in one of the fashionable hotels, whose members were men of the Imperial Court, senators and financiers—one of the most exclusive clubs of the capital. They had a suite of rooms, magnificently furnished. No women ever were admitted, and yet, when police finally raided the place, they found a large number of dresses and other female finery as rich and handsome as the Empress herself was accustomed to wear. A report was made to the Emperor. "When he saw that persons of the highest position, and bearing most celebrated names, were involved in the affair," relates Iwan Bloch, "he at once ordered that the matter should be dismissed, and said to the Procureur-General: 'We must spare our people and our country from such a scandal, which would do no one any good, and would do a great deal of harm.'" The Emperor may have remembered his own youthful escapade.

Kaiser William's court, in the days before the World War, was threatened more than once with upheavals of volcanic proportions. The iron hand of suppression, working, too, through the laws of libel, accomplished, though less completely, what the word of Napoleon III effected in France. The death of Krupp on Capri, reputed suicidal, following a newspaper "exposure" of his alleged orgies in the Mediterranean Paradise where Tiberius once had held his court of pleasure, came near blowing the lid off of German silken delinquencies.

Editor Harden's attack on Philip Eulenburg, a friend of the Kaiser's, was another bomb loaded with TNT. Dr. Bloch, whose book

211

is translated from the German, speaks guardedly in his chapters on homosexuality of "certain scandals by which the highest circles were sympathetically affected—I need recall only the names of Hohenau, Krupp, Israel, von Schenk, etc."

There appeared in America in 1919, in the heat of the post-war frenzy, a book called "Secret Life of the Kaiser," with the signature of Henry W. Fisher, and alleged to be "From the Private Papers and Diaries of the Baroness Von Larisch-Reddern of the Imperial Household."

"Prince Bismarck," it is related in Fisher's book, "used to say: 'There have been some clever warriors among the Perverse—Alcibiades, Cæsar, Peter the Great, and many Turkish Sultans, whose names I forget—but never a diplomat of distinction.'

And both old Bismarck and Herbert made it their business to tell the Emperor repeatedly that Eulenburg was unfit company for him, stating their reasons in the plainest language.

"To cap the climax the elder Bismarck added: 'One glance at Eulenburg's eyes is enough to spoil the most elaborate luncheon for me.'

"But the Kaiser took no notice and continued to associate with this man and his infamous coterie: General Count Kuno Moltke, Count Johannes Lynar, who went to prison; Count Fritz and William Hohenau, Friedrich Krupp, the cannon king, and others."

"Courtiers," the Kaiser is quoted as saying, "are like the clothes I wear: necessities. They have their fixed places in my circle; men as Eulenburg, on the other hand, are butter on the bread of our pleasure;

as for the rest, one can get along without negligée attire, but it is mighty uncomfortable in the long run."

Eulenburg inherited the domain of Hertefeld in the Rhineland, with an income of about 100,000 marks, and the Kaiser created him successively Baron, Count, and Prince. But to William and his coterie, the popular Philip Eulenburg remained "Philli."

"And," affirms Fisher's book, "after the late Nathan Rothschild —all the round table called him 'Nathie'—made the new Highness heir to a couple of million francs, the Kaiser added the title of 'Right Honorable Privy Councilor to the Prussian Crown' and sent 'Philli' to the House of Lords as his special representative."

Prince "Philli" had two daughters and three sons, and "after the first Harden trial," our authority relates, "Countess Augusta congratulated the editor on his victory over her father."

"To establish, in cold type, the relationship between Kaiser Wilhelm and the person abandoned by his children, common decency forbids," says the Fisher book. "That it continued for twenty years the scandalum magnatum of Europe's courts, despite the protests and anathemas of three Chancelors—suffices to characterize the friendship between the head of the German Empire and the most notorious libertine in Europe."

"A wing of Liebenberg Castle, communicating with 'Philli's' apartments," it is further alleged, "was set aside for William's own imperial use—in short, he showered him, up to the very day of the Harden exposures, with every favor in his power."

A further glimpse of Eulenburg is caught in the not unfriendly

213

"Memories of the Kaiser's Court" by Anne Topham, published in America in 1915, while we were still neutral and while powerful interests were still arrayed on the side of Germany:

"Certain friends of His Majesty came every year with him to Rominten. First and foremost among them was Prince Philip Eulenburg, a pale, grey-haired, somewhat weary-looking man with a pallid, fleeting smile, something of a visionary, with a nature attracted to music and art, as well as towards all that is strange or abnormal in life. He was a born raconteur, like the Emperor, but told his tales in a quiet, soft, subtle voice, with a grave face and a certain fascinating charm of manner. One could easily understand how the robust personality of the Emperor, so frank, so generous, so open-hearted, was attracted to the somewhat reserved, mysterious, gentle nature of this brilliant man, who yearly entertained His Majesty at his own home, Schloss Liebenberg, and was the repository of his thoughts and aspirations. He, however, disappeared. Rominten knew him no more. Yet probably no one was more missed than he whose name was never afterwards mentioned there. I can still see his pale face emerge from behind the red curtains of the gallery when he came to the tea-table of the Empress and sat down to entertain us with his store of literary and artistic reminiscences. He had the look even then of an ill man, whose nerves are not in the best condition, who is pursued by some haunting spectre, and some fear from which he cannot escape."

Dr. Bloch's book was written in those immediate pre-war times, when the Eulenburg and Krupp scandals were fresh. Owing to the prevalence of such a state of affairs, he affirms, "the conviction has been forced upon members of the most influential political circles that the repeal of the paragraphs of the Criminal Code relating to urnings is an unconditional necessity."

These paragraphs are based upon the edict of Justinian, A.D. 538, who seems to have been morbidly impressed with the fate of Sodom and Gomorrah, and blamed sexual inversion for plagues, famines and earthquakes. In France, the Code Napoleon reversed Justinian, and left the invert at peace, except when violence and outrages against public decency came to the notice of police—that is to say, the restrictions are the same as those that safeguard normal sexuality. Italy by the Penal Code of 1889, adopted the French view. England, stirred by the Oscar Wilde incident, has sought from time to time, like Germany, to get rid of the Justinian theory and substitute Napoleon's.

A petition asking for the repeal, in Germany, continues Bloch, was signed by "five thousand persons belonging to the circles of men of science, judges, physicians, priests, schoolmasters, authors and artists, among whom were some of the most celebrated names of cultured Germany." No suspicion of effeminacy can possibly be placed against a great number of the distinguished signers, who were acting simply to remove the scandals that were reflecting on cultured Germans in general.

"We find," observes Havelock Ellis, as profound an investigator as Dr. Bloch and as conservative—"We find prosperous commercial and manufacturing people who leave Germany to find solace in the free and congenial homosexual atmosphere of Capri; of these F. A.

Krupp, the head of the famous Essen factory, may be regarded as the type." Oscar Wilde, incidentally, was another who made the pilgrimage to Capri.

"Krupp," Dr. Ellis explains in a footnote, "caused much scandal by his life at Capri, where he was constantly surrounded by the handsome youths of the place, mandolinists and street arabs, with whom he was on familiar terms, and on whom he lavished money. H. D. Davray, a reliable eyewitness, has written 'Souvenirs sur M. Krupp à Capri,' *L'Européen*, 29 November, 1902. It is not, however, definitely agreed that Krupp was of fully developed homosexual temperament. . . . An account of his life at Capri was published in the *Vorwärts*, against which Krupp finally brought a libel action; but he died immediately afterward, it is widely believed, by his own hand, and the libel action was withdrawn."

A scandal of major dimensions, involving the nobility and intellectuals of England in some such way as the Germans have fought vigorously to avoid was threatened during the World War. Maud Allan, a music hall dancer, was suing Noel-Pemberton-Billing's paper *Vigilante* for libel because of "an attack on Miss Allan such as it was unworthy of any man to make upon a woman, according to the prosecution. The meaning of the passage complained of was that there was some connection between nameless vice and the performances at the Independent Theater," according to a London dispatch to the Winnipeg *Free Press* of May 31, 1918. During the course of the hearing testimony was introduced "to prove the existence of a book which Mr. Pembroke-Billing said had been prepared by Ger-

216

man secret agents, containing the names of 47,000 British persons, said to be addicted to vice, and held in bondage to Germany through fear of exposure." Names of men and women high in war council were mentioned as on the list, though the book was not produced in court.

Only this year (1928), also, an English authoress, Margery Lawrence, is reported in the Hearst newspapers to have "written a novel bursting with revelations of fashionable life in London—but no English publisher dares to publish the book." Miss Lawrence is quoted as having discovered in Chelsea "muscular women and effeminate young men—and worse!"—Chelsea, "the playground of Belgravia, Mayfair, and strange as the combination may seem, Suburbia." She finds a second Babylon in this Chelsea—"the art quarter from which many artists, alas, are being driven by vicious imitators, quasi-artists who use studios for everything but painting."

London, however, is guarding as effectually its secrets from open scandal as did Paris under Napoleon III.

A contemporary European Prince who assumes female costume seriously as a disguise is in the habit of breaking into the newspapers every once in a while in some scandalous escapade. In March, 1926, he was arrested in a Portuguese border village, dressed as a woman, and, according to the newspaper reports, with a quantity of cocaine in his possession. He protested by telegraph to the Queen of Spain, after which the police released him. He is Prince Louis of Orleans-Bourbon, cousin of King Alfonso, a thorn in the flesh of that monarch, and eccentric "bad boy" of Spain. His mother is the Infanta Eulalie.

It was his disguise as a woman that resulted in his arrest on crossing the Portuguese border with the cocaine, instead of concealing him from the police. He had been under suspicion, and it was known his favorite disguise was female attire. He is described in newspaper reports as being "endowed by nature to assume the habiliments of the fair sex. He is tiny, wasp-waisted, small-footed, and has large, dreamy black eyes." Among the numerous adventures that annoy and worry his royal kindred are occasional appearances on the professional stage as a girl dancer.

The assumption by the Prince of Wales of petticoats for a private theatrical performance·was of no such serious import so far as it concerned the individual, but it caused a much greater furore in Europe and throughout the world because of the vastly greater importance politically of the heir to the British throne.

Published pictures of the Prince in the rôle of the Prima Donna in the farce, "The Bathroom Door," with short skirt and red wig, indicate he was "clowning" and attempting no serious simulation of femininity—much after the fashion of college glee club boys in farcical skits.

The stage directions of "The Bathroom Door," as published, provide that the Prima Donna, at her entrance, "preceded by little thrills and bursts of song," shall be "a very beautiful woman whose peignoir is more wonderful than most people's best tea-gowns. She has on a lace night-cap. She carries sponge bag and towel. She crosses nonchalantly to the door, tries it, gives an exclamation of disgust and exits, singing." The bathroom is a community affair in a hotel, and the en-

218

tire action of the slight little piece centers about the attempts of the various guests to get in to make their morning toilet. There are two other female characters, besides the Prima Donna, one of whom, according to the cast of characters as printed in the Hearst Sunday feature section, was played by Lieut-Com. Lilly of H.M.S. "Repulse," and the other by an officer of the ship unnamed.

The performance was given on the "Repulse" as the battleship was returning with the Prince from a tour of Africa and South America.

"More or less all over the world already have been printed the photographs of the Prince of Wales, heir to the throne of England, in feminine costume with a red wig," observes the Hearst paper, concisely summing up the "scandal."

"The British Isles and the British Colonies are divided in their opinion as to whether it was an undignified and disgraceful thing for the heir to the throne to exhibit himself as a feminine impersonator.

"The publication of the photographs upset King George, and the shock almost prostrated the young man's mother, the Queen. Some of the English newspapers have scolded the Prince, while others take the view that times have changed and that a popular monarch nowadays must be a good mixer, a good dancer, able to play jazz and sit in at a poker game—and, for good measure, be able to take part in private theatricals if occasion offers."

Perhaps if the atmosphere in London were less intense, the incident would have been passed over more lightly.

"The Hon. Anthony Asquith, son of Lord Oxford and Asquith,

has been playing part of the rôle of Boadicea, the Amazonian queen, in a British film," related the Associated Press, of another rather notable but less prominent London incident. "He drove the chariot in an exciting race scene in place of Miss Phyllis Neilson Terry, who otherwise played the Queen. Miss Terry found that guiding galloping horses from a swaying chariot was beyond her strength, and Anthony Asquith understudied in it, attired in her royal robe and a wig. Recently young Asquith visited Hollywood with his sister, Princess Bibesco, and made a study of American film production."

Reminiscent of the days of d'Eon, was the female disguise of Major Yeates Brown, British aviation ace, who performed valuable secret service for his government during the World War. He lived and worked among the Turks in Constantinople as a German woman governess.

There appeared not long ago in Russia a youth who declared he was the Czarevitch Alexis, son of Nicholas, claiming he had escaped the massacre of the Czar and his whole family at the hands of the Bolshevists. Dressed as a nun, the boy went about the streets of the village of Kozmodemyansk, soliciting aid and telling his story to the priests. He had convinced certain of the holy fathers of the truth of his claims, when the police arrested him. He is described in newspaper accounts as an attractive youth of twenty-three, Alexander Savin by name.

During the Irish uprising in the days of De Valera, not long gone, the picturesque Michael Collins, extravagantly worshipped for his courage and military skill, resorted on one notable occasion to female disguise when caught in a pinch.

"When the Labor people were in Dublin," related one of his pæan-singers just after his tragic death, "we had Michael dressed up as a Sister of Mercy to smuggle him into the city, and someone chanced to question whether it was a right use to make of such a costume. There were those who began to laugh the question down; but not Michael.

" 'I think you are right,' he said very gravely. 'I can find some other disguise just as effective.'

"And he did, with the help of a boy who had been an actor and was as clever at inventing a disguise as Michael was at wearing one. This time it was an old farm-wife, with a big foot and a big waist, but a very sharp tongue. We all laughed until our eyes watered to see him go off like that, although we knew the danger of it.

"He swore that he would meet the Labor men from England just as he was, and the story goes that he kept his word. They must have thought him a queer-looking general if he did, for the wrinkles and the dirt on his face made him look seventy years old, and his whining accent was as droll as anything I ever heard."

Though no royalist—with whom we have been dealing principally in this chapter—Michael Collins was the stuff kings are made of when the people have not the obsession for a republic, and on this side the water we have a duplicate of his importance politically, who comes under our survey, though Jefferson Davis, President of the Southern Confederacy, was no warrior.

Friends of Davis denied the story at the time and those careful of his memory deny it even more vehemently today, that, following the downfall of his government and his escape from Richmond to Georgia, he was captured by cavalrymen of Wisconsin and Michigan, attired as a woman.

In a book entitled "The Trial of the Assassins and Conspirators," published in Philadelphia in 1865, containing a history of the murder of President Lincoln, with a complete transcription of all the documents and court proceedings, there is a full-page illustration from wood-block, entitled "Portrait of 'Jeff. Davis' in His Wife's Clothes" —a good facial likeness of the deposed leader of the rebellion, with full beard, bare-headed, attired from neck to ankles in female garments, heavy and coarse. He is wearing men's boots.

When he saw his cause was lost, President Davis, with his family, retired from Richmond, first to Danville, Va., and then to Washington, Ga. There, for reasons of prudence, he separated from his wife and children and his wife's sister. Capture at the hands of Federal General Wilson, stationed at Macon, was feared. Davis learned, however, of treachery on the part of some of his own Confederates, who were planning to seize the trunks Mrs. Davis had with her, which they heard contained much treasure and very valuable papers taken out of Richmond. Davis rode hard a distance of eighteen miles to rejoin his wife. General Wilson got wind of his whereabouts, and moved his cavalrymen on to the capture and a reward of $100,000 on Jeff Davis' head.

The Davis party had started for the Gulf of Mexico, hoping to get out of the United States, either to Europe or one of the Latin-American states to the south. Tents were pitched for the night near Irwins-

222

ville, a village south of Macon. All were weary, and retired to sleep. A squad of cavalry from Michigan and another from Wisconsin advanced under General Wilson's orders with secrecy and caution.

"Simultaneously, from opposite points these two parties approached the camp of Davis and his little party just at dawn, May 11, 1865. Mistaking each other for foes, they exchanged shots with such precision that two men were killed and several wounded before the error was discovered. The sleepers were aroused. The camp was surrounded, and Davis, while attempting to escape in disguise, was captured and conveyed to General Wilson's headquarters.

"Davis had slept in a wrapper," continues the eminently respectable and conservative "Harper's Encyclopædia of United States History," from which we are quoting, "and when aroused hastily pulled on his boots and went to the tent door. He observed the National Cavalry. 'Then you are captured?' exclaimed his wife. In an instant she fastened the wrapper around him before he was aware, and then, bidding him adieu, urged him to go to a spring near by, where his horse and arms were. He complied, and as he was leaving the tent door, followed by a servant with a water bucket, his sister-in-law flung a shawl over his head. It was in this disguise that he was captured. Such is the story as told by C. E. L. Stuart of Davis's staff."

Modern France contributes a military incident. In the Dreyfus affair, it was brought out that Esterhazy at one turn of the conspiracy, "after being greatly alarmed, ready for suicide or flight, had all at once become audacious, having received help from 'a veiled lady,' otherwise du Paty de Clam."

XI.   CRIME IN FLUFFY RUFFLES

FEMALE impersonation plays an extensive part in the annals of crime, and, while the looser, more enveloping dresses and veils have been employed by fully-bearded rascals for a quick get-away, records are not wanting of hardened criminals with soft skins, smooth cheeks and mellow voices who have played the woman intimately in pursuit of their calling, and played her well.

The type is exemplified in that wicked and witty book of the Restoration period, "The English Rogue." The narrator of the adventures, which are partly autobiographical and partly fictitious, relates how:

"Sometimes when we had robbed, and fearing lest we should be taken by the Hue and Cry, it was but turning my horse loose, and then would I put on woman's apparel (which I always carried in my portmantle in such expeditions) and getting up behind my dear friend, I passed unsuspected as his wife. This stratagem frequently served as a safeguard to us both. By this means, we several times robbed houses, under the pretense of my friend taking lodgings for himself and wife."

This debonaire, effeminate-looking highwayman once found himself outclassed in that respect. The concise chapter heading tells as much of the long, droll story, as we need here: "From this farmer's house he (the narrator) rides he cared not whither: on the road he is strangely surprised by a woman robber in man's apparel: he discovers it by unbuttoning her breeches to search for private pockets within: they two conclude a perpetual friendship." His gallantry, perhaps, should not be overlooked. "Pardon me, most courageous Amazon!" he exclaimed, on making discovery of his mistake.

This gentlemanly rogue, while apparently in full possession of attributes nature showers on the male (else he is the same awful liar heroic male conquerors of female virtue generally are in telling of their scores of conquests) was pretty vain of his charms in their feminine aspect.

"The slenderness of my body, whiteness of skin, beauty and smoothness of face (having no hairs thereon) added a suitableness to my garb," he observes, when he first donned the apparel of his mistress, after he was robbed of his own clothes in a bawdy house. "I must ingeniously confess, when I consulted with a looking-glass, I thought the transmutation of sexes had been verified in me."

It had not, however, as was proven when he ventured, like Achilles of old, in his disguise among many maidens—the fair scholars at a boarding school. He was accepted as a girl, but like Achilles, discovered himself to one of them, and from "Joan," as he called himself, he became to her "John."

Fiction or fact, this "English Rogue" was not at variance with type. The authentic Jack Sheppard, while not so subtlely feminine, if contemporary portraits are to be relied upon, nevertheless could look the woman well enough to break out from Newgate in female attire, and cheat the gallows for a time.

His escape was one of London's decided thrills of 1724. Sheppard, housebreaker and pickpocket, was as much a popular hero as Robin Hood had been in England—as Jesse James was to become in America. But callous, unimaginative judges had condemned him to death, and he was thrown into the hold, whence only the gallows could snatch him. One day, however, two women visited him. Whatever was the matter with the guards—silver or careless negligence—these women seem to have slipped him a small saw and a file, together with parts of their clothing, supplying between them a complete outfit for Sheppard. When they were gone, the expert housebreaker sawed and filed his way out of the condemned hold, donned his women's garb and slipped past the lodge where the turnkeys were carousing, and so to freedom. London was extravagantly happy over the escape of their hero, but his enjoyment of his popularity and his desire to emulate himself brought him finally to Tyburn.

The most popular criminal in history, is his distinction. Sir James Thornhill painted his portrait. Seven different histories of his exploits were published and eagerly snapped up. Defoe wrote a novel about him, published in 1724, the year of his escape, recapture and execution. A hundred years later, another English novelist, Ainsworth, again made him a hero of fiction.

Jack Sheppard's sensational escape from Newgate was duplicated in New York on Nov. 19, 1873, when William J. Sharkey, condemned to die for the murder of his friend Robert S. Dunn, "in broad daylight, dressed as a female, walked out of the Tombs into Franklin street and liberty," as Sutton expresses it in his history of that famous prison. Sharkey, however, was not as vain as Sheppard—he didn't meddle playfully with the law any more, and disappeared completely from history.

The escape, according to Sutton's narrative, was planned and mainly executed by Maggie Jourdan, sweetheart or wife of Sharkey, who had killed Dunn the year before in a saloon in New York in a quarrel over $600 Dunn owed him. Maggie was assisted, it was alleged, by Mrs. "Wes" Allen, wife of a burglar doing time in Sing Sing.

Sharkey had had the privilege of walking in the yard and on the tiers, but was so insolent, violent and abusive they were taken away from him, and he was confined in his cell, and could be talked to only through the iron grating. Maggie, who was of good family and pretty, was faithful, and visited him every day.

At 10 o'clock on the morning of the escape, Maggie was admitted to see Sharkey, and talked to him through the grating until past noon. At 12:30, Mrs. Allen was given a ticket of admission to the prison, though her husband had already been sent up the river. She said she wanted to see another prisoner named Flood. She stopped in front of the cell where Maggie was talking to Sharkey, conversed with them for some minutes, then went on up to a higher tier where Flood was confined.

227

Mrs. Allen stayed with Flood until near 2 o'clock, when the gong sounded for withdrawal of visitors. Maggie had left Sharkey at 1— noted by the guards as odd, since she was in the habit of staying till the last minute.

At 1:30, continues Sutton, "a peculiar-looking female passed down the corridor, through the two lower gates, and out the main entrance, passing three men, whose acuteness is presumed to be wonderful from their long and varied experience. This peculiar-looking female was dressed in a long black dress of woollen material; wore a black cloak across a pair of very broad shoulders, and had on her head an Alpine hat covered by a thick green barege veil. This veil, all the keepers allege, was kept close over her face."

They remarked afterward that there was something "suspicious" about her, but no one thought to stop her at the time. Officer Doran, who patroled a police beat outside, "watched the suspicious female, saw her run for a Bleecker street car and jump on board. The officer said that this peculiar-looking female had on a new pair of gaiters with French heels, and he was somewhat surprised to see the nimble way in which she alighted on a car which was going at the time at considerable speed."

At five minutes till 2, Mrs. Allen was walking nonchalantly out the main entrance of the prison when she was asked for her ticket. She fumbled about in her pockets but couldn't find it. She was detained, an investigation was started, and Sharkey's escape was discovered. In his cell, his clothing was found, together with his black moustache, newly shaved off and still wet with lather.

Mrs. Allen was held, and Maggie was arrested. Mrs. Allen denied all knowledge of the escape, and was released without being charged. Maggie was brought to trial, the jury disagreed, and eventually she was given her liberty.

The conductor of the street car was questioned. "Do you remember a tall woman, dressed in black, getting on here?" he was asked. "I do remember somebody dressed in black, but that woman was a man, and he got off at Bleecker street."

"This is the last trace of Sharkey," says Sutton.

Neither Sheppard nor Sharkey can be considered an ideal "female impersonator," but M. Antoine François Derues, who was making a noise in France simultaneously with the Chevalier d'Eon, more nearly fills the bill.

M. Derues, who added to his name without a great deal of authority "de Cyrano de Bury, Lord of Candeville," has the honor of being the first of a long and distinguished line of trunk murderers.

He was born at Chartres in 1744. His father was a corn merchant. "His parents died when he was three years old," relates H. B. Irving in his "Book of Remarkable Criminals," where the story of M. Derues is told most thrillingly. "For some time after his birth he was assumed to be a girl; it was not until he was twelve years old that an operation determined his sex to be masculine."

Antoine probably was not as elated over the discovery as George Sand would have been—little Aurore Dupin, it is related, used to jump violently up and down as a small girl in the hope certain missing equipment would tumble down and she would be like other little boys.

Her hope was never realized, but Mme. Sand in later life did the best she could to remedy the joke nature had played on her by taking under her protection the gentle Chopin and the pretty Alfred de Musset.

Begging pardon of the memory of George Sand for bringing her in here, in connection with Antoine Derues, let us go on to relate that the newly-discovered boy grew eventually to man's estate, and became a grocer.

But, records Mr. Irving, "not content with the modest calling of a grocer, Derues had turned money-lender, a money-lender to spend-thrift and embarrassed noblemen. Derues dearly loved a lord; he wanted to become one himself; it delighted him to receive dukes and marquises at the Rue Beaubourg, even if they came there with the avowed object of raising the wind. The smiling grocer, in his everlast-ing bonnet and flowered dressing gown à la J. J. Rousseau, was ever ready to oblige the needy scion of a noble house. What he borrowed at modest interest from his creditors, he lent at enhanced interest to the quality"—which would have been fine business had the "quality" been inclined to pay back.

Derues found himself up against it. He bought merchandise on credit, and sold it out at a bargain for the sake of the ready money. He was trying to stave off ruin until his wife's inheritance, badly en-tangled, was available.

His wife was Marie Louise Nicolais, who had done the little grocer a marvelous favor by marrying him—she being, or so it was alleged, of the noble family of Nicolai. Moreover, there was money coming to her could the estate ever be settled, but the fortune seems to have been magnified an hundred fold in the eyes of the socially ambitious grocer.

On the strength of his wife's prospects, M. Derues bought from M. and Mme. Etienne Saint-Faust de Lamotte a vast country estate for about $100,000.

M. de Lamotte, ex-equerry to the king, had run away with the daughter of a wealthy citizen of Rheims. The lovers lived together until a son was born, and then the girl was made Mme. de Lamotte to legitimate the boy.

Mme. de Lamotte was the energetic half of the partnership, and it was when she went up to Paris, in 1775, to obtain a position for their son at the Court of Louis XVI, that M. Derues entered into contract to buy the estate. The de Lamottes needed the money to further their son's ambitions, and Madame had gone to Paris with her husband's power of attorney to sell. A proctor named Jolly brought Derues and Mme. de Lamotte together in the month of May, the transaction was completed, and the grocer gave Madame a note for $5,000 to fall due April 1, 1776. The rest was to be paid in installments.

In December, 1775, M. Derues, accompanied by his little daughter, went down to look over his newly-acquired estate, and stayed there for six months, the guests of the de Lamottes. His great good humor and his piety won all hearts. The village priest, especially, was taken. M. Derues amused his new friends by dressing as a woman—his smooth face, feminine features and daintiness of step delighted especially the priest.

The note fell due, but M. Derues pleaded in an easy, offhand way the long legal process of settlement of his wife's estate, and he stayed

231

on through the summer and into November without apparent worry. Then he left for Paris.

The de Lamottes began to grow a bit uneasy, and Madame decided to go to Paris to investigate the pleasant little man's circumstances. Derues, learning of her arrival in the capital, insisted on her paying him a return visit, and spend her stay as his guest. She accepted, and brought the boy along.

They had not been long in Paris before Mme. de Lamotte fell ill. The boy's health, too, began to fail. Then, Mme. de Lamotte died suddenly, but, instead of notifying her husband, who didn't even know she was visiting at their friend's home, Derues put her body into a big leather trunk, rented a cellar for the storage of Spanish wine, employed a man to dig a big hole, buried the "wine" himself, and then took away the trunk. This trunk he later filled with china, and sent it to M. de Lamotte. The boy died a little later, but he was given regular burial, not under his own name, but as Derues' nephew.

All these preliminaries satisfactorily accomplished, M. Derues prepared to enter into possession of his estate. He went down to see M. de Lamotte, who was growing uneasy at not having heard from his wife and boy. Why, didn't he know? M. Derues had seen her at Versailles, where she had gone in the interest of her Court ambitions for her son, had concluded the sale of the property, paid over the amount in full in gold, and here was the receipt, with her signature. Mme. de Lamotte, it embarrassed him to say, had taken the money and run away with an old lover—she was a loose character, you know, her son having been born out of wedlock.

It sounded plausible to M. de Lamotte, but M. Jolly, the proctor, who was called in, wasn't so sure. The husband's power of attorney was still in the hands of M. Jolly, who had negotiated the sale originally, and without it—such was the tedious aggravation of the law—Mme. de Lamotte's signature to the receipt in full wasn't worth the paper it was written on.

M. Derues did some tall thinking, and it flashed into his mind to make use of the God-given ability to masquerade, which had so amused the priest. "He had made Mme. de Lamotte disappear, why should he not make her reappear?"

He went to Lyons. "A Lady dressed in black silk, with a hood well drawn over her eyes, called at the office of M. Pourra, a notary. The latter was not greatly attracted by his visitor, whose nose struck him as large for a woman."

He dismissed his observation, however, as only a disagreeable feature, and was not suspicious when she introduced herself as Mme. de Lamotte, and asked for a power of attorney by which she could pay to her husband the interest due on certain money received from an estate. The notary gave it to her. Derues' object in getting this paper was to show Jolly and M. de Lamotte that Madame was still alive. De Lamotte, getting the interest, would believe she actually had received the money, would swallow his disgrace, call off Jolly and let M. Derues enter unmolested into possession of his hard-earned estate.

But, while Derues was in Lyons, M. de Lamotte had bestirred his sluggish energies to go to Paris. The immediate stimulus seems not to have been anxiety over his wife and son, but rage because Derues had attempted to sell some of the wine from the fine cellar of the estate.

M. de Lamotte told the full story of his dealings with Derues to the police. By the time the little grocer returned from Lyons, the deed and Mme. de Lamotte's signature to the receipt in full had been established as forgeries. Derues was arrested. The new power of attorney given to the woman in black at Lyons was found to bear the forged signature of Mme. de Lamotte. Eventually the bodies of both mother and son were found, and an autopsy revealed the presence of corrosive sublimate.

Antoine François Derues' dainty feminine body was broken on the wheel and then burned alive.

Chicago's over-burdened annals of crime furnish an even more sensational case of female impersonation, although Fred G. Thompson, arrested in June, 1923, as the "smiling bandit queen" who had shot to death Richard C. Tesmer a few nights before, when Tesmer and his wife were putting their car into its garage, eventually was acquitted of the murder. But from June until October, the "man-woman" prisoner was a sensation in Chicago, and, by press reports, throughout the world. His looks, his acts, his attire, his habits, the events of his life were all recorded in newspaper stories, and read with the eager interest anomalies of sex usually excite.

On the night Tesmer was shot down by the "bandit queen," who had with her a male companion, Mrs. Tesmer got a clear view of the murderer's face, with a "sardonic grin, a satanic smile," which she said she would know anywhere.

Police arrested a number of female suspects, but it was not until,

234

acting on a clew that the person sought might be a man masquerading as a woman, they arrested "Mrs. Frank Carrick" in the apartment of her husband, a chauffeur, that they were confident they had run the murderer to earth. Mrs. Tesmer positively identified "Mrs. Carrick" by the smile immediately upon arrest, and insisted on the identification after the chauffeur's "wife" was ordered into the clothing befitting his sex, following a medical examination made by a woman physician attached to the police department.

"Mrs. Carrick" was arrested early in the morning, still in night negligée, a kimono. Bundled into a frock and hat, she was taken to the home of Mrs. Tesmer, where positive identification was made, and then to a police station. During the day, while detectives were busily engaged in running down clews, nature was just as busy, and by nightfall, "Mrs. Carrick" had acquired such a stubby beard beneath her powder and rouge, that it was thought best to investigate before locking her in for the night in the women's ward. The chief of police, on receiving a signed report from the physician, ordered the prisoner, to his embarrassment, to sleep among the men.

By this time, too, "Mrs. Carrick" was identified with Fred G. Thompson, a name found on a card in the Carrick home, and upon a direct question being put, Thompson admitted that was his real name.

"God gave me a double nature," he is reported to have told the police in those first interviews. "When I was thirteen years old I was chased out of my home by my father. I am thirty-two now. Fourteen years ago, I was married to Frank Carrick at Crown Point, Indiana. During recent years I appeared as a singer in a north side cabaret."

235

On the witness stand during his trial in October, he gave some further pertinent information about himself. He was born in Columbus, Ohio. "I was naturally a very quiet child," he said. "I wore boy's clothing, but I always wanted to wear a woman's clothes because I felt easier."

He told how he came to Chicago when he was fourteen and abandoned male attire. He first worked as a chambermaid, he said, and later, "because of his high soprano voice," became a cabaret singer.

"Once I tried to be a boy and put on male clothing," he testified. "The men would not believe me and told me to go home and put on proper clothes and not try to masquerade around."

Another time, determined to be male, he bought five acres of land near Chicago and tried to farm it, but the task was beyond him. He turned to masculine clothing and habits during the big floods in Ohio, helping his family out of danger.

He told of his marriage in 1912 to Frank Carrick, and related how once they were arrested and ordered to produce their marriage license, which they did.

Though his life with Carrick was happy, a dozen years later he married a girl, Marie Clark—he "sympathized with her and did not want her to go wrong." Newspaper reporters already had investigated the Marie Clark story, and had discovered that "this marriage so angered Carrick, who had 'married' Thompson, that a fight resulted, ending in all three living together in a strange compact." On the witness stand, Thompson testified he and Marie Clark did not live together as married people.

In court, "Thompson was attired in silk garments, though wearing trousers, and with his hair in braids over his ears. His trousers were of satin, his shirtwaist was open and his face rouged. He looked very much a girl, "spoke in the low tones a woman might use, nervously clasped and unclasped his hands, sobbed and told of his double life."

When asked by his attorney point blank if he killed Tesmer, Thompson answered: "No, gentlemen, I could not kill a cat or a dog." and then covered his face with his hands and wept hysterically.

The judge, after asking him a few questions on one occasion remarked quite seriously and involuntarily, "That will be all, lady."

Thompson denied from the day of his arrest he had had anything to do with the murder. He was home that evening, he said, "sick from moonshine." The police failed to break down this alibi. The strongest testimony against him was Mrs. Tesmer's positive identification of him as "the laughing, blue-eyed girl" who had shot down her husband. Thompson's eyes were gray, but that point didn't materially affect her testimony, since she saw the bandit under an electric light. The jury deliberated for two hours, and brought in a verdict of not guilty.

Thompson had been pettishly angry because the judge refused to permit him to appear in court in his beloved female finery, in which he felt so much more at ease. On acquittal he resumed feminine attire. He sought to capitalize his notoriety by appearing in a Chicago vaudeville theater, but the Chief of Police forbade it. Thompson brought injunction proceedings—unsuccessfully—appearing in court this time, "modishly gowned in a sport costume and close fitting toque." During the course of the hearing, he offered to go through his proposed theat-

237

rical performance, but the judge answered: "I'm afraid I'm not a good judge of that sort of thing." Thompson, thereafter, gradually faded from the public eye and from Chicago police annals.

A girl newspaper reporter who saw him frequently during the murder proceedings and who interviewed him when he was dressed in both male and female clothing, tells me he was much more agreeable to the eye as a woman. "In man's clothing," she said, "he gave me the disagreeable impression you get of repulsively effeminate men. In women's clothing he seemed a woman, and not a masculine woman, at that."

Joseph Wendling, the Louisville murderer of little Alma Kellner, one of the most noted crimes in American police history, masqueraded once for three days as a woman with success enough to elude penitentiary guards searching for him, whom he met on the streets of Frankfort, Ky. That, at least, was his boast on being captured.

Wendling, though convicted in 1910 of the murder of twelve-year-old Alma the year before, burning her body and hiding the charred remains in the cellar of a church where he was janitor, escaped the noose and was sentenced to penitentiary for life—"the most cowardly verdict that I ever heard of," indignantly commented little Alma's uncle. Frank Fehr, a Louisville millionaire.

At the Kentucky state prison at Frankfort, the murderer turned out a model prisoner, and despite the enormity of his crime, he was permitted to go outside the walls to work as an electrician at the capitol building and elsewhere. While working at the capitol one day in the summer of 1919, he seems to have felt a surge of the impulse

which had proved fatal to Alma, and called down upon himself a sharp rebuke and revocation of his privileges by annoying the seven-year-old daughter of a prison contractor. A short time afterward, Wendling walked out of the penitentiary with a tool box on his shoulder, passing a guard who knew him well, but who seems not to have known he was no longer trusted.

There was, of course, a great furore, which became national and even international, with some caustic criticism of the prison officials for their laxity and for making a "trusty" of Wendling. Realizing the importance of getting back their prisoner, every method known to the science of man-hunting was put into operation. Yet Wendling, with headquarters only two blocks away from the penitentiary, eluded his pursuers for three days, and this despite the fact his restless nature would not permit him to remain in hiding, but forced him to roam the streets.

He had walked out of the prison at 7 o'clock in the morning. At midnight that night this newspaper bulletin from Frankfort was flashed to papers all over the country: "Wendling was seen in this city tonight on East Main street near the state cemetery by a man who lived near the penitentiary for years and recognized him. He was dressed as a woman in a black dress and wore a white fascinator."

A shot was fired at him by a woman who saw him running away, but Wendling escaped over a bluff, and there was a general disposition to question the identity of the masquerader. However, the strange "woman" was seen again and again, and a feverish search was carried on, but the final capture of Wendling came about through his peeping into a window on the third night at a young girl, who saw him and screamed. Young girls always have been his Nemesis. He was in male attire when pursued and captured by the girl's father.

Wendling had been hiding during the period of his liberty in an attic in the capitol building, which he had espied and appropriated while working as an electrician there. He had furtively provided a woman's dress, a raincoat, fascinator and cosmetics, including eyebrow blackening. This feminine equipment he augmented after his escape from prison by stealing a small basket of laundry from a washerwoman, who had set it down to go into a grocery.

Though his masquerade was unsuccessful the first night, and he narrowly escaped capture or death on being recognized by his old acquaintance, the county coroner, he had better luck thereafter, and on recapture boasted he rubbed against the police on the streets, and they had not detected him, even though they were looking for a man disguised as a woman. His plan was eventually to escape from Frankfort in his female attire, and go west where he had found refuge for several months after Alma Kellner disappeared.

It came to light during the three days' excitement, that Wendling, in his excursions out of the prison, had, on several occasions, tried to get little girls ten or twelve years old to help him carry his tools. He was also accused of waving at female children from prison windows.

Photographs of Wendling reveal a weak, rather handsome face. The poster sent by the Louisville police department all over America offering a reward for his capture on suspicion of the murder of Alma Kellner bore a full length portrait of a natty young man who might easily have transformed himself then into a girl and so eluded the vigilance of Detective Tom Burke, of the San Francisco police, who recognized him and took him in.

Monte Guess, another Kentucky murderer, had a mania for escaping from prison—on each of two such occasions he killed a man, his complete murder record. His first victim was a guard at a reformatory for youthful incorrigibles, to which Monte had been sent as a "bad boy." He beat to death with a ten-pound metal ball the guard, who tried to prevent his escape. For this murder he was sent to penitentiary for life. He was getting away from this stronger prison with a fellow criminal, a robber from Louisville, when the two quarreled violently on a spiral stairway before they were clear of the walls. Guess stabbed the robber in the back and killed him, but claimed self-defence—"I beat him to it; it was a duel."

After several other attempts, Monte finally got through, and it was while at liberty for several days that he was seen in female clothing, walking along a country road. A physician driving along in his car noticed something peculiar about the "woman" and slowed down. Monte seems to have been deficient in technique, for the physician readily saw the pedestrian was a man. It wasn't any of the doctor's immediate business, however, so he stepped on the gas and drove on. It was not until he got home and saw a photograph of the escaped prisoner in a newspaper that he knew who it was he had encountered on the road.

Chronicles of crime are rather rich in instances of this sort. Besides Sheppard, the Newgate traditions dwell rather excitedly on Alex-

241

ander Scott, highwayman and mail robber, who was visited in prison by an oyster woman, at the instigation of Scott's wife. The oyster woman managed to exchange clothes with Scott, who proceeded unmolested to the lodge gate. He rang the bell, but the gate tender, for some reason or other, was slow in responding. Meanwhile, a guard discovered the substitution of the oyster woman for the highwayman and rushed out after Scott. The guard got to the gate just at it was being opened to let the bogus oyster woman through. He tore the veil from the "lady's" face and readily recognized his prisoner. Scott attempted a knock-down and quick getaway, and though he sent the guard sprawling, the turnkey leaped upon him and overpowered him.

William Callehan, mail thief, had better luck. He didn't get out of jail in women's clothes, but made a clean get-away in feminine attire when once without the walls.

Callehan and a companion had robbed a post-office near Windsor, Ontario. They were caught trying to cross from Windsor to Detroit. While awaiting trial in jail at Sandwich, near Windsor, they killed the jailer and escaped. Callehan, somehow procured women's clothing, and in that disguise crossed the river into the United States and disappeared. His companion, Matthew Kennedy, was recaptured, convicted, and imprisoned for twenty years.

Female disguise was one of the many methods employed to compass escape by the imprisoned Jacobites after the '15, it is related in "Chronicles of Newgate," but not always successfully.

Among others, Mr. Barlow of Burton Hall tried it. In the first instance a crazy woman, Elizabeth Powell, well known in Westminster

Market, came to Mr. Barlow with a whole suit of female apparel, but fearing it might be a trick or that he might fail in the attempt, he discovered her.

A week or two later, however, inspired by the woman's proposal, Barlow did make the attempt. Close-shaven and neatly dressed in female clothes, he came to the gate with a crowd of ladies who had been visiting their Jacobite friends, hoping to pass out unobserved with the others.

But the turnkey, on the alert since there had been too many escapes of late, became suspicious, caught hold of him, turned him sharply about, and in the struggle that ensued threw him to the ground.

"The rest of the women cried out in a lamentable tone, 'Don't hurt the poor lady; she is with child!' and some of them cried, 'Oh, my dear mother!' Whereupon the turnkey, convinced he had to do with a lady, let him go."

However, before Barlow could get clear of the prison, he had to pass inspection by a special commissioner appointed to ensure the safe custody of the rebels, and this commissioner, Carleton Smith, was not so easy as the turnkey. When Barlow saw he was detected, he offered Smith ten guineas to let him pass, but the commissioner refused, and conducted the prisoner, just as he was, before the court then sitting at the Old Bailey.

Barlow was neatly padded, his face was painted red and white, and he looked every inch a lady. He told the judge that the clothes had been brought him by his wife.

243

"The court," goes on the account, "was very well pleased to see him thus metamorphosed, but ordered him to be put in heavy irons, and the clothes to be kept as a testimony against him."

American prison annals furnish a parallel case. "Kid" Cole, serving a life term in the Nebraska penitentiary for killing a pawnbroker, succeeded adroitly one day in joining a party of female tourists, visitors to the state fair being escorted through the prison, and he added his "Ohs!" and "Ahs!" to theirs at the various sights. He easily passed all the guards and was about to emerge through the last gate with the party when a deputy warden took a hard look at him, detecting something strangely familiar about this woman, and finally recognized Cole.

The prisoner had displayed extraordinary ingenuity in getting together his disguise. "He had perfected a good-looking hat of cardboard, wire and chair linings," wrote a newspaper correspondent; "made a wig of the fine black hair used in the better upholstering jobs; swiped from the store-room of the prison theater a pair of woman's black oxfords and tinted them brown to go with the color scheme he had laid out; fashioned a pair of women's stockings out of the sleeves of a discarded brown silk jersey; made a corset of blue satin chair backing and fitted with dozens of eyelets taken from army shoes on the junk pile; carried a brown handbag; made a neat-looking gown out of mercerized brown lining for chairs.

"When and where he did the painstaking work necessary, the prison officials do not know. They say it was the cleverest effort in the history of the prison in the way of attempted escapes. Evidently the man had prepared the costume weeks in advance, and selected this date because during state fair week hundreds of country people take the opportunity to visit the state penitentiary. These are conducted through in groups of a hundred by detachments of guards. Cole dressed in a secluded corner, and as the procession passed him, joined it."

Henry Bode, modern soldier of fortune, international spy, giving his allegiance to any army that happened to be in his vicinity, numbered female impersonation among his arts of disguise.

Born in Germany, Bode came early to the United States, was brought up partly in Hawaii by a wealthy family that was educating him, and eventually joined the United States Navy. Later he became a Klondyke miner, made a fortune in three months and gambled it away in three nights. He was with the Montana Infantry in the Philippines, where he made a good record as a fighter. In the Russian-Japanese war he was in the Russian Intelligence service. General Leonard Wood used him next in the Philippine Constabulary. In Mexico later, he fought under Madera's banner.

At the outbreak of the World War, he went to his native Germany, won the Iron Cross May 19, 1915, was assigned to the Intelligence Department, and ordered to New York, to report to the German Consulate. The Consulate used him successively in the Far East, Havana, Madrid and then Mexico. While in the oil fields of Tampico, the United States entered the war. The Mexicans believed him an American spy, and when he started back across the border, the Americans seized him as a German spy, and he was sent to prison for ten years

—though Bode didn't seem to be sure whether he wanted to serve his native Germany or his adopted America.

It was while in the Russian Intelligence service, living in a bamboo hut in Corea, that his art of female disguise was effectively brought into play. Bode, drinking with a new-found friend, confessed he was a Russian spy, and the friend passed a tip to the police, who went after him and surrounded his hut.

"While they were waiting for him to emerge, a curious sight attracted their attention," narrates George Barton in his "Celebrated Spies and Famous Mysteries of the Great War."

"An elderly woman came forth, leaning on a cane, and evidently moving with great difficulty. The dress of this strange creature was fantastic in the extreme, the poke bonnet especially being a wonderfully made creation that evoked the laughter of the police.

"They asked her if Bode was in the hut, but she shook her head as though she could not understand their words, and pointed back at the house in an imbecile sort of style.

"They watched the stranger until the last edge of her poke bonnet had disappeared around a corner, and then they went into the hut. They looked at one another in consternation, as well they might, for the place was empty. No sooner had the supposed female turned the corner than she cast aside the poke bonnet and the dress, and stood revealed as Henry Bode."

Bode made good his escape, and sailed for Yokohama and then for Manila, where he was safe from the Japanese, and where he was shortly at work for General Wood.

A curious escape was effected at Sing Sing a few years ago through an amateur theatrical performance. A comedy, "Honey Girl," was staged by the convicts and presented before an audience of 1,157 persons from the outside, the proceeds going for a Christmas turkey feast for the inmates of the prison.

Pat Dealy, with twenty-four years to serve, was the heroine, and an ideal "honey girl" he made, with his wig, his rouge and his feminine fripperies.

At the finish of the performance, the visitors filed out, laughing and chatting, having thoroughly enjoyed the evening. But, as the count came near the end, it was discovered 1,158 persons, men and women, were leaving. An alarm was sounded, a quick check-up was made, and Pat didn't show. He had made a clean getaway.

The supposition was that he had gone to his dressing room, quickly altered his female make-up to some extent, so as not to be recognized as the heroine of the play, returned to the auditorium, and walked out gayly chatting like the other women. The men emerging were carefully checked, but no one thought to watch the ladies.

While on the subject of Sing Sing's "little theater," which has become a well established institution, there was one performance of a musical comedy, written and composed within the prison's walls, which broke into print through the oddity of the fact that the hero, fanatically devoted to the "one woman" idea, was played by a young man doing three years for bigamy. His gray-haired old mother, object of much sentimental interest, was a hardened holdup man doing a long stretch.

Police and courts clash frequently with men or boys masquerading as women, their intent running the entire gamut from the trivial to the grave.

In Vienna shortly after the war, an elderly woman and two girls entered a smart café one night. All were fashionably dressed, and the woman, well past forty, was conspicuous even in that gay crowd because of the low cut of her gown, which revealed a pretty and well-preserved neck and bosom. They sat at a table. The girls lighted cigarettes, but the woman startled every one by applying her match to a huge cigar, which she began puffing with relish. The proprietor, who may never have heard of George Sand, asked the three to leave. On their refusal, he called the police.

At police headquarters, the elderly lady was discovered to be a man, and he revealed his identity as a former chief justice of a high military court. He explained he "was very fond of dressing up in women's clothes, as it gave the idle people in the cafés something to talk about." Despite his rank as "Excellency" he was fined and warned to desist from further female masquerading in public.

England, a few months ago, enjoyed a sensation in the capture of a giant female "ghost" that had been haunting the lovers' lanes around Curry-Rivel for a year, terrorising many a swain and his damsel when she swooped down on them with her six-foot stature. A posse, headed by the landlord of the village inn, effected the capture.

The "ghost" turned out to be the Rev. Arthur H. Read, the local preacher, disguised as a woman, "to see whether men were immoral enough to flirt with him," explained the press dispatches.

248

"Men, I take my hat off to you," he proclaimed oratorically, rising to the occasion of his capture. "I can truly say that you never stood so high in my esteem as now. The heart of English manhood is sound as ever.

"I visited many areas in my disguise. Only once did an immoral man molest me. That was at a far-away seaside resort. I sat on the sea front, and all at once I felt a man leering at me. It was a terrible feeling, and I moved away quickly."

Read had obtained the women's clothes, the newspaper reports continue, without the knowledge of his wife and grown-up children, from garments sent in to be sold at rummage sales.

"I wondered whether the world was as bad as it was painted," he told the villagers immediately on his capture, "and whether men and women were worse than they were a generation ago. I decided to disguise myself and investigate. It was difficult, for my height was against me. But by pressing a hat down tight on my head and stooping as much as possible, I seemed shorter.

"To find the attitude of the ordinary man to the ordinary woman, going along on city streets or country roads at night, I made my tours, making no advances to any one. To my surprise and satisfaction, though I walked many miles, no one gave me any trouble."

The villagers could not return the compliment. Too many of them had been scared almost out of their wits by the gigantic "female ghost." Lovers ran from their lanes, windows were locked, children were afraid to go out after sundown. It was in one of the pleasant spots sweethearts frequented that the preacher was captured.

One masquerader in feminine attire the police do not molest is Ed Valley, who lives on an island in Lake Superior, between the United States and Canada.

"Valley wears women's shoes, ear-rings and lace goods, and a careful scrutiny will reveal the unmistakable lines of a corset," according to a writer in the Milwaukee Journal. "When he goes to bed he is dressed in a lacy nightgown. The man keeps himself very much aloof, and the natives have never been able to solve the mystery of his apparel, although he has lived on the island longer than most of its other inhabitants.

"There are numerous explanations for his actions, but one account stands the test of time. He is said to have had a love affair in his youth that ended tragically with the death of his sweetheart. In memory of her he wears the lace goods and high-heeled shoes, the story goes. The islanders say the style of the shoes is that of a bygone day, undoubtedly contemporary with the girl he loved.

"The shoes have high French heels, yet Valley carries himself with perfect poise and walks about as gracefully as any girl. He makes the shoes himself. There is a sharp contrast in the color arrangement. If he wears tan tops he has white laces and if he has white tops the laces are black. His favorite shoe is a three-color combination—a black patent leather bottom, tan top, with white laces. The toes are extremely pointed. The average woman would have great difficulty walking in them. At the foot of Ed Valley's bed is a pile of women's shoes numbering more than fifty pairs. These have all been worn by him and each pair has been manufactured by himself.

"On some days he wears overalls, but generally he has a pair of trousers that reach just below the knees. This costume sets the high top shoes in bold relief. He is never known to attire himself in dress-up clothes. The man earns his living by constructing boats."

Valley's one strong masculine trait, as described by the writer, is a corncob pipe which is invariably in his mouth, when he is seen by the islanders, who thoroughly respect him, and the tourists.

At Camden, New Jersey, Mrs. Hattie Joseph sued for divorce from her forty-four years old husband, who, she said, always slept in silk underwear. "My husband never slept in anything but silk," she told the judge. "No remonstrance of mine could stop the habit. When he would run short of various garments he would go into backyards at night and steal them off clothes lines. Several times he was shot at, but always would return with new unmentionables." Those were the days before the makers of men's underwear had the courage to put their silken garments on the market.

The wife of Robert W. Scofield, an electrical engineer of the Borough of Queens, New York, sued for separation from her husband.

"Shortly after our marriage," she set out in her complaint, "I began to miss my silk underwear. After searching for it, I would find it hidden in desks and other places in my husband's room. I never could leave any of my clothes around the house. Once I went to a masquerade with a girl friend and an hour later my husband arrived attired as a woman. He had ridden on street cars and elevated trains dressed like that. On April 1 last I returned home after a movie and found him in bed with some of my clothes on. His face was rouged; he

251

wore my gold wedding ring, my earrings, and my best dress was hanging on the closet door. He had been wearing that."

She and a woman friend alleged he always "wore women's silk lingerie and corsets," and would parade through the house in feminine attire, including long silk hose and high-heeled pumps, admiring himself in the mirrors.

In a raid on a Greenwich Village Bohemian "tea shop," police arrested, among nine women and five men, a dancer known as "Ruby," also as "Rosebud"—"a scented beauty who wore light silk underwear, a corset, silk stockings, black pumps and a maroon colored opera wrap," wrote a newspaper reporter.

"When the prisoners reached the station the women and men were separated and the women taken into the matron's office to be searched. That is where Ruby went too far, for in a few minutes the matron, flushing with indignation, came dashing back to the desk sergeant and announced that Ruby was a man."

"Ruby," on investigation, was found to be a chorus man in a musical comedy up-town. He lost his job with the show, though the police magistrate dismissed the victims of the raid.

Robert Meyers, a negro female impersonator, member of an ebony theatrical troupe, was arrested in Buffalo and sent to jail for thirty days on plea of guilty of stealing two dresses from a colored lady friend. Silk stockings, powder puffs, paints and cosmetics were found in Meyers' room.

In a raid on a flashy negro resort in Louisville, a natty young buck known as "The Sheik" was arrested, attired in vivid pink pajamas, with hair combed woman fashion and wearing a huge diamond pin on his breast. He was wanted by the narcotic squad.

When bobbed hair came into fashion for women, the "bobbed-hair bandit" began to operate, first in Brooklyn, and then rapidly all over the country. One of the early suspects in Brooklyn turned out to be Raymond Stanley, a young man masquerading as a woman, arrested on a petty larceny charge.

Over in Yonkers a policeman added to the gayety of the bobbed-hair bandit pursuit by assuming female disguise himself, in hopes of running across her on her night prowlings and winning her confidence. He was Patrolman Robert Bush. He kept his eye peeled for male bandits, too, and for "mashers."

In another New York village, Highland Falls, the Chief of Police himself donned female attire to catch a "masher." The village is near West Point, and complaints were made by women that a soldier had been annoying them. Cristoff succeeded in making himself into so attractive a flapper that, sure enough, he was accosted. The flirtation hadn't proceeded far, however, when the policeman slugged the soldier and put him under arrest. The soldier turned out to be a corporal out for a good time.

To help a worthy cause, another New York policeman, J. J. Byrne, assumed a crude, burlesque disguise, and as "Aunty Jay Walker" helped pedestrians across Fifth avenue, lecturing them the while on the sins of jay-walking.

A man appeared in the District Attorney's office in Los Angeles and gave his name as Cardenon Augustus Harms. He told a queer story, not unmixed with pathos. He wanted to know his exact status legally and to clear up his jumbled affairs.

"The District Attorney's office was especially interested in the case," according to a newspaper report, "because of the fact that for many years Harms appeared in public in feminine garb and was accepted for a girl. He declared that he had lived and had been reared as a girl because his mother told him he was a girl. It was only after he grew to manhood and wanted to earn his own livelihood that he revolted against the idea that he was a girl, threw off his parental injunction and set himself up as a man. The transformation is said to have taken place several years ago at Reno, Nevada, where he had lived for many years. In a frank statement Harms is said to have declared that he was married last November to Miss Rena Mae Conklin and that they had carefully considered all phases of their marriage before taking their step. He declared that their marriage is on a higher plane than the ordinary union."

The latter statement might be construed as indicating his mother may have had some psychical reason for her choice for him, or it might have grown out of a confused diffidence because of his long masquerade as a girl.

In San Francisco, "Mrs. Esther Egan" got into trouble because her ankle was too thick. A woman in a hotel lobby noticed the defect, and permitting her eye to dwell on Mrs. Egan's skirt when it tightened as she walked, she noted further that the calf was a little too muscular and sinewy. So she called the police. When the officers arrived, "Mrs. Egan" had gone to bed. Forcing their way rudely into her room, the policemen found her wig on the dresser and a head quite masculine above her feminine nighties. They allowed her to dress—"a neat satin frock, velour coat, fur trimmed, one red rose on the shoulder and red beads." "Mrs. Egan" turned out to be Paul Le Baron, wanted for peddling narcotics.

In another California hotel, at San Jose, a man in female attire was arrested on suspicion. After being finger printed, he turned out to be Edward Tyson, a mulatto, with a record for burglary and robbery, with prison terms.

He had registered the day before as a man under an assumed name. But next morning, there came down in the elevator a stylishly-clad woman of Spanish appearance, whom the clerk couldn't recognize as among the guests of the little hotel. On closer inspection, he fixed him as the "Edward Lefridge" of the register, and called the police, who completed the identification.

Returning to Los Angeles, we encounter Miss Anna Butcher, who, went by the name of Frank Butcher in the city jail and was "embarrassed by the male attire lent him by another prisoner."

He hadn't committed any grave offenses, so far as the police could learn. For ten years, he had worked in various homes as a housemaid. "Five a week and board and room is better than anything I could get as a man," he told the police, "and besides, I like to do housework." A little touch of feminine vanity was his undoing. Miss Anna Butcher appeared at a beauty parlor and wanted her hair marcelled. The operator wasn't long in discovering she was working on a wig. Also, Anna had a slight stubble on her face. The operator called the police.

A pretty girl was seen on the streets of San Francisco, apparently chewing gum, but closer inspection revealed a quid of tobacco slightly protruding from her rouged lips. One of those busybodies who are always calling the police intervened, and at the station the girl turned out to be a "female impersonator of stage and screen stars," and gave his name as John Reed Erskine. The police were wide-eyed in their admiration of the exquisite style of his clothes, the beaded eyelashes and general professional make-up. The tobacco was the only discordant note in the symphony of beauty.

Police at Winchester, Kentucky, were called upon by shocked pedestrians, returning late at night and passing a billiard room, to investigate the moral right of a couple of pretty flappers to shoot pool. Patrolman Mal Tarpy loaded the college boys into a taxi, so that they wouldn't get into any further trouble, and chased them back to their dormitory.

Though Thomas W. Spurgeon's only female vanity was a pair of blue and gold girl's garters, they led to his arrest in a New York street car, and to the solution of sixty-seven burglaries. Spurgeon had crossed his legs, and his wide, bell-bottomed trousers revealed the garters. Two detectives, chancing to be on that car—one of those ten-thousand to one shots, as they say in horse-racing—had heard the day before a description of that very pair of garters, bought by a boy for his sister, and stolen from him.

Sometimes the police are called too late.

" 'Cherchez la Femme' is the watchword of the Berlin police in their investigation of the mysterious murder of Lieutenant Von Plue-

256

skow, who was found hanging in his room at Potsdam, his feet, hands, and elbows strapped," read a Berlin dispatch to the London *Daily Express* on an August morning shortly after the war.

"The lieutenant wore a woman's corsets and long white gloves. On the table was the picture of a beautiful French woman. Friends of the victim who had visited him in his room shortly before his death say the picture had not been there before. Detectives are working on a vengeance theory. It is believed several murderers had a hand in the tragedy."

In New York, Dr. Jose A. Arenas, a physician-dentist from Cuba, shot his ex-mistress Ruth Jackson and her lover, Ignatio Marti, with whom she had gone to live, and then killed himself.

"The autopsy left no doubt that Dr. Arenas was a case of status lymphaticus," Dr. Benjamin Schwartz, first assistant to the Chief Medical Examiner, is quoted in the *New York Times*. "I made a most complete report because of the scientific value of the autopsy. As is true in such instances the body showed practically no hair on the cheeks and only straggling hair on the chin and upper lip. The skin was delicate and smooth. The legs were arched, as might be the case in a woman. The doctor was most unmasculine in all respects.

"This confirmed my first deductions after seeing the body on Saturday night in the doctor's furnished room with alcove bed room adjoining. You will remember that as soon as I had seen him I revealed that he was wearing corsets. These cases of status lymphaticus are intensely interesting. In them the blood vessels are very small, and the lymphatic element is greatly in excess. They die suddenly, as

257

from ruptures of blood vessels. Many of them are degenerate. Most of them are criminals. All of them are liable to commit crimes of passion. Among them are found a large percentage of drug addicts."

The Jackson girl, wife of a Toledo automobile salesman, had been living with the doctor for some time when, ten days before the tragedy, she had gone to live with Marti, "a healthy, normal lad." She had discovered something of the doctor's abnormality, and had learned vaguely he had killed somebody in Cuba before coming to New York. On one occasion, he had cut up her stockings in a frenzy—"it is highly probable that he derived pleasure from thus destroying the woman's stockings," was the autopsy report. Marti and the Jackson girl had called to get her clothes, when Arenas opened fire.

"Samuel McCarty, thirty-four, attired himself in a woman's corset, a pair of red silk bloomers, flesh-colored stockings and gray dancing pumps. Then he knotted a window cord about his neck and hanged himself." Thus tersely reports the New York *Telegraph*. "He left no note to explain his act."

Paris, too, contributes its suicide—or murder. One morning in 1926, Raphael de la Chapelle, an official in the Ministry of Agriculture, was discovered "hanging from a stout hook in the ceiling of his drawing-room. He had been dead for hours. His hands and feet were securely bound. A stout scarf had been used as a noose. As the body dangled from the hook, it was reflected in a full-length mirror standing against the wall.

"What interested the police much more, however," continues a Paris correspondent to the Philadelphia *Inquirer*, "was that Monsieur

258

de la Chapelle, brilliant, able and conscientious official of the Government, was dressed in women's clothes! Down to the last detail, his garb was that of a fashionable woman, pretty enough to be vain and young enough to be fastidious, even to the stockings of sheerest silk, the many-colored garters and the lacy lingerie."

M. de la Chapelle was a married man and the father of two daughters, but for months had lived alone in the apartment where he was found. To this apartment, a modiste had been sending the daintiest of lingerie addressed to "Mme. Cartier," and when the police began to trace down Madame to find out what she knew of the death of the young government employee and especially about his hands being tied, they found she had suddenly disappeared from the night life of Montmartre, where she had been conspicuous in its gayety. Comparing descriptions and photographs, the police concluded the lives of Monsieur de la Chapelle and Madame Cartier had been strangled out simultaneously by the same rope.

"Madame Cartier, otherwise Monsieur de la Chapelle, had many men friends while playing at being queen of the night life of Paris, but none of them knew her well. As dinner companions, dancing partners, theater guests or fellow-revelers at the cafés, Madame liked men, but when she left Montmartre for the night (usually early in the morning) she left that life behind and bade them not to follow her. In the studios, La Cartier is remembered for her elegance, her wit, her camaraderie, her tolerance, and her looks."

An intimate girl friend of Madame Cartier told detectives that while she did not know her chum was a man she frequently suspected

259

it, and knew Cartier was not her real name. Other girls were found who knew Madame well enough to know she had assumed her name, but were not aware La Cartier was a man.

The unsolved mystery of de la Chapelle's death long troubled the police.

XII. PINK GARTERS FOR THESPIS' SOCK

JULIAN ELTINGE, in the prime of his art, was the most fastidious female masquerader in the theater since Edward Kynaston.

Had Eltinge lived in the days when the boy actress was a necessity, the days before women were admitted to the stage, he probably would have developed into a great and serious player of female rôles, instead of limiting himself to the lightly satiric.

He had, in the flush of his success, a great desire to try Juliet, but plans actually under way never materialized. Eltinge realized that he was more or less of a freak, who must limit himself to fun-making. Sarah Bernhardt could do Hamlet, and Maude Adams L'Aiglon, and command respectful critical attention, whatever their limitations in comparison with men of equal genius in the rôles, but Eltinge could not do Juliet—though such was his art, at that time, that he undoubtedly would have been one of the finest Juliets on the stage.

For Eltinge possessed a real genius for impersonation. He not only could wear female clothes, and wear them better than nine-tenths

261

of the women of the theater, but he could catch the little psychological tricks of women, and project them across the footlights. There was always a touch of mocking satire, done with the conscious art of the delicate caricaturist. Had he elected to be serious, he had both the brains and the art—to say nothing of the assured physical advantages —to put his characters across.

Though always the comedian, Eltinge restored female impersonation to an art, from which it had fallen into the coarsest and most obvious slap-stick and buffoonery after the passing of the Restoration "actresses," Kynaston and Nokes and Hart. Hart's friend, Lacy, set the pattern—or rather fixed it, for this sort of buffoonery was common in Shakespeare's time. Even today, whoever essays Falstaff, be he so dignified, almost sanctified a figure as Otis Skinner, must appear ridiculously clothed as Mother Prat, to be teased and tormented by Mrs. Page and Mrs. Ford and soundly beaten by Mr. Ford. Eltinge brought back beauty, grace, subtlety, and, most of all, the genuinely feminine ring.

Though immensely popular for a decade and more, and as frantically favored by women as was Kynaston, Eltinge's career has been singularly free from scandal. Tales of his athletic prowess may or may not be the usual protective covering press agents are in the habit of throwing around female impersonators, but it is certain Eltinge conducted himself through some dizzy mazes of popularity more like a clear-headed athlete than a temperamental prima donna—or even a temperamental tenor.

He was born in Boston in 1883, and while still in his teens was participating in amateur dramatics in heroine rôles. In 1904, he appeared professionally, or semi-professionally, in "Mr. Wix of Wickham," and then went professionally into vaudeville, playing for five years throughout the United States and Europe. An engagement at the Palace theater, London, opening May 14, 1906, started the buzz of excitement, setting him apart from all other female impersonators.

His overwhelming popularity, however, dates from his tour of the United States in 1908-9 with the Cohan & Harris Minstrels—a monster minstrel show George M. Cohan staged to prove that minstrelsy was a real art and could be made as entertaining and engrossing as any other sort of up-to-date musical show, not excepting the Ziegfeld "Follies," then in the second and third year of glorification of the American girl. Cohan proved his point, even though the big minstrel show was so heavily saddled with expenses—nearly every minstrel man of prominence in America being on the pay-roll—that it could not break even. However, Cohan charged his big show to "advertising" for himself and partner, and considered the money well spent because of the enormous sensation it created.

Of all the features, Eltinge was the superlative. Young, extraordinarily handsome, with a slim body, a well-developed white chest, little feet and hands, he was a brilliantly beautiful woman in the men's show. He did not appear in cork, but in the pink and cream make-up of a woman of breeding and fashion, devoid of hauteur, and a "good fellow."

He sang a series of songs, changing from one dazzling costume to another more dazzling, as the program proceeded. It was the day of the dawning of daring female dress—the ending of the Victorian era and the first gliding steps into our present period of near-nudity on the stage and boulevards. The skirts were becoming shorter and shorter, but the real sensation was the Directoire gown, slit up one side to reveal the feminine leg above the knee as the skirts swished. Eltinge's gowns and hosiery and hats were in the very height of the new fashion, and their perfect cut, gorgeous material and the grace with which he wore them made his feminine auditors gasp and their hearts flutter.

It was due to Eltinge that this show was as popular with women, who have never been able to get up any great enthusiasm for minstrel shows, as it was with men. The men in the audience liked Eltinge for his great good nature and his satirical flings, but it was the women who were infatuated with him.

After the minstrel tour, Eltinge was made a star in a musical comedy, "The Fascinating Widow," a college play in which he appeared in both female and male rôles, a student masquerading as a female heart-breaker. It wasn't much of a show in itself, but Eltinge's exceptional ability kept it popular for three years. It is largely due to the press agenting of this show that Eltinge has the reputation of being a star in his youth in college theatricals.

"The Crinoline Girl," "Cousin Lucy," "Her Grace the Vampire," "Countess Charming" and "His Night at the Club," all built on the same general lines—the male finding good reason to appear in female guise—followed, bringing Eltinge's career down to about 1920. His later appearances have been principally in vaudeville, and he is still

(1928) clever as a female impersonator, though the flash and dazzle that were his in youth are gone.

Eltinge has been a good business man, and is now possessor of a ranch some thirty miles out of San Diego, well up in the mountains, where he is a genial and liberal host to his friends, theatrical, literary and artistic. On his ranch he prefers to be known as Bill Dalton—that's his name, William Dalton. A theater in New York is named for him, but in his rôle as female impersonator and not as amateur cow-boy—the Eltinge. He is, or has been, part proprietor, along with his old friend and manager, Al Woods.

Eltinge's revival of the art of female impersonation and his sensational success, of course, started a whole swarm of men flocking to the stage in women's attire. Some idea of this superabundance may be gathered from an article in the theatrical weekly, "Variety," of date March 8, 1923, a decade and a half after Eltinge set the fashion:

"There are more female impersonators in vaudeville this season than ever before, according to the vaudeville booking men. Three impersonators on one bill at a split-week house recently is viewed as a record.

"The numerical strength of the impersonators was heavily swollen following the war, when recruits from the ranks of the many service acts entered vaudeville and remained. The disintegration of the service act and the laying aside of the uniforms seemingly did nothing to deplete the ranks of impersonators, who re-formed into two-act combinations, single and the latest craze, 'working in front of a band.'

"An idea of the number of aspirants for the wig and the skirts may be gleaned from statistics compiled at one of the large middle western naval stations during the war. When a call was issued for aspirants for feminine attire for an entertainment, 125 responded."

This latter bit of statistical information throws some light on the wisdom of the move we have already commented on, of depriving our budding sailors and soldiers of normal female prostitutes. For, while many of our boy-actresses of the stage have not been inverted, the great majority of males who desire to masquerade as women have more than a normal share of the feminine in their nature, and the records of the English boys' schools and of prisons all over the world are sufficient to indicate what the big percentage of one-hundred-twenty-five boys eager to array themselves in petticoats might do to one training station.

Of the legions who have invaded the stage, the one whose genius most nearly approached Eltinge's was Bert Savoy. Savoy appeared with a partner, Jay Brennan, who dressed in normal male clothing and was the "feeder" of the popular team of Savoy and Brennan—that is to say, Brennan led up to the jokes, which Savoy cracked. After the death of Savoy, who was killed by lightning while walking along the Long Island ocean beach with four friends during an electrical storm, Brennan annexed another partner, Stanley Rogers, of nothing near the talent of Savoy, but the team of Brennan and Rogers has gone along with apparently little diminution in popularity.

Savoy's studies of the female were radically different from Eltinge's. Eltinge has always appeared as a young woman of refinement, good breeding, education, "class"—if wicked, she was only a

266

trifle so—just enough wickedness to serve as sauce. Savoy's epochal creation was a prostitute—a red-headed street walker, with a wit of razor sharpness, but with no malice in her "wise-cracks." She had a mythical friend "Margy," a girl chum as brazen and mischief-loving as herself, and it was the comic exploits of Savoy's red-headed vamp and this Margy that Brennan coaxed out of him, to the huge delight of the audiences. Rogers uses the same material, but he lacks Savoy's genial good-humor and effervescent personality that lessened the shock of the vulgar, clever wickedness.

Savoy's loud-mouthed, over-dressed harlot was as excellent a bit of artistry as Eltinge's "fascinating widow," just as one of Lautrec's denizens of the brothels of Paris matches—and more—a court lady by Watteau.

Savoy's dramatic death by lightning suddenly concentrated his wide popularity, and many and eloquent were the tributes paid him. This one by Edmund Wilson, The Dial, August, 1923, is probably most vividly expressive of his art and of the place he occupied in the contemporary theater:

"One instrument in the great jazz band of New York has suddenly been silenced: Bert Savoy is dead. But the comic character he created will never be forgotten by those who saw it. When he used to come reeling on the stage, a gigantic red-haired harlot, swaying her enormous hat, reeking with corrosive cocktails of the West Fifties, one felt oneself in the presence of the vast vulgarity of New York incarnate and made heroic. Well, we have heard the last of Margy's wise-cracks and the thought is a genuinely sad one. Still, in the brash

267

nights of the city, between Reisenweber's and the Montmartre, we shall sometimes be haunted by the accents of a gasping raucous voice, hard-boiled, shamefully obscene, but in a continual tremor of female excitement: 'I'm so glad you asked me that, dearie! You don't know the half of it, dearie! You don't know the half of it!' "

A classic example of Savoy's humor was his story of the preacher who reprimanded Margy for playing jazz on the piano on Sunday. The minister asked her sorrowfully if she knew the Ten Command-ments. Margy said she didn't, but believed she could pick out the tune if the preacher would hum it.

Savoy varied the dressing of his strident strumpet with the changes in fashion. His gowns were a burlesque of the gayest craze of the moment, exaggerated but kept feminine. Great jewels, ten times the size of whatever happened to be worn, would flash from his red wig or his fingers or his breast or his ankle. His loud, fantastic garters were works of art.

Savoy came by his flashy street walker naturally. His first stage appearance, as a boy, was in a curio museum in Boston, where he did a chair dance. He alternated with a "cooch" dancer, whose move-ments he learned perfectly to imitate. He and this dancer formed a partnership and plunged into the carnivals, where they were not very successful financially.

Then followed some knocking about the country as a chorus man and in vaudeville. With a vaudeville outfit, he played a servant girl, injecting into the rôle a good deal he had learned from his "cooch" dancer friend, and it was this girl he later made famous as the wisecracking red-head. He did the mining camps of Montana as a female impersonator, and then went to Alaska, where he played the barrooms all up and down the Yukon. He returned to the States and went east as far as Chicago, where his fortunes began to improve.

The Russell Brothers, knock-about comedians, who often played in skirts, roughly burlesquing women, took Savoy on as an understudy, and it was while he was playing Jim Russell's part in a farce called "The Female Detective"—during an illness of Jim's—that Jay Brennan, then in a vaudeville team of dancers, became acquainted with him. During the next summer vacation in New York, the two got together and concocted the act for vaudeville, which eventually became a feature in "The Passing Show of 1915."

After that, Savoy and Brennan had no difficulty in getting spots in the limelight of the biggest shows—"Miss 1917," the Ziegfeld "Follies" of 1918, the Ziegfeld Roof, "Hitchy-Koo," "Cinderella on Broadway" and "Greenwich Village Follies." It was when on vacation after finishing with the latter show, that Savoy was killed. A friend, Jack Vincent, a chorus man walking with him, was killed by the same bolt. Brennan was to have been of the party, but had gone to a health resort to recover from nervous strain.

Stanley Rogers, who took Savoy's place as Brennan's partner, was a protégé of Savoy's. Bert found him doing a single act as a "vamp" in a small vaudeville house. When a touring company of "Greenwich Village Follies" took to the road, Rogers was put in the parts Savoy had played in New York and the larger cities. Brennan, after Savoy's death, trained Rogers in the business of his old team-mate, and, after a tour in vaudeville polishing him off, the new team joined "The Ritz Revue" and later went into "Artists and Models."

Savoy married in Chicago. His wife got a divorce from him, alleging cave-man tactics. Then, a few years later, she sued him for breach of promise, alleging he had proposed to her but failed to re-marry her.

Another American, who has won considerable fame in the music halls of London and Paris, is Francis Renault. He not only presents types of femininity, but imitates particular stars—Ruth St. Denis, for example, and Geraldine Farrar and Alice Delysia. Renault is credited with a remarkable soprano voice, far above the average of the female impersonators, permitting his duplication of the opera stars. His figure is such as to make him acceptable as an imitator of even so lithe and graceful a female dancer as Miss St. Denis.

Karyl Norman, singer of southern songs, and Alyn Mann, credited with the juvenile grace of a young high school girl, are others who have emerged to a plane a little above the multitude of youths seriously trying to compete with girls in the matter of looking and acting like females on the stage.

Nor should Jackie Coogan be forgotten, the wonder infant of the screen. Jackie is growing up now, and may never again relish being a girl even in the name of art. But in one of his pictures, a filming of "A Dog of Flanders," in the rôle of the little Flanders boy, facing the world alone with his dog, he was called upon to masquerade as a girl in order that he might attend the birthday party of the heartless landlord's daughter. Just as Jackie was the handsomest lad on the screen, so was he the prettiest little girl at the party.

270

Europe has now, and has had in the recent past some female impersonators comparable in art with Julian Eltinge, but it is a significant fact that when European writers are discussing them, they use Eltinge as the standard of comparison. In England Eltinge is known from his personal appearances in the London music halls, and on the continent he is familiar from his moving pictures.

Berlin has Middendorf, whose art of counterfeiting a woman is so perfect that a lawyer friend put it to use in a trial in court. The woman owner of a hotel was in trouble due to an accusation that she had let her place be frequented by persons of bad character. She was near conviction, when her attorney called an elegantly gowned young woman, whom the judge questioned seriously and politely. "Now I ask for acquittal of my client," said the lawyer when the judge had finished. "The witness is not a woman at all, but a man. If an astute court can't tell the difference between a man and a woman, how can it expect my client to distinguish good characters from bad on sight."

The judge good-naturedly saw the point and discharged the innkeeper. The witness was Middendorf.

In Buda-Pest flourished Aranka Gyvengy, who is said to have played female parts, minor rôles, in the state theater for twenty-three years without the public knowing of his sex.

Stiv-Hall, of the Paris variety theaters, is credited with the same sort of power the critics attribute to Francis Renault—perhaps to a higher degree. Yvette Guilbert, Theresa Judic, Sarah Bernhardt, Rejane, Patti and Clèo de Merode are in his repertoire. "His voice has such an extensive range, and is so supple, that he once proposed to record on phonograph disks imitations of all the principal singers of the day," says O. P. Gilbert, from whose book we have also borrowed the note about Gyvengy.

Gilbert also lists Chretienni, who "dressed as a lorette, performed at the Jardin de Paris, and whose seductive leers were calculated to turn the heads of young men of twenty"; Stuart, a soprano, of the Alhambra, Paris; Gyp, who "could make up as a woman, so far as outward appearance went, but could neither sing, act, nor dance"; Ristori, the violinist and dancer, "and a gymnast who only dons female attire for the purpose of surprising his audience"; Nielda, now dead, "able to impersonate women fairly well"; Sergi, who was, "to all appearance, a tall graceful young woman with a good soprano voice"; Bertin, who "gave some fairly good imitations of women," but who has not returned to the stage since the war, and Barbette, a wire-walker.

Barbette, concludes Mr. Gilbert in his discussion of the men-women of the contemporary stage, including Eltinge, to whom he assigns first importance, though he has seen him only on the screen— Barbette "resembles an American girl, and no one suspects him to be a man until, at the end of his performance, he takes off his wig. Amongst acrobats it is no unusual thing to find slim young men posing as a girl; in their case, their identity is not revealed, and their names in the program are fanciful cognomens which give no indication of sex. It may be remarked that a large proportion of these male impersonators of women are American or British, and but seldom French or Italian, or still more rarely German or Swedish."

Mr. Gilbert's statement of the slim young men in acrobatic acts passing for girls can readily be believed by any one who saw the Griffin Twins, exceedingly graceful and finished young artists in acrobatic poses, who accompanied Harry Lauder as a supplementary vaudeville act on his latest American tour. There was much murmuring and guessing in the audience as to the sex of these lads, whose faces, hair and trim figures gave the impression of girls in their opening number in which they were attired in close-fitting black suits, somewhat in the fashion of Elizabethan days—an impression dispelled later by the muscles of their naked legs and arms in a Greek warrior pose, and reaffirmed in later pictures.

Many contemporary male stars have appeared on the stage in female clothing without trying, in the least, to give the audience the impression they are feminine. As we have pointed out, anybody essaying Falstaff must, for a few moments, become a "female impersonator."

The most fearful theater tragedy of modern times occurred when the star was thus arrayed—and a grotesquely tragic figure he cut trying to stay the disaster.

It was the Iroquois theater fire in Chicago, the afternoon of December 30, 1903, wherein 602 people, mostly women and children, lost their lives in eight terrible minutes of shooting flames and wild panic.

The hero was Eddie Foy, and he was in his dressing room making up for the burlesque part of Sister Anne for her scene with the trick elephant in "Mr. Bluebeard." A chorus number was on when some

273

draperies caught fire, and the flames began to leap briskly in full view of the crowded audience. Excitement started out front, but the girls kept bravely on, though little bits of the flaming draperies were falling onto their flimsy costumes. Foy rushed to the stage, and attempted to allay the excitement, now growing into panic and soon to become a pandemonium. The saving of many lives is credited to his coolness and nerve, though nothing human could prevent the catastrophe. Foy was the last to leave the stage in the comic petticoats of the ridiculous Sister Anne.

In his youth, when boisterous burlesque was rampant, De Wolf Hopper played a coy Juliet to Marshall P. Wilder's Romeo. Henry E. Dixey won his spurs in "Adonis," wherein he burlesqued a country girl. Neil Burgess was famous as the Widow Bedott, a cross between broad burlesque and serious interpretation of the middle-aged, sometimes sentimental heroine.

Hutton in his "Curiosities of the American Stage" believes George Holland's presentation of John Poole's travesty of "Hamlet," March 22, 1828, "was about the beginning of what, for want of a better term, may be styled 'legitimate burlesque' in the United States." Holland himself played Ophelia, doubling with the First Grave-Digger.

In 1839, William Mitchell made his advent, and the boisterous merriment started in earnest. Fanny Elssler was a sensation of the day in "La Tarantula," so Mitchell put on "La Mosquito." Hutton quotes from the play bill:

"First time in this or any other country, a new comic burlesque ballet, entitled 'La Mosquito,' in which Monsieur Mitchell will make his first appearance as *une première danseuse,* and show his agility in a variety of terpsichorean efforts of all sorts in the genuine Bolero-cachucacacavonienne style. . . . The ballet is founded on the well-known properties of the mosquito, whose bites render the patient exceedingly impatient, and throw him into a fit of slapping and scratching and swearing delirium commonly called the 'Cacoethes Scratchende,' causing the unfortunate being to cut capers enough for a considerable number of legs of mutton. The scene lies in Hoboken."

Mitchell performed his dance in an exaggerated make-up of Miss Elssler, and "burlesqued the charming and graceful Fanny with comic humor," according to William K. Northall, a writer of the day. "The manner of his exit from the stage at the conclusion of the dance was irresistibly comic, and the serious care with which he guided himself to the side scenes, to secure a passage for his tremendous bustle, was very funny."

Mitchell delighted New York for a decade, and then his popularity began to wane, with William E. Burton and John Brougham wresting from him his laurels. Burton played Lady Macbeth and also Queen Bee, a gypsy woman, in a piece called "St. Cupid." In this company was Mark Smith, popular as Mrs. Normer in a play of that name, which Mitchell had introduced, and as Norma in a play called "Villikens and His Dinah."

Burton and Brougham, the latter famous as the author of the comic pieces, "Pocahontas" and "Columbus," lasted in popularity, too, about a decade, and then came Miss Lydia Thompson, setting the new style of extravaganza. This was in 1868, and the youngsters of that generation have come down as the veterans of this, or, at least, the generation just past.

Harry Beckett, one of these rising geniuses, later to become the great low comedian of Lester Wallack's company, was considered extravagantly funny as Minerva in Lydia Thompson's "Ixion"; as the Widow Twankey in "Aladdin," as Maid Marian in "Robin Hood" and as Queen Elizabeth in "Kenilworth."

James Lewis, another of the youngsters, did "cruel injustice to the character of Lucretia Borgia. . . . The palace of the Borgias was set as a modern apothecary's shop, where poison was sold in large or small quantities, and Mr. Lewis excited roars of laughter as a quack doctoress, with great capabilities of advertising herself and her nostrums." Lewis was also a hit as Rebecca in "Ivanhoe" and Oenone in "Paris."

To that period, too, belongs Daniel Setchell's "Leah the Forsaken."

The twin-star of Harrigan and Hart was beginning to rise. "Harrigan's plays grew out of the vaudeville sketches in which he as the male character and Hart as the female, impersonated the types of city life which delighted the audience of the Theatre Comique with their humor and fidelity to life," records Dr. Arthur Hobson Quinn in his new and complete "History of the American Drama," and Hutton throws further light on this pair and their tendency to masquerade for comic effect, by setting out that "N. C. Goodwin burlesqued a burlesque at Harrigan and Hart's first theater, when he played Captain Stuart Robson-Crosstree to the Dame Hadley of Mr. Harrigan and the Black-eyed Susan of Mr. Hart."

Clyde Fitch was growing up. "At Amherst College, which he entered in 1882, he pursued his self-determined course, wearing clothes which were the theme of campus comment but winning his recognized place as one of the leaders of the dramatic interests of Amherst." Again we are quoting Quinn's history. "He not only acted such parts as Lydia Languish in 'The Rivals' and Peggie Thrift in 'The Country Girl,' but he directed Wycherley's play, painted scenery and designed costumes."

Toto, the popular clown, occasionally dons skirts absurdly voluminous, for some bit of grotesquery. Fred Stone, a graduate of the sawdust ring, who adapted the art of clowning to musical comedy, indulges now and then in similar buffoonery. One of the Mosconi Brothers, expert dancers, inventors of the "Gigolo," did a swiftly acrobatic burlesque of Suzanne Lenglen, the tennis champion. There is no attempt at genuine impersonation in stunts of this sort.

In a gambol of the Lambs, the foremost theatrical club of America, there was put on a spectacular musical revue, written by Roy and Kenneth Webb and staged by Hassard Short. Thirty actors were included in the cast, and among the rôles assigned, as published in the New York *Telegraph*, were Richard Barthelmess as "Cleopatra"; Rudolph Cameron as "Carmen"; Teddy Gibson as "Camille"; William Gaxton as "Zaza"; George LeGuere as "Lady Macbeth," Stanley Ridges as "Tosca," Burton Churchill as "Scarpia," Effington Pinto as "Salome," and Joseph Santley, a young man who has donned skirts occasionally for comic effect in his own musical shows, as "Du Barry." The skit included male rôles, too, such as "Antony," the

277

"Toreador" and the "Devil." In another gambol, George Raisley was cast for "Juliet," Shakespeare's love-sick maid, drafted into a burlesque sketch called "Four Dames and a Guy." Female impersonation, more or less serious, is not an unusual feature of the Lambs' gambols.

"Chic" Sale, comedian, numbers in his gallery of grotesque character creations, largely rural, a female village character of middle age, burlesqued and satirized, as are all his personages, but decidedly a characterization, too.

Female actresses are beginning to appear on the stage in Japan, as they did surreptitiously in England in the days of Charles I, with a bold open invasion threatened, as in the Restoration era. Hitherto, feminine rôles have been enacted by boys.

"Signs of the times" in Japan are indicated by a controversy the Minister of Education had with the colleges. It was brought to his attention that the playing of female rôles by boys in the boys' schools was having the injurious effect we have suggested as resulting from a lusty young army deprived of prostitutes. The boys in girl's attire did not lose wholly their assumed charm when the play was over.

So violent an opposition came to abolishing the drama altogether from the colleges, however, that the Minister compromised. He agreed to permit the boys to assume girls' rôles so long as they did not dress in girls' clothing. A similar ruling was made in the girls' schools. The young ladies could appear in boys' rôles, if necessary, but they must not wear boys' clothing. The danger to their girl chums in the masquerade was too great.

Of late, the American stage has had quite an influx of Japanese female actresses—not only acrobats, but singers, dancers and readers of lines, who demonstrate a talent that will make their native stage important when they attain full freedom back home.

China has not only a stage of men exclusively, but has a system of private entertainers, who resemble the singing and dancing youths of Greece and Rome. "The boys have been carefully brought up for this occupation," records Havelock Ellis, "receiving an excellent education, and their mental qualities are even more highly valued than their physical attractiveness. After the meal the lads usually return home with a considerable fee. What further occurs the Chinese say little about."

Throughout the Orient, this employment of effeminate boys as entertainers in preference to genuine girls, is more or less prevalent— girls are used, too, but are little esteemed, while the boys sometimes are richly and even regally honored. In Lahore and Lucknow, in Richard Burton's time, were to be seen on the street, "men dressed as women, with flowing locks under crowns of flowers, imitating the feminine walk and gestures, voice and fashion of speech, ogling their admirers with all the coquetry of bayaderes."

Some future Burton, after strolling through Boston Common or walking around Columbus Circle, New York, may have a similar report to make to posterity, except he cannot say with truth the chorus boys wear gowns that publicly. Otherwise, the description fits.

The boys Burton saw in Afghanistan are perhaps nearer the modern American mark—"each caravan is accompanied by a number of boys and lads almost in woman's attire, with kohled eyes and rouged

279

cheeks, long tresses and hennæd fingers and toes, riding luxuriously in camel paniers."

A comic attempt to make the entire Chinese race even more effeminate than the Jew Weininger savagely accuses his race of being, occurred in America during our Chinese labor excitement. Arthur Train tells about it in an article in *The Pictorial Review,* December, 1921, entitled, "Of the Making of Fool Laws There Is No End":

"An ingenious member of the legislature of a State in which the factories act prohibited the employment of girls under eighteen, recently proposed an amendment to the law (evidently with the idea of preventing competition from Chinese labor) that thereafter 'all Chinamen' should 'be deemed girls under eighteen!' "

London had a mild flurry not long since, akin to that of Tokyo. The British censor refused to license a play called "The Gay Young Bride," declaring, according to press dispatches, he would not issue a permit for a play wherein a man impersonated a young woman. The argument was advanced that numerous female impersonators had played the halls, but the Lord Chamberlain pointed out he had no jurisdiction there, excepting as regards playlets. He said his only objection to the play under consideration was the masculine characterization of a young woman.

British aspirants are not discouraged, however, by limitation of their talents to the lowly halls. London was amused in October, 1927, by the ambitions of Cuthbert Smith-Wilkinson, a character about town, whose late wife was known as "the best dressed woman in the world."

"Do you think some show would put me in the chorus to start me toward my ambition of becoming a female impersonator?" he is quoted in a London dispatch to American newspapers as having written to a newspaper man.

"Elizabeth Asquith—daughter of the former Liberal Premier—once told me: 'How well you would look in a white dress and blue sash', when she saw me acting at a charity show as a lady.

"I have appeared on the stage with leading actors and actresses at such performances. I am tall, have a good appearance, can sing a little, and do a few dance steps. You won't throw my little letter in the fire, will you?"

He is described in the press dispatch as being six feet, two inches tall, and possessed of a "warm tenor voice."

Female impersonators in amateur dramatics have become almost as much of an institution in American colleges as football heroes, and every year sees the lovely girl-boys touring America with the approval —or, at least, without the disapproval—of the college faculty—all for the honor of Alma Mater!

When the Princeton Triangle Club produced "Napoleon Passes," a New York critic wrote enthusiastically of "the rhythmic dancing of a Tiller ballet of Princeton lads," and suggested interesting Mr. Ziegfeld "in the glorification of the American college boy."

On a rotogravure page of the Chicago *Tribune* in December, 1927, were flashed half a dozen handsome pictures of boys in stunning female attire, participating in "Feature That," played by the Haresfoot club of the University of Wisconsin, and "The Same to

You," by lads of the University of Michigan, both scheduled for Chicago during the mid-winter holidays. These citations are made only as samples of a custom prevalent in the universities of first importance.

It is seldom these college boys create anything more than the passing stir of their participation in their particular show. An exception was Lionel Ames, University of Michigan star of a play called "Cotton Stockings Never Made a Man Look Twice," who got newspaper publicity that even a Julian Eltinge might have envied. Whoever was press-agenting the Mimes that year—the university's dramatic club— used professionals methods, broadcasting Ames' photographs everywhere, and concocting stories such as having his pretty legs insured for $25,000. Then, the "dashing soubrette" of "Cotton Stockings" and "In and Out," got married, and apparently has not made capital for the professional stage of his wide-spread amateur publicity.

Another of the college boys who won more than average renown was Halsey Hills, and his extra fame came about because he was a football hero, too—a quarterback at Dartmouth. His glory as an athletic hero came after he was thoroughly established as a singer, eccentric dancer and impersonator of female rôles in the annual college dramatics. He had tried for football honors for three years, without ever being any farther advanced than a scrub. He wasn't taken very seriously on the gridiron, probably because of his dramatic achievements. But, his chance came in his senior year, when he was chosen to stop a gap in a game against Vermont. He did it so effectively, that he was sent in regularly against Harvard, where his play was so brilliant that he blazed out as a national hero. It was then the newspapers began printing stories about his astonishing duality—the prettiest girl and the most heroic boy in the school. They compared him with Eltinge—as newspapers always do a new female impersonator—pointing to Eltinge's record in the ring as an amateur boxer.

In the Princeton Triangle's "Napoleon Passes," the "prima donna" was also an athlete, Phillips R. Holmes, a former Cambridge University rower. The athletic touch is always a good "press yarn."

A college boy in a co-educational school who won in a curious contest against girls was Emmett Goldman, senior at Auburn college, Alabama. He was voted "Queen of the May" against three girl aspirants for the honor, and, according to the press dispatches, his girl friends who had backed him, "promised to bedeck him faultlessly for the festival."

Let's close the chapter on a professional note—an operatic note, at that. "While on a train en route from Chicago to Boston, with other members of the Chicago Opera Company," the newspapers were printing in January, 1923, "Harry Cahill, interpreter of the company, attired himself in the clothing of Hazel Eden, one of the sopranos, and proceeded to vamp William Beck, a baritone. The flirtation went along splendidly until Beck discovered the deception and said unkind things to Cahill, as a result of which he is nursing a sore jaw, which came into contact with Cahill's fist."

XIII. THE BOY WITH THE "MONA LISA" SMILE

THE tantalizing mystery of "Mona Lisa's" smile may be that it is no woman's smile at all, but a boy's.

This is a better guess than Freud's, that it is the smile, not of La Gioconda, but of Leonardo da Vinci's pathetically wanton mother, forever illuminating the subconscious of her talented bastard son.

For, if the Gioconda smile has had its innumerable successors, so had it also its antecedents, and the first on record is not on a woman's lips but plays mysteriously around the mouth of a bronze half-naked boy hero of Israel—the David of Leonardo's master, Verrocchio. The same enigma is there, the same subtle, amused perversity.

The smile is to be found also on the faces of two other young men, John the Baptist and Bacchus, both in the Louvre.

"From the locust eater of the Bible," writes Muther, "Leonardo made a Bacchus, an Apollo, who with a mysterious smile on his lips, and with his soft thighs crossed, looks on us with infatuated eyes."

The Saint John is from the same model as the Bacchus—they might be interchanged, indeed, without hurting the religious sense of the most devout Christian or the esthetic sense of the most joyous pagan.

Moreover, there is in the Louvre a "Madonna, Child and Saint Anne" of Leonardo's and the Saint Anne has such kindred facial and bodily features, including the smile, that she probably was painted from the same young male model—she has the same naked feet as the Bacchus, with long, strong, beautiful toes.

"The figures are androgynous," writes Freud of the Bacchus and the Saint John. "They are pretty boys of feminine tenderness with feminine forms; they do not cast down their eyes but gaze mysteriously triumphant, as if they knew of a great happy issue concerning which one must remain quiet; the familiar fascinating smile leads us to infer that it is a love secret."

Freud's reading of the secret of the smile is a little gratuitous, but his main contention that the figures are androgynous is an irresistible conclusion of any beholder.

Verrocchio's David, too, is androgynous. This boy hero, who has just cut off the head of Goliath—the ghastly trophy is lying at his feet, and he is still holding a short sword in his right hand—is not only wearing the enigmatic smile that was to be transferred a quarter of a century later to the face of the pretty girl wife of Francesco di Bartolommeo di Zanobi del Giocondo, but he is resting his left hand on his shapely hip in a way that annoyed Scott, giving "a flippant attitude very much at variance with the subject."

The boy's breasts are as rounded as a well developed virgin's, his waist is small, his hips maidenly. His arms and legs, however, are slender and sinewy, and the whole impression, despite the feminine suggestion of head and torso, is of extraordinary strength—this youth actually slew Goliath—maybe he could bend a horseshoe in his hands, like lead!

Verrocchio took for his model for David, guesses Symonds, "the first Florentine prentice who came to hand," and of this boy the David is "a faithful portrait."

The bronze was executed when Leonardo, just turned twenty, was a pupil in the studio of the master—an exceptionally handsome lad, moreover, whom Verrocchio, so fond of his boy apprentices that he remained a bachelor, adored next to his supreme favorite, Lorenzo di Credi.

Leonardo was destined to develop shortly into the handsomest man of his time—with "beauty of person," records Vasari, "which was such that it has never been sufficiently extolled" and with a "grace beyond expression."

This Renaissance Apollo, however, was not destined by the gods for the solace of adoring ladies.

"The act of procreation," he observes in one of his many notes still extant, "and everything that has any relation to it is so disgusting that human beings would soon die out if it were not a traditional custom and if there were no pretty faces and sensuous dispositions."

This paragon of beauty was as fastidious about his clothes, which must be of the richest fabrics, as he was cool to female charms, and yet such was his physical strength that he was "able to bend one of the iron rings used for the knockers of doors, or a horse-shoe, as if it were lead"—Samson, Hercules, the great Conde!

Matchless as were his beauty and his strength, they were surpassed by the power of his intellect and by his skill as painter, sculptor, architect and musician. Philosopher, he was, and inventor, and naturalist, and mathematician—perhaps the most versatile intellect the world has ever harbored.

"While in Milan," relates Vasari, "Leonardo took the Milanese Salai for his disciple; this was a youth of singular grace and beauty of person, with curls and waving hair, a feature of personal beauty by which Leonardo was always greatly pleased."

Vasari also knew "Messer Francesco de Melzo, a Milanese gentleman, who, in the time of Leonardo, was a child of remarkable beauty, much beloved by him, and is now a handsome and amiable old man."

Freud delved deep into all the Leonardo literature—and there are scores of volumes and many manuscripts extant—and reports:

"It has always been emphasized that he took as his pupils only strikingly handsome boys and youths. He was kind and considerate toward them, he cared for them and nursed them when they were ill, just like a mother nurses her children, as his own mother might have cared for him. As he selected them on account of their beauty rather than their talent, none of them—Cesare da Sesto, G. Boltraffio, Andrea Salaino, Francesco Melzi and the others—ever became a prominent artist." (Salaino is the Salai of Vasari, and Melzi the Melzo.) "Most of them could not make themselves independent of their master and

287

disappeared after his death without leaving a more definite physiognomy to the history of art. The others who by their productions earned the right to call themselves his pupils, as Luini and Bazzi, nicknamed Sodoma, he probably did not know personally"—it may be observed that both Luini and Sodoma repeated the "Mona Lisa" smile.

Moreover, records Freud of Leonardo, "while he still lived as an apprentice in the house of Verrocchio, he with other young men were accused of forbidden homosexual relations which ended in his acquittal. It seems that he came into suspicion because he employed as a model a boy of evil repute."

In Verrocchio's studio—and the master cannot be wholly acquitted of suspicions that lay upon his pupils—Leonardo "executed certain heads in terra cotta of women smiling," but whether the smile of "Mona Lisa" or the Bacchus or the Saint John or the David of Verrocchio, it is not set down.

Freud, pasting all these and other bits of information together, including his famous dream of the vulture, and submitting the whole to his method of psychoanalysis, discovers his favorite mother complex operating.

Leonardo was the illegitimate son of a wealthy notary and a peasant girl. His father married a rich young lady about the time of his birth. This marriage was sterile, and when Leonardo was five years old, he was taken into the home of his father, with the wife's consent, and legitimatized. It is presumed he spent the first years of his infancy with his mother, who married a peasant. The smile of his mother, the deserted peasant girl Caterina, Freud believes, persisted in Leonardo's

288

subconscious, and "as he became a painter he endeavored to reproduce this smile with his brush and furnish all his pictures with it."

But that doesn't explain the identical smile on the face of Verrocchio's David, a work of art Freud, despite all his painstaking research, seems to have overlooked.

May it not be, rather, that Leonardo himself was the beautiful, effeminate, yet strong model for David—"the first Florentine prentice who came to hand?" Yet not chosen haphazard, for Leonardo's beauty of person, strength of arm, and feminine delicacy is compatible with the conception a boy-lover like Verrocchio would have of the Jewish lad, who lamented over Jonathan: "Thy love to me was wonderful, passing the love of women."

And may not the "Mona Lisa" smile be Narcissian?

Leonardo, who cared nothing for women, but preferred to be with the handsome boys in his studio, labored nevertheless for four years on this portrait of the third wife of a man for whom he cared little. Nor was there any consideration of money. It has been conjectured by the commentators of Vasari that "evidently he found in the Gioconda exactly that type which was most sympathetic and interesting to him, for the Lisa is the incarnation of the Leonardesque smile."

It is not impossible that she may have been "sympathetic and interesting to him" because she resembled him—because she possessed startlingly the smile that had fascinated him when Verrocchio spread it about the lips of David—not impossible, nor improbable in view of the self-worship these men verging on the feminine exhibit. The Abbé de Choisy is the well-defined type.

Yet Lisa's smile troubled him. He worked four years on the portrait, and then left it unfinished. During the sittings, he "took the precaution of keeping some one constantly near her, to sing or play on instruments, or to jest and otherwise amuse her" that she might smile —the smile that was almost his ideal, yet not quite.

When an old man, Leonardo did a portrait of himself, still extant. His face is wrinkled and he has a long flowing beard, which does not, however, conceal his shaved upper lip nor his lower. From under the wrinkles and the beard emerges a suggestion of the face of Bacchus and of Saint John. An earlier bearded portrait, by another hand, reveals the similarity still more strikingly. This latter face is about to break into a smile—a smile that well might be La Gioconda's on the face of Bacchus.

But, if the Narcissian theory be too fanciful—and I believe it more tenable than Freud's psycho-analytic melodrama of a mother's perpetually illuminating smile—the facts do not exclude another.

If Leonardo was not the model for David, some other boy in the studio of Verrocchio certainly was, and his smile may have had a fascination for the young Leonardo as strong as it had for the master. Was this model "the boy of evil repute" who got Leonardo into trouble?

Or, perhaps, he was the one pupil whom Verrocchio loved even above Leonardo—Lorenzo di Credi, that gentle soul who bore tenderly the remains of the master to his grave, and who, long afterward, when the fanatic Savonarola was inflaming Italy with his preaching and proclaiming "that in houses where young maidens dwell it is dangerous and improper to retain pictures wherein there are undraped figures," threw into a bonfire, lighted by the holy monk on Shrove Tuesday for the purpose, all his studies and drawings he had made from the nude figure. It was the famous Bonfire of Vanities, wherein perished many other works of art, sacrificed by painters worked into a frenzy similar to Lorenzo's and by patrons of painters, along with books, statues and musical instruments—"a most lamentable destruction," observes the daring Vasari, in the shadow of the Inquisition, "and more particularly as to the paintings."

But, it is hard to believe that either "the boy of evil repute" or the gentle Lorenzo could have continued in the potency of his smile from 1476, when the David was completed, until 1504, when Leonardo ceased work on the "Mona Lisa." I prefer the Narcissian hypothesis.

The androgynous David of Verrocchio was by no means a novelty in sculpture. Rather, it conformed to classic type, as established by the Greek masters.

Greek sculptors immortalized the boys they loved, not only in the effeminate male figures of young athletes, Bacchuses, Ganymedes, Mercurys and Apollos, but in the slim, slender-hipped, small-breasted nymphs, Dianas, Graces, and Venuses. The names of the boy models are lost, but their figures persist eternally in marble and bronze.

In his fascinating "Eros," Emil Lucka sets out vividly the esthetic of the Greek sculptors—and the painters, too, though the boyish Venus of Apelles rising out of the sea faded in Nero's time, and all the other canvases are but a tradition.

"The Hellenic ideal of beauty was almost invariably realised in the male form. One has but to remember the peculiar hermaphro ditism of antique sculpture which, although it may rouse our enthusiastic admiration, is so hopelessly foreign to our inherent nature. Both Dionysus and Apollo are represented with male and female attributes, and the female figures approach the masculine not only in their bodily proportions but also in the cast of their features. The Greeks excelled in the representation of the hermaphrodite, a being which came very near to their ideal of the human form. We find this ideal invariably co-existing—even in the Renaissance and in our days—with homosexuality. Only the form of the growing boy presents both male and female lines, the blending of which was the dream of classical Greece. The Greeks hated the extreme, not only in relation to sex and human form, but in connection with every other sphere of life. . . . The Greeks of the classical period disdained woman; she was for them inseparably connected with base sensuality. . . . To the Greek mind, woman was the embodiment of the dark side of love, and it was merely the logical conclusion of this conception when, at a later period, she was regarded as the devil's tool."

These boys the sculptors delighted to honor, and, as Greece set the artistic standards, as well as the philosophic, that held Europe in thrall down nearly to our own day, a huge percentage of our sculpture is androgynous.

Michelangelo, the one mighty genius of the Renaissance working in marble who could have broken the spell of the classic ideal, not only failed to do so, but helped fix the charm more securely.

Michelangelo, even more certainly than Leonardo da Vinci, was a slave to male beauty. Like Shakespeare, he wrote sonnets to a youth he adored, Tommaso dei Cavalieri, and his effeminate canvas "Ganymede" was painted for Tommaso and probably celebrates his charms. Other sonnets he wrote to Cechino Bracci, a young boy who died at seventeen. These poems to handsome lads are very much in the spirit of certain of the verses of Walt Whitman's "Calamus."

Michelangelo's "romance" with Vittoria Colonna, late in life, has been used in many efforts to offset the tales of his boy loves, but "this very plain woman with a large masculine nose" and nearly as old as himself, is taken no more seriously as a mistress passionately adored in the flesh and blood than Dante's Beatrice or Petrarch's Laura. She, like them, was only a symbol.

The sculptor's "contempt for women, without which the spirit of classical Greece is hardly thinkable," observes Lucka, who has, again, threshed out the whole matter expertly, "formed a parallel to his male friendships."

Lucka thus sums up his art: "Nearly all Michelangelo's youthful male figures—with the exception, perhaps, of the gigantic David— deviate from the decidedly masculine and approach the mean, the human in the abstract; thus they seem to us imbued with a quality of femininity; they even exhibit decidedly female characteristics.

"I have in mind first and foremost the youths depicted on the ceiling of the Sistine Chapel (the most soulful adolescent figures in the world), but also Bacchus, St. John, Adonis, and the figures in the background of the Holy Family at Florence. Cupid and David Apollo (in the Bargello) are almost hermaphroditic, and even the Adam, and

293

the unfinished Slaves in the Boboli Gardens exhibit female characteristics.

"Without going further into detail, I would draw attention to the modelling of the breasts and thighs, which positively raise a doubt on the question of sex. (I am referring to the two youths above the Erythrean Sybil.) Seen from a distance, they create the impression of female figures, while the youth above Jeremiah is a perfect Hellenic ephebos.

"On the other hand—with the exception of two of his early Madonnas and, perhaps, Eve—he has not given us one glorified female figure; all his women are characterised by something careworn and unlovely; some of his old women—most strikingly the Cumæan Sybil—are depicted with absolute masculine features, masculine figures and gigantic musculature.

"His ideal was the Hellenic ideal, a form that was human but neither man nor woman; all extremes, but also all peculiarities and everything personal, were, if not completely suppressed, at any rate pushed into the background.

"We regard this ideal, which is alien to our inherent nature, with a feeling akin to contempt; for the modern ideal is male and female; but it nevertheless was of great moment in the obliteration of sex and the accentuation of the purely human. The Platonic love of young men (and also Michelangelo's) was in its essence pure love of humanity, love of the perfect human body and the perfect human soul, whose greatest harmony was achieved in the adolescent. Moreover, the superior mental endowment of the boy made an intelligent conversation—so highly appreciated by Platonists and Neo-Platonists—possible, whereas with a girl a man could only jest."

This girl-boy ideal sprang up—or, at least it was given definite character—in the days of Plato; and by Plato, through the "Dialogues" it was fixed, and given a philosophical importance from which the world has never since become quite free.

Plato, who learned at the feet of Socrates, that a beautiful boy is to be preferred to a girl, whatsoever her charms, and Sappho, who taught her girl friends that love among themselves was holier than love profaned by the male element, utilitarian and only for reproduction, are the fountain heads of wisdom from which inverted genius has quaffed comfort in all succeeding ages. Their philosophy has even had its appeal for the sexually normal. It was a part of Sappho's ideal to let the human race perish—though she herself was mother of Cleis, a devoted and well-loved disciple. Certain non-inverted philosophers, like Tolstoy, would extinguish mankind, not by sterile embrace, but by abstinence.

As Lucka has pointed out, Plato's contempt for women became vaguely infused through Christianity, and "she was regarded as the devil's tool." Communities of holy men sprang up in the arid intellectual darkness of Europe, disdaining women, but, unfortunately as too many records demonstrate, unable to control sinful desires.

When art began to appear in the monastic era, it was as effeminate —or, if you prefer, as sexless—as the art of classic Greece. Greek influence may have had its effect, unconsciously or subconsciously, for Greece was the light of the world in matters artistic as well as philosophical, and the very abhorrence of paganism may have led to uncontrollable imitation—the fascination of the wicked, to which the monks, because of their asceticism, were peculiarly susceptible. Witness their temptations by the Devil, and their fervor in recounting and dwelling on their sins, much more readable than their dull repentance therefor.

Anyhow, the Medieval Christs are almost invariably effeminate, and the Byzantine Virgins resemble young men attired in gorgeous drapery. The handsomest youths of the monasteries served as models for both the male and the female figures, just as they were to do well into the Renaissance.

It was not until the time of Raphael that the Madonnas began to take on consistently the appearance of live, human women—Raphael's loveliest Virgins were posed by his pretty mistress, "La Fornarina," of whom he has left so delightful a half-nude secular portrait. Margherita, she was, the baker's daughter, living next door, and her pretty feet playing naked in a fountain led to her surprise and capture by the ardent young painter, and her ultimate canonization as the "Sistine Madonna." Arletta's feet, you may remember, twinkling in a forest stream, made her the mother of the mighty bastard, William the Conqueror—Bathsheba's white body glistening with the water of her bath under an oriental moon fired the imagination of King David, and led to the death of her husband and the birth of Solomon. "La Fornarina" put an end to the male Madonnas.

Male models continued in the studios as originals for female pictures for a considerable period after the advent of women, however, just as boy actresses persisted on the stage. Most of the figures were

296

draped, so that an adolescent male apprentice was as good for all practical purposes as a girl. Sometimes even when partial nudity was required a male model was made to serve—the shoulders and arms of Guido Reni's Cleopatra belonged in life to his favorite male model, and there is little distinction between this painter's almost wholly nude Andromeda and the equally nude Christ at Baptism. The face of his David, moreover, is almost identical with the face of Andromeda, though the body is somewhat more masculine than Christ's—strangely enough, in view of other painters' conception of David. But then, too, Michelangelo's David is almost the only young figure he did which is decisively male. The androgynous figure again appears in Guido Reni's Michael, the archangel, who has a face more feminine even than Cleopatra. The nude Saint Sebastian, again, face and body, is a repetition of Andromeda.

St. Sebastian, incidentally, throughout the history of art is more often than not effeminate. In Lorenzo Costa's painting, this saint, entirely nude except for a narrow waist drapery hiding only the sex organs, is so nearly a woman that the label is necessary to distinguish him as a man, except for the inevitable arrows. Costa's model for the saint would have made an ideal female impersonator.

Guido Reni's versatile model—male or female at the painter's will—was his color grinder and general studio assistant.

"Color grinder," in those early days, was sometimes a term of camouflage. For example, when the painter Giovan Antonio de Bazzi accepted a commission in a distant city, he stipulated that not only his own expenses be paid, but also the expenses of "certain boys, color

297

grinders and other assistants by whom he was attended." Bazzi is more familiarly known to history as Sodoma, a name he seems not to have resented in those days of utter frankness.

His was a gay and frivolous nature, laughing at scandal, and therefore inviting it among scandal-mongers. Most of the stories on which his nickname rests have been refuted, but he has probably been over-whitewashed in the zeal of his exonerators. The fact that he was singled out in an age of studios buzzing with catamites for the unenviable distinction of his sobriquet, and the further fact that he passed his fancy name on to one of his disciples, Giomo del Sodoma, are smoke enough to indicate considerable fire.

Wherever Sodoma went, he was accompanied by a whole retinue of handsome boys. He was inordinately vain of his personal appearance, working "by fits and starts only, or when fancy took him," says Vasari, contemptuously—the general attitude of this historian to this particular painter—"caring for nothing more earnestly than the dressing of himself pompously, wearing a doublet of brocade, a short cloak all covered over and decorated with cloth of gold, head-gear of the richest fashion, a gold chain and other fopperies of similar kind, best suited to Jack-puddings and Mountebanks."

Once, decked out in finery like that with a color scheme of flaming yellow, Sodoma, with the aid of a tall mirror, introduced his own portrait into a story of Saint Benedict—of much more interest and value to future generations than the boy saint himself. Sodoma's black hair is long, flowing and luxuriant, and his garb, while not a woman's, is fantastically effeminate.

298

"He reminds us of one of the eccentric decadents of the last century," writes the modern art historian Pijoan, "with the same affectations of estheticism only with less art."

Sodoma's Saint Sebastian is considered by most critics his best work. While not so extreme in its approach to the female form as Lorenzo Costa's, still, as Pijoan correctly observes, "the nude body is a beautiful example of the androgynous type and is slightly bent. In spite of the subject it has a certain sensuality, for we have here rather a modern Ganymede or Hylas. The head of Il Sodoma's St. Sebastian has a beauty never to be forgotten"—and this head is decidedly feminine.

Which of Sodoma's handsome retinue posed for St. Sebastian, it would be interesting to know—anyhow he posed again, most undoubtedly, for the nude female figure, unnamed, but much more fascinating and artistically important than the Christ, in "Christ in Limbo." It is not, however, Sodoma himself in front of a mirror—as the Bacchus and Saint John in the Louvre might be Leonardo da Vinci.

One of Sodoma's disciples became his son-in-law—Veroni, called "il Riccio." He married Faustina, from whose mother the gay dandy was separated for many years.

By running a fine-toothed comb through the annals of art in all the aged, so much material of the sort we have been discussing could be gathered, that a supplementary volume the size of this would not hold it.

Gainsborough's "Blue Boy" may be cited incidentally and hurriedly. Though painted by an artist of unquestionable virility, this portrait of a young ironmonger of immense wealth, a warm personal friend of Gainsborough, has in itself telltale features that suggest comparison with the David of Verrocchio and the young men of Michelangelo. This spirit of the portrait has set psychologists reviewing the friendship of painter and model, with no results beyond vague speculation.

The Greek period in art and the period of the Renaissance are not unmatched today. Dr. Talmey, who withholds the names of patients and correspondents, quotes a letter written by "an artist painter who is about to marry":

"I can tell you that homosexualism has always been an abhorrence to me, and that the sole reason for my desire to wear gowns is purely feminine love for what is beautiful and picturesque. In my relations to the other sex, I am just as normal as any other man."

That is the most charitable view for any of us to adopt when we meet fantastically-dressed young men with eyebrows arched and penciled and lips rouged in our journeys through the art colonies.

Of many literary artists of genius we have already spoken. But a few more must be noted to make the record substantial.

Cellini, who, like Michelangelo, was also a writer, and whose Autobiography quite overshadows his bronzes in importance, has been accused of giving away so strongly to a temperament similar to Michelangelo's as to have been thrown into prison—as possibly was Leonardo da Vinci before his trial because of relations with "the boy of evil repute."

Aretino, poet, critic and warm personal friend of Titian's, for

300

whom he sat sometimes as model, was of temperament similar to Cellini's.

Winkelmann, who, like Oscar Wilde, attempted to lead the modern world to the Greek ideals, was murdered by a cook, "a wholly uncultivated man," says Havelock Ellis, "a criminal who had already been condemned to death, and shortly before murdering Winkelmann for the sake of plunder he was found to be on very intimate terms with him."

Oscar Wilde, whom we have perhaps discussed sufficiently in the chapter on Shakespeare, was destined from his cradle for his spectacular career—and those who believe in pre-natal influence may go even behind the cradle. When he was born his mother, Lady Wilde, was so disappointed that he was not a girl that she dressed him like a girl anyhow, and treated him like one. In his maturity, when he was writing, he usually wore a white gown with a monkish cowl, imitating Balzac—it is in cowl and gown that Rodin did his sensational figure of the French novelist. Wilde wore his auburn brown hair in frank imitation of the feminine. He is said to have dressed his hair after a particularly effeminate bust of Nero in the Louvre.

Shakespeare, too, invites a little further attention at this point. Having identified certain of his "actress" friends, we now propose to throw out a hint to the next investigator as to the identity of the poet himself. If anyone is troubled with the assignment of the definitely homosexual Sonnets to the writer of the dramas, why not detach the Sonnets, and ascribe them to Richard Barnfield?

"An Elizabethan lyrical poet of high quality," we quote from

301

Havelock Ellis, "whose work has been confused with Shakespeare's, Richard Barnfield, appears to have possessed the temperament, at least, of the invert. His poems to male friends are of so impassioned a character that they aroused the protests of a very tolerant age. Born in 1574, he published his first poem, 'The Affectionate Shepherd,' at the age of twenty, while still at the University. It was issued anonymously, revealed much fresh poetic feeling and literary skill, and is addressed to a youth of whom the poet declares:

'If it be sin to love a lovely lad,
Oh then sin I.'

"In his subsequent volume, 'Cynthia' (1595), Barnfield disclaims any intention in the earlier poem beyond that of imitating Virgil's second eclogue. But the sonnets in this second volume are even more definitely homosexual than the earlier poem, though he goes on to tell how at last he found a lass whose beauty surpassed that

'of the swain
Whom I never could obtain.

"After the age of thirty-one Barnfield wrote no more, but, being in easy circumstances, retired to his beautiful manor house and country estate in Shropshire, lived there for twenty years and died leaving a wife and son."

It is up to somebody to search the Sonnets of Shakespeare for the Barnfield cypher.

Dr. Ellis takes little stock in the theory that Shakespeare was inverted. "All that can be said," he observes, "is that he addressed a series of sonnets to a youthful male friend." But Ellis believes that

302

other great Elizabethan dramatist, Marlowe, possessed homosexual tendencies, and one of his most telling arguments is that "Marlowe's poetic work, while it shows him by no means insensitive to the beauty of women, also reveals a special and peculiar sensitiveness to masculine beauty." It is precisely this enthusiastic appreciation of Adonis above Venus in Shakespeare's frenzied ballad turned hotly out of the classic—an enthusiasm that surpasses Marlowe's—that makes me believe, even above the arguments from the Sonnets, that Shakespeare created his dramatic heroines for his male stage friends.

In Marlowe's drama of "Edward II," Dr. Ellis finds more concrete evidence that the playwright may have been guilty of the charges brought against him by a gallows-bird.

Nicholas Udall, author of the first English comedy, "Ralph Roister Doister," the immediate predecessor of Marlowe and Shakespeare, was definitely charged with crimes against the boys of Eton, where he was headmaster. He was tried, confessed, and was imprisoned.

The Baconians may take what comfort they may get from the fact that Francis Bacon seems to have had the temperament necessary to write the Sonnets. Dr. Ellis quotes a writer of the time who is precise in his accusations of Bacon, "and even gives the name of a 'very effeminate-faced youth' who was his 'catamite and bedfellow.' " Ellis points out that women play no part in Bacon's life, and "Bacon's writings, it may be added, equally with his letters, show no evidence of love or attraction to women; in his 'Essays' he is brief and judicial on the subject of Marriage, copious and eloquent on the subject of Friendship, while the essay on Beauty deals exclusively with masculine beauty."

If a man, Queen Elizabeth was more fortunate than many distinguished subjects, who were barred, out of deference to decency, from masquerading thus publicly in the skirts and bodices they must have craved.

Virgil has been under suspicion on the strength of certain fervid lines to young swains in the Eclogues. If the mouth of calumny speaks truth, the poet must have had a congenial gossip's familiarity with his friend Augustus.

Tasso and Ariosto, those other epic poets of a later Italy, have aroused similar suspicions with certain of their poetic lines.

The German poet Kleist wrote the most florid letters to his young friend Ernst von Pfuel, who afterward became Prussian war minister. "You bring the days of the Greeks back to me. . . . When you used to bathe in the Lake of Thun I would gaze with the real feelings of a girl at your beautiful body. It would serve an artist to study from. . . . Go with me to Anspach, and let us enjoy the sweets of friendship. . . . I shall never marry; you must be wife and children to me."

Lord Byron, against whom was urged every sin, natural and unnatural, including incest and murder, did not escape charges of the Scythian wickedness. "I have been informed," writes Dr. Ellis, "that some of his poems nominally addressed to women were really inspired by men. It is certain that he experienced very strong emotions toward his male friends. 'My school friendships,' he wrote, 'were with me passions.' When he afterward met one of these friends, Lord Clare, in

304

Italy, he was painfully agitated, and could never hear the name without a beating of the heart. At the age of twenty-two he formed one of his strong attachments for a youth to whom he left £7,000 in his will."

Goethe, says Ellis, is reported to have written elegies of homosexual character which still remain unpublished.

Tennyson's love for his youthful friend Hallam, as revealed in "In Memoriam," is expressed at times so fervently as to set the scandal hounds on his trail, but Dr. Ellis is of the opinion that, "although such strong friendships may involve an element of sexual emotion, they have no true and definite homosexual impulse; homosexuality is merely simulated by the ardent and hyperesthetic emotions of the poet."

Ellis links with the Tennyson-Hallam friendship the kindred case of Montaigne and Etienne de la Boëtie.

These poetic friendships, when finally purified of all sexual dross, become, perhaps, the classic fire of Milton's passion for Lycidas, which I fail to find anywhere under suspicion. Nor, do I find Shelley, despite his girl features, suspected for "Adonis" or for any of his exploits, as wild and scandalous as those of his friend Byron.

Swinburne has interpreted the soul of Sappho in verse better than any woman has ever done, and better than any other man. Like Byron, he flaunted sins, real and alleged, in the face of a shocked public for the thrill of the shock, and laid himself and his circle of literary and artistic friends open to the suspicion of feminine frenzies.

Edward Fitzgerald, deathless for his version of "Omar Khayyam," though married, was devoted to his male friends, and when the one he most loved died, W. K. Browne, he "used to wander about the shore at night longing for some fellow to accost him who might give some promise of filling up a very vacant place in his heart." This fellow he finally found, Joseph Fletcher, a giant fisherman, six feet tall, and to him Fitzgerald gave the fanciful nickname of "Posh," and seems to have become almost abject in the worship of him. "Posh" is described by Fitzgerald as "a man of the finest Saxon type, with a complexion *vif, male et flamboyant,* blue eyes, a nose less than Roman, more than Greek, and strictly auburn hair that any woman might envy. Further he was a man of simplicity of soul, justice of thought, tenderness of nature, a gentleman of Nature's grandest type." There were lovers' quarrels, however, since "Poshy," as Fitzgerald got to calling him, doesn't seem to have been properly devoted, and he caused the poet any amount of unhappiness.

Paul Verlaine, the French poet, was not happier in his poet friend, Arthur Rimbaud, and a tempestuous quarrel led to Verlaine's imprisonment.

The case of Walt Whitman is assuming Shakespearean proportions. Whitman lost a government job and was shunned by many good people for certain expressions in "Leaves of Grass"—especially the section known as "Calamus," difficult to obtain unexpurgated—and during his late years and since his death, many and learned psychologists have been busy with his case, not only in America and England, but also, and especially, in Germany.

No poet writing in English has sung so eloquently of boy love, unless it be Shakespeare, and not even Shakespeare equals him in vivid frankness. While Whitman was still alive, John Addington Symonds wrote him and asked what he meant by certain endearing expressions, and received from Whitman a reply that the implications of the questions "quite daze me" and that "that the 'Calamus' part has ever allowed the possibility of such construction as mentioned is terrible."

Certain of the psychologists, however, pass lightly or ignore this letter, alleging it to be decidedly at variance with the whole spirit of "Calamus," and speculating Whitman answered Symonds more diplomatically than truthfully.

" 'Manly love' occupies in his work a predominance which it would scarcely hold in the feelings of the 'average man,' whom Whitman wishes to honor," says Dr. Ellis, examining the whole of "Leaves of Grass," and not exclusively the "Calamus" section. "A normally constituted person, having assumed the very frank attitude taken up by Whitman, would be impelled to devote far more ardor to the subject of sexual relationships with women and all that is involved in maternity than is accorded to them in 'Leaves of Grass.' Some of Whitman's extant letters to young men, though they do not throw definite light on this question, are of very affectionate character, and, although a man of remarkable physical vigor, he never felt inclined to marry."

If not our American Samson or Hercules, the muscular Whitman may eventually qualify as our Leonardo.

Walt Whitman will re-establish—if anybody—the cult of boy love in the modern world. He is the first priest of thunderous authority who has stood before the altar of Venus Castina since Plato. He is no dainty, dilettante acolyte, like Oscar Wilde. His voice is the voice of the prophets of old days. Aided and abetted by reformers intent upon eliminating natural sex impulses from our civilization, the philosophy of "Calamus" may match for power the philosophy of "Phædrus."